D0205163

WITNESS FOR PEACE

The Seattle School of Theology & Psychology
2501 Elliott Ave.
Seattle, WA 98121
theseattleschool.edu

WITNESS FOR PEACE

A Story of Resistance

ED GRIFFIN-NOLAN

WESTMINSTER/JOHN KNOX PRESS
Louisville, Kentucky

Book design by Publishers' WorkGroup

First edition

Published by Westminster/John Knox Press
Louisville, Kentucky

PRINTED IN THE UNITED STATES OF AMERICA
2 4 6 8 9 7 5 3 1

Library of Congress Cataloging-in-Publication Data

Griffin-Nolan, Ed.
   Witness for Peace : a story of resistance / Ed Griffin-Nolan. — 1st ed.
      p.   cm.
   ISBN 0-664-25179-X

   1. Nicaragua—Politics and government—1979–   2. Witness for Peace (Organization) 3. Counterrevolutions—Nicaragua—History—20th century. 4. Volunteers—Nicaragua—History—20th century. 5. Volunteers—United States—History—20th century. 6. United States—Military policy. I. Title.
F1528.G74   1991
972.8505'3—dc20   90-22812

To two people who inspire me more than they know:
Robert L. Greene
my uncle and friend
and
Jahaan Reza
whose life is a testimony that people can choose love even when
governments teach hatred and division.
With love.

CONTENTS

FOREWORD

On a clear fall weekend in October of 1983, I sat with two dozen other people in a room at a convent in Philadelphia. Each of us had heard disturbing reports from Nicaragua—tales of violence, torture, rape, and other atrocities. And each of us knew that these terrors were being financed by our own government, through an armed force that came to be known as the contras.

I had been to Nicaragua the year before, hosted by evangelical Christian friends whose medical workers on the Nicaragua/Honduras border had been among the victims of the fighting. These friends pleaded with us to go back to our own country, the source of this suffering, and to try to stop our government's policy of terror toward Nicaragua.

In that room in Philadelphia, each of us felt convicted by such pleas. Among us, we had a couple of centuries' worth of experience in peacemaking, nonviolent direct action, and work for justice. We knew that the situation in Nicaragua cried out for our response and that something had to be done.

Others, many of whom are mentioned in this book, had already begun to think and pray and act on such a response. In that room, we dreamed big dreams about the possibilities and began to work out the small details. We faced our own doubts, the nearly over-whelming logistical obstacles, and differences of opinion about the best shape for what we were setting out to create. We had no budget and no office.

We were going to ask people to pay their own way into a war zone. We would be asking U.S. citizens to risk, in some cases, jobs or reputations—and we knew that each would have to face the fact that they might be risking their lives.

The idea seemed both daring and foolish. Was it brilliant or naive? Would anyone sign up, or would this idea just die in that Philadelphia convent?

Almost eight years later, four thousand people have traveled to Nicaragua with Witness for Peace. They have prayed, stood with the grieving, documented atrocities, recorded stories, attended funerals, harvested coffee and beans—and have returned to the United States to talk about what they have seen and heard. Witness for Peace has become one of the most effective networks of opposition to U.S. policy in Central America. Those who joined have had their own lives transformed, as this book testifies.

Witness for Peace stands as one part of a movement of resistance that altered U.S. policy and, many believe, may well have prevented a U.S. invasion of Nicaragua. Witness for Peace takes its place in the long history of nonviolent action for peace.

This book documents the project's rich history—the stories, the testimonies, the personal faith and fears. It details enough of the internal workings of the organization, including debates and dissension, to enlighten anyone interested in how such a movement comes to birth. It stands as an encouraging testament to the fact that even logistical nightmares and internal wranglings can be overcome.

Witness for Peace: A Story of Resistance is an honest reflection that doesn't gloss over the organization's weaknesses and the difficulties it underwent. But Ed Griffin-Nolan also paints a picture of the strength and dedication of the many very ordinary citizens who make Witness for Peace work.

It is a story that needed to be told. And Griffin-Nolan, who served for a time as coordinator of Witness for Peace in Nicaragua, has the perspective, experience, and commitment needed to tell the story. He traces the evolution of an idea to its culmination as a movement. It is a story that is sometimes heartbreaking, but always filled with hope. It is a reflection on a rare historical relationship between the people of two nations whose governments pronounced themselves "enemies."

This book is really a testimony: the remarkable saga of a very risky project that became one of the most powerful experiments in nonviolence the world has seen. The political influence of Witness for Peace in the U.S. policy debate over Nicaragua was substantial, but its personal impact on the lives of those who became involved will undoubtedly prove even more long-lasting.

Finally, Witness for Peace is a venture of faith, rooted in a spiritual commitment. That reality decisively shapes its nature and character and contributes to its long-range power in people's lives. Witness for Peace became a kind of altar call for many, and none of us who responded will ever be the same again.

JIM WALLIS

ACKNOWLEDGMENTS

This book would not have been possible without the concern and caring of dozens of Nicaraguan families who opened their hearts and their homes to me over the course of nearly four years. Whatever understanding of their reality these pages may convey is largely due to their patience and love under the most trying of circumstances. I am especially grateful to Doña Juana Moran of Paiwas and Florentina Perez of Lagartillo.

Hundreds of Witness for Peace volunteers, delegates, and staff people shared their time, memories, photographs, press clippings, and diaries, and much of that material makes up this book. More people than I can mention here provided hospitality as I traveled through Nicaragua, Central America, and the United States conducting interviews. Thank you.

My thanks to Nancy Eckel for suggesting I attempt this project, and to Jim Wallis, David Sweet, Dick Taylor, and Phyllis Taylor for encouraging me to continue. Photographer Paul Dix accompanied me on several journeys through Nicaragua and allowed me to see the country we both love through his very special eyes. Anne Woehrle and Herb Gunn read two drafts of the manuscript and their comments helped enormously with the rewriting. Betsy Nolan of the Betsy Nolan Literary Agency provided extremely valuable advice, and Walt Sutton of Westminster/John Knox Press skillfully maneuvered the manuscript through a rapid production schedule.

My parents, Carol and Ed Griffin, provided me with love and support from the very beginning, and saved the day by coming to Syracuse to take care of Daniel at deadline time.

Finally, my deepest thanks to the friend who has always been my family, Liz Griffin-Nolan, and the little boy who graces our lives, Daniel Edward.

PROLOGUE

Richard Boren hugged the floor of the tiny hut, listening in darkness to angry shouts and machine-gun fire moving closer. Spanish voices and shooting echoed all around.

A thirteen-year-old girl and her mother, who had invited Richard to spend the night in their home, huddled with him and shared in the desperate waiting, not knowing what would happen next. Rockets fired from the nearby hillside landed with a thud and a blast. Smoke from burning homes and sheds burned their nostrils—for all they knew the whole village was going up in flames. For Boren it was his first time under fire; for the Nicaraguan farming community of Mancotal, it was the third time that the contra army had singled them out for attack.

Boren was the only foreigner in Mancotal on the night of March 1, 1988. The people living there were war refugees, farmers who had left their land and settled there as the contra war intensified in recent years. Richard, a thirty-one-year-old from the United States, had come to investigate a report that a group of contras had kidnapped more than a dozen men from the area in the past week. Now he was about to be swept up in that same wave of kidnappings, about to become a victim of the crime he had come to investigate.

The blasts were deafening. The shouts of the men were right outside. Reina, the little girl, panicked and jumped up, terrified. She fell next to Boren, not making a sound. He reached over and felt blood pouring from her leg. "Oh, my God," he whispered to himself. "She's been shot."

Blood seemed to cover everything—it was spewing from her

15

knee. The door crashed open. Bullets penetrated the flimsy walls. Shouts. "Get out, you dogs, you sons of bitches, everyone out!" Reina kept bleeding uncontrollably. Boren pulled a sleeping bag from his backpack and wrapped it around her leg. It was too dark to know if it was doing any good. He needed some light, and she needed a doctor quickly.

The shouts from outside were fierce. "Out of there, rabid dogs [a pejorative name the contras use for the Sandinistas], or we're coming in."

"We're civilians, only civilians," he tried to shout above the roar from their assault rifles. The threats were punctuated with machine-gun fire. "If I don't go out," Boren thought, "they're going to kill us all." Slowly he made his way across the room through the smoke and darkness toward the door. He cupped both hands on his head and stepped out into the night.

When he emerged, the three contra soldiers who were doing the shouting were taken aback by the sight of a tall white man with closely cropped hair. They aimed their rifles at him. Boren spoke to them in Spanish: "There's a little girl in there bleeding. Let me help her."

"Come with us." The soldiers pushed him toward a path away from the house.

"She'll die if someone doesn't help her," he protested. It was to no avail. They were just following orders. They trained their rifles and ordered him to walk.

The shooting ended. Boren had no way of knowing, but four residents of Mancotal, and two contra attackers, lay dead or dying in the darkness around him. He knew only that Reina had been shot and was losing blood rapidly. His captors marched him down a path to see their leader, who was deciding what to do with another group of prisoners. The prisoners were local farmers rounded up for "recruitment" or interrogation.

Boren could feel his heart pounding as he and nearly a dozen others were ordered to start marching north. He looked back at the scene where minutes earlier he had awoken to the most frightening moments of his life. Flames leapt from burning buildings. Smoke rising from the burning houses was silhouetted against clouds lit by a full moon.

Nine days would pass before he learned the fate of the little girl. In that time, all but two of the prisoners vanished. Boren and a man called Victor Rodriguez were the only ones still being held. Reina

Ramos never left his mind, but in his captivity something else came to preoccupy him—the safety of his fellow captive.

Boren enjoyed a measure of protection as a U.S. citizen. The guns carried by the men who held him were supplied by the U.S. government. The bullet that had penetrated Reina's leg was most likely "made in the U.S.A." The radio signals the contra squad emitted as it snaked through the mountains of Jinotega were monitored carefully at the headquarters of the National Security Agency in Fort Meade, Maryland. The men who gave orders in the contra ranks had been trained in Fort Benning, Georgia, only a few hundred miles from the North Carolina town of Elkin where Boren grew up.

Boren, as his captors sensed from the moment he emerged from the house, was a special case. Rodriguez, however, was one more of thousands of Nicaraguan campesinos taken prisoner by the contras in the six years since they had begun their war. Contra captives were used as beasts of burden or guides, and many were killed for their political beliefs or involvements.

In the strange moral calculus of America in the 1980s, the death of Rodriguez would make him just one more dead campesino in a war in which scores of Nicaraguans died unseen and unheard by the world. Any harm that befell Boren, however, would become an international incident. His captors had to know this. Over the next eight days Boren struggled to save Rodriguez, to extend to him the immunity granted Boren by his U.S. passport.

How Richard Boren came to be in the community of Mancotal on the night of the attack is the story of a religious and political organization called Witness for Peace. On the night Reina Ramos was shot and Boren and Rodriguez were taken, more than thirty U.S. citizens working with Witness were spending the night in forgotten rural settlements sprinkled throughout Nicaragua. Three groups of twenty people each were preparing to travel to the Central American country to spend two weeks in the war zones as part of a rotating presence, to experience and understand the impact of their country's actions on people living, as one founder of Witness for Peace phrased it, "at the other end of the gun barrel."

The presence of these rather ordinary Americans, who were motivated by conscience, religious conviction, or both, was becoming increasingly controversial as Nicaragua became a topic of national debate in the United States. They had been attacked verbally by contra supporters in the United States and threatened physically by the contras in the field. Twice before they had been taken prisoner.

CIA Director William Casey had been heard to curse the presence of such people as an obstacle in his agency's path, impeding the war he wanted to carry out in Nicaragua. Contra leader Arturo Cruz fretted that Witness would be the undoing of his efforts to win sustained U.S. backing. The presence of dozens, then hundreds, and eventually thousands of Witnesses for Peace in the Nicaraguan war zones constituted a headache for U.S. strategic planners contemplating an invasion of Nicaragua. Witnesses' testimonies upon their return home challenged the official version of Nicaraguan events and added fuel to the greatest debate on war and peace to take place in the United States since the Vietnam war.

It started with a simple concept. A group of religious people believed the presence of unarmed U.S. citizens near the Nicaraguan/Honduran border would deter attacks by the Honduran-based contras. The presence was to be both nonviolent and faith-based. Participants committed themselves to constantly seeking ways to act as peacemakers in the mountains of Central America and the battlefields of public opinion back home.

People of conscience in the 1980s confronted what has been called a "confessional moment" with regard to Central America, a moment in which they must either do something or else abandon the claim to be the heirs of their own religious and moral traditions. Church people, members of solidarity groups, academics, and activists of many stripes had marched miles and miles, signed endless petitions, been jailed, and held vigils and rallies to stop the bloodbath taking place in El Salvador. When it was revealed that the United States was sponsoring a proxy army and unleashing its own secret forces against Nicaragua, they heard a cry for more risky forms of peacemaking. A national security establishment unwilling to be bound by laws, the Constitution, or the will of the people had to be confronted directly and consistently.

Witness for Peace went beyond the protests and practiced stubborn resistance. They announced that they would camp out in the war zones until the fighting stopped. They began with a small group in the town of Jalapa. As the war expanded and more Nicaraguan communities asked the Witnesses to be present with them, their actions spread to all corners of Nicaragua. As the U.S. government's determination to continue the war grew, acts of protest and resistance back home multiplied.

When the war was invisible, Witness did all it could to shine a light on it. When the contras adopted a strategy of deliberately attacking civilian targets, Witness sought out the testimony of the victims and publicized their words as widely as possible. When the threat of invasion loomed, Witness threatened to block the runways at bases in the United States and to position themselves near the targets in Nicaragua. When the Reagan administration sought public approval for the war by embracing the contras as freedom fighters, Witness joined with other groups to denounce, based on what they had seen with their own eyes, this "big lie."

When the administration pursued a policy of "low-intensity conflict" designed to avoid the shedding of American blood, Witnesses courted the prospect that their own blood might be shed as they traveled and lived in ever more remote villages. At the end of the 1980s, when the shooting war receded from our headlines and public attention shifted elsewhere, Witness continued to accompany the Nicaraguan people, to be present in the seesaw process of reconciliation and reconstruction.

Witnesses lived with and shared the dangers of ordinary people in the rural areas of Nicaragua that the contras had converted into war zones. They involved themselves directly in the lives of Nicaraguans who were being targeted by the contras and by the U.S. government. They worked and prayed with the Nicaraguan people in the midst of a profound and risky social transformation and tried to be an echo of their hopes for justice and aspirations for progress. They heard the victims' cries and tried to convert their own sorrow and outrage into a human blockade to stop the flow of weapons and words of war directed from Washington at the poor of Central America.

Like Richard Boren struggling to stanch the flow of blood from Reina's wounds or wrangling with his captors to safeguard Victor Rodriguez, Witness for Peace tried to use a bit of the safety and privilege given them by accident of birth to shield their Central American brothers and sisters from Washington's wrath.

Gilberto Aguirre, a leader in Nicaragua's Baptist church and ecumenical development work, says with gratitude that Witness for Peace has saved lives. Sixto Ulloa, the Baptist lay leader who helped launch the organization, says Witness convinced the contra forces to end their siege of Jalapa in 1983. Many people today believe the efforts of Witness and like-minded groups prevented an all-out U.S. invasion of Nicaragua.

Evangelical pastor Jim Wallis describes the encounter of U.S. people of faith with their Central American counterparts as part of the "transformation of the American churches." The breadth of the transformation of communities of faith remains to be seen, but the depth of conversion for the thousands who made the journey and the many thousands more who were deeply touched by them is a power for peacemaking that will not easily dissipate.

The impact of exposing so many privileged North Americans to how the other half lives and dies will live beyond the 1980s and the debate on contra aid. The thousands of Richard Borens who have learned how it feels to be unable to sleep because a nation eighty times larger and a million times more powerful is deciding whether or not to make war on you have had an experience that clarifies issues in a way no amount of study and reflection can do. Growing to love the people our government would have us hate energizes for creative action for peace. Those who have gone and seen for themselves have come home to reflect, with their own communities, on what it means to be a person of faith and conscience in a society drunk on its own power.

America had never seen quite such a thing. It is one thing to protest war—it is another thing to move in with the victims.

Nearly four thousand Witnesses like Richard Boren have gone to Nicaragua to see for themselves what was going on, to listen to the victims like Reina and tell them that they want their two peoples to live in peace. Hundreds of Nicaraguan families like Reina and her mother have opened their homes to visitors from the country that was financing the war that was bringing them so much misery.

The Witnesses have labored to bring the story of thousands of Reinas back to the U.S. people, especially through faith communities. For their efforts to bear witness to what they saw and heard, thousands of people have been put in jail, lost their jobs, forfeited careers, upended their marriages, and convinced their siblings, colleagues, children, and parents that they have lost their minds. Congressman Edward Feighan of Ohio calls them "modern-day profiles in courage."* Countless lives have been changed—all to try to stop a war the Witnesses felt their country should never have started.

As the '80s came to a close, organizers could claim the Witness for Peace network had grown in just a few years to more than forty thousand supporters. Witness for Peace grew out of something very (North) American—a desire to get a job done—and evolved into a joint effort of U.S. and Nicaraguan people of conscience, a movement

*Cleveland Plain Dealer, June 12, 1984.

to challenge basic assumptions about the use and abuse of U.S. power. It started as a response to the cries of the Nicaraguan people, and it became a transforming experience for thousands, an experiment in creative nonviolence, and one of the most important and dramatic citizen efforts to stop the Central American war.

As peace comes to Nicaragua and the political pages of our newspapers turn to other topics, the ties that have come to bind these two peoples will linger. Makers of the next third-world war may find the going just a bit more difficult as a result.

Politicians who count on ignorance and apathy for support of militaristic politics may be surprised at the response from the public. Preachers who try to ignore the next war may find congregations a bit less content to sit back passively now that a new way of peacemaking has been pioneered.

Something new has happened in the history of U.S. political and religious communities. Witness for Peace is a dramatic manifestation of changes occurring in the relationship between U.S. communities of faith and the national security establishment. People of faith have discovered through their own experience that petitioning for peace is not enough. A new spirit of peacemaking is alive, a spirit that calls us to active, loving intervention on behalf of the victims of our own nation's conduct. Witness for Peace is a response to that spirit.

This is the story of the Richard Borens and the Reina Ramoses —the story of Witness for Peace.

1

ON THE BORDER
OF WAR

WANTED

Non-violent Christian women and men, immoderate in opposition to militarism and foreign intervention, for peace mission
to Nicaragua-Honduras border. Must speak fluent Spanish,
have previous rural living experience in Third World, be of
sound mind and body, and be prepared spiritually to stand
and if necessary risk death alongside a people threatened with
armed invasion by forces trained and outfitted in the U.S. Sub-
sistence salary. Must be over 21.
                    —draft of a Witness for Peace recruitment ad

The secret was getting out. On April 3, 1983, the *New York
Times* ran a major story detailing U.S. involvement with Nicaraguan
counterrevolutionaries staging cross-border raids on civilian and military targets in Nicaragua from camps in Honduras. Ten days later, a
congressional subcommittee evoked President Reagan's wrath by
voting to bar any assistance to the contras unless explicitly approved
by the entire Congress. The CIA had already begun ignoring a similar
prohibition passed months earlier.

On April 27, eighteen months and $19 million after the CIA be-
gan training and funding the contras, President Reagan told the U.S.
people for the first time that he wanted to use their tax dollars to
carry on a war against Nicaragua. Addressing Congress that day, he
took his Nicaragua policy out of the closet, went on the offensive, and
promoted the contras to the rhetorical rank of "freedom fighters."

The president had decided to begin a battle for the hearts and
minds of the public.

The U.S. government was already committed to the war. The Defense Department had been forced to confirm that a $5 million radar base had been left in Honduras, still functioning, after recent military exercises, and reports circulated that the bill for CIA Central America operations in the past two years had reached $50 million.

At the United Nations, Nicaragua charged that the United States was using the contras to provoke a Nicaraguan-Honduran border war. Evidence was mounting to support this claim.

To people in the northern Nicaraguan countryside and towns near the Honduran border, the war had never been a secret. The cost there was not in dollars but in human lives. Already nearly six hundred Nicaraguans had died in a war that had initially appeared to be the work of aimless marauders. By April 1983, it was clear the violence was more than the work of hoodlums. A sizeable and well-equipped army, led by exiled officers from the National Guard of the previous regime, was readying itself on the Honduran side and had already launched major incursions into Nicaragua.

The contras had the town of Jalapa in their sights. Jalapa, ten square blocks of wood and cinder-block homes, was the largest town near the border. On March 23, contras attacked the morning bus on the winding dirt road from Ocotal. Battles between contra troops and Sandinista militias could be heard most nights in the northern Segovia mountains. On March 28, an ambulance was attacked on the road to Jalapa and its driver was killed and a nurse wounded.

On the night of April 8, the contras all but destroyed El Porvenir (the future), a tobacco farm that sat right on the border. Civilians and defenders were wounded in the shelling, which forced the eventual evacuation of the farm, one of the most productive in the country.

The contra commander who led this and many other raids was a man with the impolitic pseudonym of "Suicida" (suicide). Suicida had no time for the niceties of public relations. To a reporter touring his Honduran camp a few days earlier Suicida had boasted that his goal was to "cut the head off the Sandinistas."

In a conversation with *Washington Post* reporter Christopher Dickey, a contra leader mused about Suicida that "there are people who learn to kill and who love it."*

A war led by men like Suicida could not long remain a secret. His cause was hatred and his tactic was terror. The soon-to-be-

---

*Former contra leader Edgar Chamorro, as quoted in Christopher Dickey's *With the Contras* (New York: Simon & Schuster, 1985), p. 16.

infamous contra chief had been roaming those hills for months, laying waste to farms and homes and killing men, women, and children, often with sadistic techniques. Prisoners received no mercy, and even his own troops were subject to arbitrary beatings and summary execution. Survivors told stories of rapes that husbands, daughters, and sons were forced to witness, and of executions in which young boys were forced to pull the pins of hand grenades hung round their fathers' necks. Suicida, a former National Guard sergeant who had served a brief sentence for a 1970 murder, was an expert at terror.

Suicida's siege at El Porvenir would have been just one more attack gone unnoticed in one more day of secret warfare, except for the busload of gringos that showed up less than a day after the shelling stopped.

On the afternoon of April 9, a yellow school bus pulled into what remained of the settlement. The tobacco warehouse was in cinders and smoke still rose from the gauze that shielded the tobacco fields. Spent shells lay all over the ground, and huge holes were dug out where the mortar shells had hit. Many of the brick homes, newly rebuilt following an earlier attack, had been hit again.

The militia guarding the rubble and the few remaining civilians stared as thirty dazed North Carolinians piled out of the bus. The group, representing ten religious denominations, had flown to Managua the night before for a one-week fact-finding tour. When they heard of the attack on El Porvenir, they decided to set out in the early morning in hope of reaching the border region that day to see for themselves. They had been on the bus since 4:00 A.M. El Porvenir was the last of three stops. The six-hour ride from the capital, the 100-degree heat, and the emotional devastation of their visit to war-ravaged communities had left the group exhausted.

Jefferson Boyer was among those who climbed out of the bus to view the devastation and meet the people who had survived it. Boyer knew the area well; as a Peace Corps volunteer a decade ago, he had worked just across the mountains on the Honduran side of the border. He knew firsthand the pains of life for Central American peasants, particularly those with a social and political commitment. His friends, including two priests, had been among those killed by the Honduran military in a massacre at Los Horcones in 1975.*

*Penny Lernoux, *Cry of the People* (New York: Penguin Books, 1982), pp. 110–114.

The trip filled Boyer with a sense of being back home. But home wasn't the same as it had been. Signs of war were everywhere.

As the group wandered from building to building, Boyer talked to a few soldiers, youngsters who had come to work the crops and were now defending the farm. One of them pointed to a zinc-roofed hut on the horizon, across the border. It was Suicida's headquarters. Through binoculars Boyer could see khaki-clad contras strolling about.

"Why aren't they shooting now?" he asked.

"Because you're here," the soldier replied.

It was after 3:00 P.M. A three-hour ride still separated the group from the relative safety of Ocotal. "The bus driver is getting very nervous," said Gail Phares, a former Maryknoll sister who organized the trip for CITCA, the Carolina Interfaith Task Force on Central America. "It's not a good idea to be on that road after dark." It was an uncharacteristic understatement for Phares, who ran such study tours with the same loving but stern hand she once used as a young schoolteacher in the distant mining town of Siuna, in Nicaragua's northern rainforest, two decades ago.

That was before the war. Now her main concern was getting a busload of exhausted gringos safely back to Managua. The sun sets quickly in Central America. Suicida's commandos were within a few miles. It was time to say goodbye to El Porvenir.

Boyer and some of the others were already thinking about staying. "It really got to us," he says. "The tobacco warehouse had gone up in smoke, the gauze was on fire, [and] all the buildings."

The visitors were ordinary, middle-class Americans from the United States. They were mostly churchgoers from North Carolina: eight pastors, a few academics, a housewife, one congressional aide, and a retired IRS employee. Their average age was over forty. Most of them had children. Most were seeing Central America for the first time. The Nicaraguans did not want them to leave. They brought the group to a tin-roofed house on the edge of the property. Blood coated the floor, and a child's pair of shoes sat in the middle of the room. More bloodstains marred the walls.

A young mother stood trembling in shock inside. Her three children and her mother had been taken away in an ambulance that morning. An infant, two toddlers, and their grandmother were all injured in the overnight attack. She didn't know if they were dead or alive. The fear and anguish on her face told the delegation more about the war in Nicaragua than a week of meetings or years of reading.

Evelyn Mattern, a Franciscan sister, wrote of that moment in a poem:

Only the three tin roofs remain
from the barns burned up by bombs.
We can guess what has been, though,
from what is left.
Only the blood remains
on the soft brown wood
of the small dark house
where a neighbor wails strongly
for three small children who are gone,
eaten by the flaming metal.

The driver was calling them. They started slowly toward the bus, saying goodbyes, shaking hands, embracing these people they had just met, making pledges not to forget. The woman began to cry. Men and women of the delegation cried with her. Boyer held her. "What the hell are we doing?" he called out to no one in particular. "We can't just leave these people."

Yet the bus was about to leave. "I knew that the most important thing that group of people could do would be to get back to the United States and to tell the story of what had happened," said Phares. That didn't make leaving any easier.

"Holding that woman was the most empty gesture I've ever made in my life," remembers Boyer. "I said, 'cuidese, señora' [take care, ma'am]." The bus driver wanted to go. Boyer went to the back of the bus and broke down. Phares tried to comfort him. "To this day," Boyer said solemnly five years later, "I think we failed those people. We should have stayed."

That day, looking at the faces of his companions, he could see they were all feeling the same combination of rage, helplessness, and a measure of culpability. The eyes of the woman who was trembling inside that house would not leave them. Their government had provided the mortar shells and trained the men who aimed them at that house. The bus engine came to life and the odor of diesel fuel mixed with dust as the driver hurriedly put them back on the road south, away from the border.

Inside the bus, Phares kept repeating just one thing. "Somehow," she said, "we have to find a way to stop this war." Boyer thought back on the soldier's words. The contras, funded by the United States, would not dare attack while U.S. citizens were in town. In his anger he blurted out, "If the United States is funding this, then let's put fifteen hundred . . . volunteers here to stop this fighting. If all it takes to stop this killing is to get a bunch of Americans down here, then let's do it."

"We kinda laughed at first," says Boyer, "but out of that we started talking about having a vigil." By the time they were back on the paved road and darkness had set in, the mood on the bus shifted from horror and outrage to anger and determination, and as the night settled, an exhausted sense of hope.

Back in Managua, Phares told Sixto Ulloa what had happened and raised the idea of a peace vigil on the border. Ulloa, a radical, teetotaling Baptist, was a founding member of CEPAD, the Evangelical Committee for Aid to Development, and now directed the agency's international relations. A flowery speaker who loved earthy parables and new ideas, Ulloa lit up when he heard the idea. He imagined it as a prayer vigil for peace at the very heart of the war. Sixto immediately set to work arranging meetings with government and church leaders.

By this time the imaginative Carolinians had in mind an invasion of one thousand U.S. Christians. Over the next week they met with leading government figures Ernesto Cardenal, Sergio Ramirez, and Interior Minister Tomas Borge.

It was a hard sell. The meeting with Borge took place beside a pool at a fancy house in the hills outside Managua. When the group presented the idea, Borge, a short, stocky, enigmatic man who can be kind and poetic or tough and crude, leaned back with his cigar in the air for just a moment. "I myself would go to that place on the border and risk my life there. But I won't permit any North American to die in that place. It would be wrong for us to allow any one of you to receive a bullet that was meant for us."

The ever-optimistic Phares remembers that he also suggested that perhaps in another place, where the situation was a bit more controlled, such a vigil would be possible.

Ulloa then set up a meeting with Daniel Ortega, then head of the governing junta. Ortega's response was less ambiguous. "One thousand people? Why not five thousand?" The Sandinistas had always felt that the more international visitors who came, the better, but they did not yet fully understand the implications of this proposal. Nor did those who were doing the proposing.

After meetings in which CEPAD and Baptist church leaders endorsed the effort, Phares and company roared homeward. On the plane they drafted a flyer calling for a vigil during the July 4 holiday.

They wanted one thousand people from all fifty states to go to the border and hold a well-publicized vigil in plain sight of the contras. The contingent would then fan out all over the United States to alert religious communities and the media to the injustice of this creeping war. The original draft of the flyer proposed inviting a cast of luminaries, including a folk singer by the name of Bob Dillon (sic).

Through the muggy Southern spring of 1983, Gail Phares, Jeff Boyer, and the others confronted the task of organizing an international pilgrimage within two months. They sought a national organization to sponsor what was now being called Action for Peace in Nicaragua, but no existing peace group, Central America organization, or denomination could carry the ball. It was too much, too soon, and a bit crazy to boot.

After one fruitless trip to Washington, Boyer and Gil Joseph, a history professor, came back discouraged. Without national support, they told Phares, "we can't do it."

She said, "Let's think about it for a day." Twenty-four hours later, they decided to do it themselves.

They organized a battery of volunteers who worked the phones at the CITCA office day and night for weeks. "I have no idea what the phone bills were those two months," says Boyer, "but it paid off." Working with networks such as the American Friends Service Committee and Clergy and Laity Concerned, with numerous regional and local task forces concerned with Central America, and with the New York–based InterReligious Task Force on Central America, they recruited, screened, and trained 153 people from forty states, people willing to go to the border and risk their lives to "stand with the Nicaraguan people."

FOURTH OF JULY IN JALAPA

Three months and thousands of phone calls after the first trip, the largest group of North Americans to come to Nicaragua since the Marine invasions of the 1920s stood outside Jalapa in a vigil with Nicaraguan Christians, many of them victims of the ever-more-public contra war. One hundred fifty-three people came together on short notice. People with tight schedules found themselves somehow making time. People who didn't have the money found friends or institutions willing to sponsor them. Their purpose was to call attention to the war and demand an end to U.S. sponsorship of the contras.

The CIA and the contras had stepped up their war since April.

El Porvenir was deserted. Suicida had come back with fifteen hundred troops and artillery support from the Honduran army and had overrun the settlement. His troops had kidnapped, tortured, and beheaded three campesinos.

The nearby village of Teotecacinte, a flat town of one-story wooden houses laid out on two dusty main streets, had suffered eight days of contra mortar bombardment. On June 23, a mortar shell killed four-year-old Suyapa Gutierrez as she ran from a bomb shelter to retrieve her pet chicken. She became the first child to die in the battle for the town. Refugees dragging their few possessions poured into Jalapa day and night.

The war was spreading to other regions of the country. On the deadly stretch of road known as Zompopera, in Jinotega, contras ambushed and killed fourteen people, including two nurses and a German doctor.

The peace vigilers first spent two days in Managua interviewing government, church, and opposition leaders, visiting churches and social projects, and trying to understand complicated Nicaraguan political and social realities. They read scathing criticism of the government from *La Prensa*, the opposition daily newspaper, and heard praise from worshipers at a Catholic church. The newspaper had been subjected to government censorship; the parish had lost two hundred members in the war against General Anastasio Somoza and now, the contra war.

The time in the capital was chock-full of information and inspiration. They attended worship with Gustavo Parajon, a medical doctor, Baptist pastor, and Nicaragua's most prominent evangelical leader. After the 1972 earthquake Parajon had convened the founding meeting of CEPAD under a mango tree in Managua, and since then more than eighty evangelical denominations had joined the agency. Evangelicals in Nicaragua were a minority, perhaps 10 percent of the population, but their fervor made them highly visible.

Dr. Parajon infused CEPAD with his own humility and commitment to service. He began his reflections with some very earthy and prophetic words for the travelers. "Some of you," he began, "are suffering from diarrhea. In the next few days, many of you will become ill. You will drink the water in our countryside, and unfamiliar organisms will wreak havoc on your intestines. You will suffer, you will be uncomfortable. If you are not careful you may get dehydrated.

"But you will recover. In a day, three days, a week or two at most, it will be something you remember and never wish to repeat. You will recover because you come from a first-world country with advanced medical care, and, thank God, you have access to that medical care.

"Remember when you are feeling those pains that here in my country diarrhea has been the number one cause of death for infants."

He then explained, with a physician's knowledge of detail and a pastor's sensitivity to suffering, how a baby dies of diarrhea: the physiology of parasite infection, the desperation of a loving parent as the child slips away, and how easily antibacterial treatment can reverse the infection and undo the damage. And how, when no medicines are available, the illness goes unchecked, dehydration deprives the tiny body of nutrients, and malnutrition robs youngsters of a chance in life or of life itself.

Parajon then gave his own testimony of support for the process of change going on in Nicaraguan society. "This is how more than half of our babies used to die," he said. "This revolution is bringing health care to the rural areas. It is bringing clean water, health education, and medicine to those families who were forgotten before, and to those babies who used to die with no name. Now babies will no longer die in infancy, but will live out their normal life span." He then read from Isaiah the prophet, speaking of the time when

> the former troubles are forgotten
>   and they are hidden from my sight.
>   For behold, I create
> new heavens and a new earth.
>   Isaiah 65:16–17 (NEB)

Parajon's testimony was a window into the process by which committed Christians and committed revolutionaries have been finding common ground in Latin America. As he related his experience, the visitors got a glimpse of how Nicaraguans had invested their own faith in the attempt to create a new society. Many of the delegates had read tracts on liberation theology, but in meeting people like Dr. Parajon they began to see how faith, brought into contact with a social reality, prompted action for social change on the part of believers.

While much was still lacking in Nicaragua, the words of Parajon and others convinced this group and many to follow that the Nicaraguans had the spirit to try to create "new heavens and a new

earth," where landlessness, illiteracy, and malnutrition might be
ended.

>   [W]eeping and cries for help
>   shall never again be heard in [Jerusalem].
>   There no child shall ever die an infant . . .
>   [The people] shall build houses and live to inhabit them,
>   Plant vineyards and eat their fruit;
>   They shall not build for others to inhabit
>   Nor plant for others to eat. . . .
>   My people shall live the long life of a tree,
>   and my chosen shall enjoy the fruit of their labor.
>   Isaiah 65:19–22 (NEB)

The group would return to Isaiah 65 again and again, not just
for hope, but also as a reminder of the challenge ahead:

>   They shall not toil in vain or raise children for misfortune. . . .
>   They shall not hurt or destroy in all my holy mountain,
>   says the LORD.
>   Isaiah 65:23, 25 (NEB)

The Sandinista experiment impressed many visitors from all
over the world. Literacy training, health care and preventive health
care, land reform, the creation of cooperatives for the landless and
the unemployed—these were the shining lights of the revolution that
were being held out for them to see and embrace. And many did so.
What they saw contrasted sharply with the view from Washington
and the U.S. press: a Nicaragua filled with prisons and secret police,
breathlessly exporting subversion to its neighbors at the behest of its
alleged patron, the Soviet Union. In meetings with government officials, they were impressed by the enthusiasm and dedication of the
revolutionary leadership, though many were unsatisfied with an-
swers to their questions on the treatment of Miskito Indians, a time-
table for elections, and the growing militarization of the countryside.

At 4:00 A.M. on July 5, the group awoke, ate a rice-and-beans
breakfast, and then climbed aboard the buses for the long ride to
embattled Jalapa. Billboards and slogans painted on rocks along the
roadside reflected the confused state of affairs in the country.

"Christ lives, and is coming soon!"

"All Arms to the People!"

"We are all the Revolution!—Social Christian Party."

"Young Christian Revolutionaries Celebrate the Fourth Anniversary of the Revolution."

"Our Guns, Our Tanks and Cannons Preserve the Peace."

"Mufflers Repaired."

Near the Managua airport, a billboard for Aeroflot, the Soviet national airline, stood next to a Diner's Club billboard. This revolution was certainly going to have a style of its own.

Back home it was the Fourth of July. Barbecues, picnics, and fireworks were the order of the day. The economy was picking up, in the view of mainstream analysts. Few people in the United States knew what was going on in Nicaragua, or even where it was. It was the dawn of Ronald Reagan's "morning in America": before Lebanon and before the Iran-contra revelations. Social activism was a dirty word in many social strata, akin to unpatriotic behavior. More than a few of the 153 Action for Peace vigilers were considered crazy by their families and friends.

Outsiders would ask again and again over the years, what kind of people would do such a thing? Not only were they risking life and limb by traveling to Jalapa, but they shared a belief that somehow by doing so they could rouse their neighbors into action to stop a war that most of them hadn't even heard about. They seemed to think that by their own courage, audacity, and creativity they could outfox the most popular president in decades.

Gerry Conroy was a Glenmary priest and organizer based in Atlanta who had been involved with farmworkers and cooperatives throughout the South. Bob Bonthius and Fran Truitt, a pair of retired ministers who had just built their dream home on the Maine coast, had spent most of the '60s and '70s involved in the civil rights movements and training organizers and social activists. Evelyn Mattern, the Franciscan sister who made both the April and July trips, was a poet and a pastor.

Father Fred Daley, the vocations director of the Syracuse, New York, Roman Catholic diocese, had seen a slide show on Central America a few years back and had been looking for an opportunity to visit the region ever since. Mary Ellen Foley was an activist Sister of Mercy from New Hampshire, an example of the post-Vatican II generation of Catholic sisters involved in social action. She was the key contact for a letter-writing and phone-calling network of religious women throughout New England.

Christine Clark, the pianist at the Hyatt Regency Hotel in Baltimore, was a member of Clergy and Laity Concerned (CALC), an ecumenical group born out of resistance to the Vietnam War. Jim McLeod was a Presbyterian pastor working with Central American refugees in

Texas. Joe Moran, who did the press work, had worked for years as a priest and development worker in Honduras and Guatemala.

Most of them were middle-aged and came from the middle class, and all but a few were white and lived at or above the median income. It was a very religious group. Nearly fifty were ministers, nuns, priests, or lay pastoral workers and another twenty-six were teachers. All but a few were active members or leaders of their churches. The group included a few lawyers, engineers, and carpenters, half a dozen artists and writers, and even an "equestrian trainer." Had they been on line to board a charter flight to Hawaii, no one would have blinked an eye. They were just the sort of people who don't have to care about others far away.

They referred to themselves as "ordinary Americans," but they were mostly leaders, visionaries, people who kept up with current events and who made lives out of challenging the status quo.

Frances Brand, eighty-two years old, was a veteran traveler. She could be mistaken for Doonesbury's Lacey Davenport: purple dress, red T-shirt with a peace dove, a brooch with her initials pinned on the shirt, and a conical straw hat with pastel-colored felt flowers in the hat band. "Brandy," as her friends call her, works as a portrait painter. Since Revolutionary War times, men in her family have joined the army. The man she married, and Brand herself, had each done their stint in the service. She is a member of the Daughters of the American Revolution as well as the NAACP in her hometown of Charlottesville, Virginia.

Dick Taylor, a Quaker Catholic from Philadelphia, sat next to Brand as the bus climbed steadily up the Pan American highway. He became more curious as he chatted with her. Finally he asked her bluntly, "What are you doing here?"

"I love my country," she answered, "and I can't bear it when it does stupid or selfish things."

Then there were "the usual suspects": a few prominent names identified with the "religious left" and Latin American solidarity movements, such as writer Gary MacEoin and Rev. William Sloane Coffin. In Managua, Henri Nouwen, the Dutch author and theologian, joined them.

While the majority of participants were men, most of the leaders were women. Maryknoll sister Peggy Healy and Beverly Keene, a Presbyterian laywoman, handled mountains of logistical tasks, urged on by the indomitable Baptist, Sixto Ulloa. Ulloa had been the most visible promoter of the event within Nicaragua, though much of the nitty-gritty detail, as is true within most religious organizations, fell to the women. Religious sisters from Brazil, from Spain, from Mexico, and from the United States served as hosts and guides, along with six English-speaking Nicaraguan diplomats conveniently expelled from the United States by the Reagan administration.

The logistics alone were exhausting. "The war was the easy part," said Healy. "If we had thought through what it was going to take I never would have said yes," she remembered years later. Nearly everyone ended up with some sort of intestinal bug because the supposedly purified water they drank in Jalapa had been kept in contaminated drums.

The skies opened up the night the group arrived in Jalapa. One bus got stuck in a river and had to be pulled out with a military truck. The arrival was planned for 5:00 P.M., but it wasn't until 8:00 that everyone was in Jalapa. Nonetheless, people came out into the streets to receive them. Buses had to be pushed, and people sloshed through the muddy streets in the dark to get to the reception. "The whole town came out" is the way Boyer describes the reception.

They were greeted by a huge reception in the town's one and only theater, followed by a prayer service. It was an event such as Jalapa had rarely witnessed. Some Jalapans, recalling the sight of the caravan of buses waddling up the road and disgorging dozens of floppy-hatted, camera-toting, mostly fair-skinned English speakers into the town's square, likened the event to a Marine invasion. More than a few Jalapans later acknowledged that they avoided the group, fearful that they were a cover for CIA infiltrators.

The next day, on a basketball court behind the high school where they slept, the group joined with a group of Nicaraguans, mostly women, for a prayer vigil. They sounded two themes, one from the prophet Isaiah and the other from Thomas Jefferson. Gary MacEoin later described the vigil as "an extraordinary outpouring of human solidarity."

Dick Taylor, one of the bilingual members of the group, stood wrapped in a chasuble with "Peace" written on it in Spanish and English and read from Isaiah 58:

> If you cease to pervert justice,
> to point the accusing finger and lay false charges,
> if you feed the hungry from your own plenty
> and satisfy the needs of the wretched,

then your light will rise like dawn out of darkness
   and your dusk will be like noonday . . .
you will be like a well-watered garden,
like a spring whose waters never fail.
                                    Isaiah 58:9–11 (NEB)

The group presented the Jalapans with gifts, including medicines, baseballs, and a facsimile of the Declaration of Independence. They asked pardon for failing to live up to the revolutionary ideals of the United States. "For killings and kidnappings funded by us—forgive us and pray for us" was the antiphon at the prayer service.

What had been planned by the North Americans became a spontaneous Nicaraguan service when a Nicaraguan campesina's trembling voice answered solemnly, "You are forgiven."

Tears and silence fell. Sefilda Hernandez told the story of her seventeen-year-old son who was killed defending El Porvenir a month ago. Another mother told of her two sons who had been killed by the contras. One of them was found without a head.

As the stories continued, the group grew still. The vigil lasted three hours in a blazing tropical sun. The Nicaraguan women responded to the mention of each name of a lost loved one by saying "Presente," meaning that the person's spirit lives on. The North Americans, overwhelmed by the suffering, asked each time for forgiveness. And the mothers, their pain still fresh, forgave them.

Henri Nouwen reminded the group that the women were not asking just for their grief but asking them to act so that the same thing wouldn't happen to other mothers. Nouwen later said that he had "never been so deeply touched as when those women looked at us and said, 'You are forgiven.'

"Even though our country—our government—was part of the death of their children," Nouwen said, "they wanted us to know that we were forgiven. We embraced them—and suddenly I saw something that we very seldom see in life: the most heartrending suffering and at the same time an incredible hope. . . . They gave us hope. They were comforting us. They were trying to tell us not to settle in our guilt, not to make it self-flagellation. They wanted us to be free from that guilt and forgiven so that we could speak for them and for peace, so that the war would stop."

Stella Martinez, sitting five years later in her tiny restaurant in Jalapa, still remembered feeling hope that these people, if they saw the reality of Nicaragua, would be able to turn the United States around. "The lies end when the truth arrives," she said, and she sensed that these people were willing and able to see the truth.

Maria Rios Sevilla, who lost three children in the war, wanted the moral support of knowing her people were not alone. Years later she remembered the vigil's impact. "I still think it's something that helps. Only with unity do we defeat injustice."

The day was full of ritual. One group marched around the courtyard, unfurling banners announcing their desire for peace. Others planted U.S. flags, Nicaraguan flags, and the flag of the United Nations. Patriotism seemed almost as important as fidelity to their religious beliefs. Jeff Boyer hadn't felt so patriotic in years. "I felt proud of these Americans—they wanted to see this firsthand, and they weren't going to back off."

The solemnity wore thin at times. David Sweet, a professor of Latin American history who had spent a fair amount of time in Nicaragua, describes one phase of the border vigil. The group had just joined hands with the Nicaraguans and sung "We Shall Overcome."

"We went for a walk along the edge of this *milpa* (cornfield). Somebody had planned that we should plant a tree of peace. Nobody could find a tree (all the available trees were, not surprisingly, already planted), so somebody pulled up a corn stalk—a rather limp, mature corn plant which we were going to plant symbolically up there.

"Planting corn for the Jalapans seemed to me a bit much . . . anyway, this big group of more than a hundred is walking single file, and all of a sudden I realize that the group is walking across a recently planted cornfield, where there are all these little plants.

"I ran up this hill, shouting, This is a milpa! Get off there! Get off the corn! Of course nobody really knew what a cornfield looks like in Central America, plants clinging to a hill, growing between rocks and grass. It's not all straight rows. And here we are going up to stick this goddamned dying corn plant in the ground, and meanwhile we're trampling half the cornfield!"

Forgiveness once again carried the day. Yet Sweet, who is not a Christian, found himself moved by the spirit of sharing. The vigil itself he called "imaginatively, thoughtfully, lovingly conceived."

The suffering of the Nicaraguans, the personal contact, the depth of religious feeling among the Nicaraguans, and the sense that the Nicaraguans were striving to improve the lot of the poor embedded in the visitors an awareness that they must do more to stop this war.

Henri Nouwen's time in Nicaragua, and primarily his meeting with the people living at the border of the war, left him unable to write for months. It called him to rethink the gospel and faith that had been central to his life and ministry for decades. He later wrote: "When I moved to Latin America I was teaching spirituality and prayer. I had it together on that level and I decided to stay out of anything close to politics or economics. But gradually I realized that I couldn't avoid the political, economic, and military mess that is there to be seen. Suddenly I had this image that indeed Christ himself was called political, subversive, and was crucified as a competitor of the worldly king."*

LONG TIME COMING

In one-to-one meetings, the Nicaraguans shared their stories. They ate together, prayed together, exchanged embraces and photographs, and joined in a covenant to work for peace. These encounters provided the emotional and spiritual fuel that propelled Witness for Peace forward.

While still in Jalapa the group began conspiring to return. At least a dozen people, in separate conversations with Nicaraguans, raised the desirability or practicality of an ongoing border witness. On the ride back to Managua, their energies ran high and ideas for keeping the presence going buzzed through the four big buses.

While the circumstances of this meeting were particularly personal, the meeting of North Americans and Latin Americans on political and religious grounds had been going on for decades. In one sense, Witness was born of a unique combination of circumstances. Yet for many years Latin American Christians had been calling U.S. church people to responsibility for their country's actions, and U.S. church people had been responding.

In the previous fifteen years, Latin America had become an ever more important place for those, particularly Christians, seeking to understand and live out an integral life joining religious belief and political commitment. Latin Americans had produced a theology of

*Henri Nouwen, "A Call to Peacemaking," from a talk entitled "A Journey Interrupted," delivered in Washington, D.C., on July 27, 1983, at a service of worship arranged by the U.S. Catholic Mission Association. Published by World Peace Makers, Inc., The Church of the Saviour, Washington, D.C.

liberation, a renewal movement of "base communities"* involving millions, and strong statements and actions by church leaders, including the Catholic bishops' statements at Medellin in 1968 and Puebla in 1979.

Their actions, at times heroic, most times unnoticed, provoked violent, brutal government and military repression. Throughout the continent a segment of the church was being converted from the side of power to a church on the side of the poor. This segment was becoming a church of catacombs and martyrs.

The testimony of that church inspired and called people in the United States to action. It was this testimony and an understanding of how U.S. actions contributed to Latin America's woes that led Henri Nouwen to reflect, in many talks over the coming months, that what he calls "the spiritual destiny of North America" is intimately linked with the spiritual destiny of Latin America. Nouwen's journey took him back and forth between the United States and Latin America, and his experience in some ways mirrors the development of Witness for Peace.

Nicaragua, a poor country rich in symbolism and in testimony of faith, was the first Latin American revolution with large-scale and explicit involvement by Christians. As such it held a special role. Revolutionary Christians throughout Latin America saw Nicaragua both as an example and as a beacon of hope. U.S. Christians seeking to change their own society saw Nicaragua as an experiment and a sign of hope and felt responsibility to stop their own government's efforts to crush it.

The trip provided ordinary U.S. Christians the chance to see and meet, in the flesh, people whom they had read or heard about for years. Thumbing the pages of books, or listening to visiting pastors and missionaries from the pulpit, North American Christians had become aware of base Christian communities, of revolutionary Christianity, and of a theology that spoke of liberation and working toward the reign of God here and now.

---

*"Base Christian communities," as they have come to be known in Latin America, are small groups of believers who come together to study scripture and faith and how they apply to their lives and social context. These communities have developed mostly among the poor, function largely with lay leadership, and incorporate many concepts associated with various strains of liberation theology into their practice. For a more detailed explanation and a bibliography on the subject, see Philip Berryman, The Religious Roots of Rebellion: Christians in Central American Revolutions (Maryknoll, N.Y.: Orbis Books, 1984).

In Nicaragua they were thrust into the midst of Christians, from the most humble campesinos to government ministers, who not only professed faith in such a theology but had struggled for years to put it into practice. In Jalapa, they met members of base Christian communities who had been forced to abandon their work and eventually their homes and to flee to Jalapa. Many had seen their friends, family members, and members of their church killed for their work. In Managua they met government officials, such as Housing Minister Miguel Ernesto Vigil, who struggled for years to overthrow Somoza, and whose sons were now at the border defending the revolution.

The entire contingent met with U.S. Ambassador Anthony Quainton, who listened politely to them. Grace Gyori of Chicago showed the ambassador pieces of shrapnel from a mortar shell of U.S. manufacture that she had scooped up from the ground. Jorge Lara Braud, a theology professor, termed U.S. policy in Nicaragua "legalized murder," and Sloane Coffin publicly requested that Quainton resign in protest.

Quainton was unnerved, but recited the Reagan administration's list of complaints against the Sandinistas, including charges of repression, arms shipments to El Salvador, persecution of the church and the Miskito Indians, and the danger of the installation of Soviet military bases. The ambassador characterized what they had seen on the border as a civil war, Nicaraguans fighting Nicaraguans. Quainton said the United States was not interested in imposing its will, merely in generating dialogue.

It was a dialogue of the deaf. The ambassador and his audience were talking about two different countries. It was like a splash of cold water for the peace pilgrims, who had seen, in a matter of days, enough of Nicaragua to make them question every official U.S. Government statement of what was happening there. That night in the darkness, the 153 held a candlelight vigil outside the embassy gates, singing "Ain't Gonna Study War No More."

They were a group to be reckoned with. Over the course of the remaining day and well into the night, small groups met to hammer out plans to make the vigil permanent. As many as forty people started the meeting, and a task force of nine persevered until dawn. They envisioned placing ten to twenty people in the border areas of greatest tension. A core group of three permanent vigilers, accompanied by rotating delegations, would work on tasks given them by the community and be prepared to go to the scene of any attacks and report back to the media and the church movement.

"The idea was to send U.S. citizens to go and live with the people being victimized by U.S. militarism," remembered David Sweet. "They would share the risk, engage in biblical reflection. Their presence would say that 'the United States shall not do things to other people without U.S. citizens going there.' "

The task force outlined a plan to find, train, and support such a contingent and asked the InterReligious Task Force on Central America to take on the project. The next day at the Mexico City airport Sweet, Alaskan carpenter Paddy Lane, and Texas pastor Buddy Summers scribbled a draft proposal to be circulated, promoting a permanent border presence.

None of the vigilers could have imagined the forces they were up against or the power of their own faith and energies to ignite a response in their fellow citizens and coreligionists. They would need lots of faith. As they vigiled in Jalapa, the National Security Council met in Washington and decided to increase the pressure on Nicaragua by raising the visibility of military maneuvers and increasing aid to U.S. allies in the region. Even as they flew home, fighting spread to the previously quiet area of San Juan de Limay, and five soldiers were killed in a contra ambush. A week later the CIA's plan to arm and support a contra army of twelve to fifteen thousand became public, and President Reagan sent the aircraft carrier *Ranger* to Nicaragua's Pacific coast.

On August 10, a contra ambush of a civilian bus in Jinotega left fourteen civilians dead. That same week the contras attacked San Rafael del Norte in Jinotega and killed more than a dozen people.

Back in the United States, the masses were hardly standing at attention waiting for orders from the border vigilers. The Reagan administration was doing everything it could to keep the contras stocked and the U.S. people in the dark. A CBS/*New York Times* poll released that month showed only 13 percent of the public even knew which side their government was on in Nicaragua. Even those who were becoming aware of Nicaragua did not always share the viewpoint of the Witnesses. In that same summer of 1983 the Veterans of Foreign Wars became the first national private organization to openly begin its own contra aid fund.

Faint whispers of peace could be heard. On July 17, just off the Panamanian coast, the presidents of Colombia, Venezuela, Mexico, and Panama drafted what became known as the Contadora agreements, an attempt to resolve the Central American wars by minimizing outside interference. And on July 28, after a secret session and three days of debate, the U.S. House of Representatives decided against further aid to the contras. The vote was 228–195.

The end of the aid marked the beginning of what was to become the decade's major foreign policy debate, in which Witness for Peace was to play a major role. The administration had already begun to pass surplus equipment to the contras in order to keep them going if Congress should cut them off. The CIA predicted the contras would be in control of one-third of Nicaraguan territory by Christmas.

The returned Witnesses were not to be deterred. The memories of mortar fire, of the victims' testimonies, and the knowledge that their own country was responsible, stoked the fire burning in them. In the coming months, dedicated handfuls sprinkled all over the map worked to put together a holy antiwar crusade of a scale unheard of since the '60s and unrivaled in audacity.

Thus far more than seven hundred Nicaraguans had died in the war.

The question was no longer, Can we make a difference?

The question was, How?

2

ALTAR CALLS

Your presence here in Nicaragua is a living sign of a firm and lasting bond which has grown between the people of the U.S. and the people of Central America.
— Sister Peggy Healy, writing to
Action for Peace participants in July 1983

Jalapa struggled for its survival through the middle of 1983. Between guard duty, burying the dead, and tending the wounded and the coming crops, townspeople wondered if the Witnesses would return as promised. In Managua, Sixto Ulloa waited with considerably less patience.

In the months following the July vigil, the war spread and fears of a U.S. invasion intensified. CIA commandos destroyed most of Nicaragua's fuel supply in a series of attacks on oil storage tanks on both coasts. Dive bombers attacked the Managua airport. More than one thousand contras belonging to a new unit, the Jorge Salazar task force, made their first appearance deeper inside the country, in the mountains of Central Zelaya, killing peasants in newly formed cooperatives. Bodies with throats slit and signs of torture were appearing with frightening regularity.*

While Ulloa called frantically for the peace troops to arrive before the invasion, the Witnesses were scrambling just as frantically to get their show on the road. Ulloa, fresh from the experience of

---

*According to the account in Bob Woodward's *Veil: The Secret Wars of the C.I.A. 1981–1987* (New York: Simon & Schuster, 1987), CIA Central America chief Dewey Clarridge drew up the plans to attack the fuel depots, "but not with half-assed amateur contras in operational roles. The CIA would run and coordinate it." The CIA was also responsible for the mining of Nicaraguan harbors the following year, according to Woodward (pp. 281–283).

watching his own people organize a revolution and certain the Witnesses had almost infinite resources, did not easily comprehend that
the U.S. peace movement did not yet have a rapid deployment force.

His impatience matched David Sweet's vigor. Sweet sent a tele-
gram to Ulloa on July 13, informing him that "the Permanent Border
Witness Project is on the march." Ulloa wrote to all the participants
at the end of July to thank them for coming and to suggest that they
"share together, in another peace vigil, not only of 150 people but
many more. Just as you showed [unrelenting] dedication and energy," he wrote, "in spite of fatigue and illness during your days in
Nicaragua, we pray that you will continue to amplify the voice, not
only of the Nicaraguan people, but of all Central Americans who des-
perately desire peace without further bloodshed."

The returnees were frenetic about "amplifying the voice."
Thousands upon thousands of column-inches and hundreds of
photos told their story in local, regional, and national newspapers (in
addition to the *Newsweek* article during the trip). Almost every participant gave radio and TV interviews upon returning. Sloane Coffin
wrote an essay for the *New York Times* entitled "Nicaragua Is Not
Our Enemy." And from a thousand and one pulpits and church base-
ments from Maine to California, pastors and lay people told their stories and appealed to their congregations to join them to help stop the
killing.

The three-page proposal drafted in the Mexico City airport circulated among peace groups and religious communities. The "Project
Witness" proposal, as it was then called, lamented the failure of
"sporadic protests" to stem the tide of U.S. militarism and envisioned
a "brigade of between five and ten people willing to face death if need
be, in a northern Nicaraguan community such as Jalapa."

> The commitment of these people to share will be, on the one
> hand, simply to share the lot, the mortal danger, of the people
> living in that border region—living with them in their homes,
> and working alongside them in their daily lives. . . . On the
> other hand, they will be available to go immediately to the
> scene of any acts of violence . . . and make full reports.
>
> The use and abuse of American military power will
> therefore be under continuing scrutiny by non-combatant
> pacifist Christian and other American observers whose com-
> mitment is to confront militarism directly and personally, and
> some of whom may themselves fall victim to it.
>
> These witnesses will in turn communicate their experi-

ence of destruction directly to the American people, and in a manner calculated to heighten our sense of responsibility for it—thereby opening the way to direct opposition to militarism through the democratic political process.

No one knew how many people would buy into such an idea, but Sweet was pulling out all the stops to find them. "He was the original Witness for Peace evangelist," recalls Stuart Taylor, a Southern Presbyterian pastor who numbers among Sweet's converts. Sweet was as unstoppable as he was gregarious. A hulking six-foot-two Californian with bristling eyebrows and fiery eloquence, he had spent half his time in recent years in Mexico City and had earlier lived and worked in Brazil. To some he was a dead ringer for Tom Selleck; to others he looked more like a taller version of Ernie Kovacs.

The child of a labor reporter who grew up in an avowedly secular, leftist Midwestern household, Sweet found himself in mid-life captivated by the convergence of Christianity and revolutionary thought in Latin America. He had gone to Jalapa in July representing the "Ecumenical Committee of U.S. Citizens Living in Mexico," a Christian organization. Sweet never calls himself a Christian, explaining, "I consider 'Christian,' like 'communist,' a term of honor. I prefer to see myself as an 'admiring fellow traveler' of revolutionary Christians."

"Project Witness" (earlier known as "Project Jalapa") became Sweet's passion. He was as instrumental in bringing the idea to birth as any one person. "Without him this never would have happened," says Grace Gyori, who volunteered to organize the efforts in the Midwest.

David Sweet stormed around the United States like a tornado, touching down and stirring flurries of activity in town after town. He was on the lookout for Witnesses willing to go live in Jalapa, for people to finance their trip, and for anyone to help get the word out about what these as-yet nameless and faceless Witnesses would learn and experience.

Witness became "what I did with my summer vacation" for at least a dozen hard-core believers. While Sweet tore up and down the map looking for recruits, organizers all over the country got to work contacting networks of kindred spirits. Bob Bonthius and Fran Truitt branched out from their woodlot by the seashore in Ellsworth, Maine, and became ambassadors and fund-raisers within established ecumenical agencies. They turned to their respective denominations plus Clergy and Laity Concerned (CALC).

CALC jumped on board, triggering the involvement of Rev. Bill Webber, a well-known theologian, author, and former president of New York Theological Seminary; John Collins, a twenty-year veteran of the civil rights movement; and CALC activists nationwide. The labors of the "Maine Connection," as Truitt and Bonthius liked to be known, also led to the incorporation of "Witness for Peace, Inc." in Ellsworth and the first Witness for Peace newsletter.

In Jesse Helms country, Gail Phares was building on solid ground. Several delegations of North Carolinians had been to Nicaragua (seventeen of them on the July vigil). CITCA began to raise money for Witness for Peace before it even had a name. "We weren't afraid to ask people to do things," remembers Phares. She was nudged along by Sixto Ulloa, who called again and again during August with a plea—"we need two hundred people—tomorrow."

Grace Gyori and her family had just moved back to Chicago after fifteen years as missionaries in Guatemala. She began to spread the Witness idea in local churches, with the help of twenty-one Illinois and Indiana participants in the July vigil. Gyori found that people never involved in Central America work were drawn to Witness. The concept of a nonviolent presence in the middle of a war attracted students and faculty from a number of colleges tied to the peace churches, including Goshen College, Denison University, and Eastern Mennonite College.

Dick Taylor contacted Jim Wallis and Joyce Hollyday of Sojourners community, a young and vibrant evangelical ministry based in Washington, D.C., which combined conservative theology with a radical view of social and political issues. Sojourners magazine became a major vehicle for recruitment and publicity. Dennis Marker, a media and political whiz kid who had run election campaigns and worked in the Carter administration, had just joined the Sojourners community. Marker was turned loose along with Joyce Hollyday to develop a media strategy for the Witness project.

Jim Wallis toured the country that fall talking about Witness for Peace and calling for volunteers to go to the border. Henri Nouwen embarked on a similar evangelizing crusade, traveling from New York to Philadelphia, Washington, Chicago, Seattle, San Francisco, Los Angeles, New Orleans, and elsewhere to "call the Christian community to peacemaking in regard to Central America and to protest any form of United States intervention in Nicaragua." In Texas, Buddy Summers became a full-time volunteer and, when the National Steering Committee was formed in August, he was its first chair. He convened the earliest telephone conference calls, which included Jim McLeod, Paddy Lane, David Sweet, Fran Truitt, and Dick Taylor.

Participants hooked into a series of conference calls that began with a prayer and ended up costing thousands of dollars. Few of the key organizers even knew one another before the July trip. They all knew something had to be done. But no one was yet sure just what they hoped to accomplish or how they would go about it.

They came home from Jalapa with competing visions. Some emerged so moved by the coming together of faith and politics in Nicaragua that they wanted Witnesses on the ground to communicate the uniqueness of the Nicaraguan revolutionary process to U.S. churches. Others saw the continuing trips to Nicaragua as a launching pad to move people to work back home for a change in U.S. policy. Still others interpreted the idea of a border presence as a physical deterrent to contra violence, a protective shield of U.S. citizens standing between Nicaraguans and U.S. bullets.

The Nicaraguan government had its own idea—political tourism. Quite simply, it wanted planeloads of U.S. citizens to see the country and the revolution for themselves.

The ad hoc group commissioned David Sweet and Jim McLeod to revisit Nicaragua. Sweet had his own idea of what was to be done, derived from his years as a social critic and historian. He saw Witness as a new way to work on fundamental change in the United States. "Somehow," he reminisced years later, "somehow if you got U.S. citizens—intelligent, articulate U.S. citizens—to experience what it is like to live . . . on the receiving end of U.S. militarism and to communicate that experience back to this country, somehow, it seemed to me that you could begin to make a dent in this culture here [in the United States]."

It was an elegant idea, suited to a visionary, but an idea destined to become but a hitchhiker on a fast-moving vehicle. First he had a more practical challenge at hand.

Sweet almost failed to sell his idea to the people who mattered most—the Nicaraguan government. In August, traveling on a borrowed American Express card, he returned to Nicaragua to negotiate with CEPAD, other church partners, and the government, the particulars of "Project Witness."

The Nicaraguan government was the biggest stumbling block. They were afraid someone would get killed and the Reagan administration would use the death of a U.S. citizen as a pretext for military action, even an invasion. Sweet discussed the issue during a long evening with Rene Nuñez, a behind-the-scenes Sandinista leader. Nuñez, a sober, dignified man who spent seven years in Somoza's jails where his back was broken under torture, chain-smoked Marlboros and listened intently.

He and his wife, Leana, a government official responsible for relations with religious groups, had been thoroughly briefed on the project, and the word was that the highest leaders looked upon it favorably. They thought they were getting a program of political tourism with a religious flavor, a program to bring U.S. citizens, in great quantities, to see the reality of the war and to go home and insist that the United States stop fighting Nicaragua.

For both the Nuñezes, this was the first contact with an organized expression of Gandhian nonviolence. The project, as Sweet explained it, seemed less tangible and less immediate than they had expected. Sweet wanted Witnesses to live in the war zone, to communicate that experience back home, and by their witness somehow to change the "political culture" in the United States to one that no longer waged war on its smaller, independent-minded neighbors.

The discussion went on into the night. The sticking point was the same issue raised by Borge in April—the risk. In order to share the risk, Sweet insisted, the Witnesses must be assured they would receive no special protection; the government felt a responsibility to protect foreigners on its soil. In order to report on the war, Witnesses must be free to travel, Sweet argued; in the government's view that only increased the risk.

There was also a difference in political cultures. For decades the Sandinistas had struggled against all odds in conditions of strict security. Their numbers were so small and their apprenticeship so costly that to lose one member either to prison, death, or exile was a great setback. To hear of people who, as a method of social change, intended to deliberately put themselves in vulnerable situations took some getting used to.

In the end they agreed that Witnesses would be free to travel to the same extent as foreign journalists. There would be no special protection, but they would check with local authorities before going to very dangerous areas. The government also agreed to leave the direction of Witness for Peace to the Witnesses and to CEPAD. While they saw the obvious benefits of an effort that would convert thousands of U.S. citizens into advocates for their cause, they saw the wisdom and necessity of respecting the political independence of the Witness.

They might never have taken Witness and this flaky, inspired idea seriously had it not been for the relationship with CEPAD, the success of the July vigil, and David Sweet's winning way.

In the midst of the meeting, as Rene and Leana Nuñez pressed the idea of tours and downplayed the idea of such a risky presence, David reached into his knowledge of Latin American history and found some common ground. He compared the peace movement's sporadic action to date to the "focos" of guerrilla activity that had failed throughout Latin America a decade earlier.

"We are in a prolonged struggle, a prolonged war," he explained. The term "prolonged war" was lifted from the revolutionary theory that had given its name to one faction of the Sandinista Front: Guerra Popular Prolongada—GPP: Prolonged People's War. Witness, he hoped, could spark the nonviolent equivalent of such a war. The war Sweet described seemed an odd war indeed, a war with no visible front and no weapons except sustained nonviolent action.

Until the United States changed, Sweet argued, no third-world peoples were safe. The importance of this struggle made sense to Rene and Leana Nuñez. The spirit was catching. By the end of the meeting, Sweet had two more converts. The Sandinistas relinquished any reservations about the project and embraced it wholeheartedly.

That done, Sweet went about his other evangelizing tasks. He spoke to a Baptist meeting, preached at a street-corner Pentecostal revival, and explained the Witness idea in his thundering, near-perfect Spanish on a radio show with Ulloa.* In meetings with the Maryknoll Missioners and Sister Luz Beatriz of the Antonio Valdivieso Center, he sought their counsel and enlisted their support for the development of the Witness.

He also got swept up in the invasion fever gripping the country. An unlikely academic, he lived with all the verve and unpredictability of an urban guerrilla. "I remember David Sweet came running into the house," recalls Ani Weibe, a Catholic sister who had just moved to Nicaragua after ten years in Brazil. "He was all charged up, begging us to go to the border. He had come down to set up for October but had decided that they needed to get people up there

*CEPAD officials expressed concern that the name "Witness" would generate confusion with the Jehovah's Witnesses, who appeared to many as supportive of Somoza while he was in power. The Spanish name of Witness for Peace, then, became "Accion Permanente Cristiana por la Paz" (Permanent Christian Action for Peace), rather than a direct translation. Many, including Father Miguel D'Escoto and President Ortega, still referred to the yellow-shirted volunteers as "Testigos por la Paz."

[Jalapa] now." She was impressed with his passion but had other work to do.

By the time Sweet and McLeod flew home, they had worked out agreements for a long-term presence with both the government and CEPAD. The Maryknoll sisters offered their support, and a relationship was begun with the Antonio Valdivieso Center, a religious reflection center primarily identified with prorevolution Catholics. Before leaving, Sweet promised that Witness for Peace would have its first border team in place by October 1 at the latest.

Sweet and McLeod reported to the ad hoc committee, now made up of Bob Bonthius, Fran Truitt, Paddy Lane, and Dick and Phyllis Taylor. The committee met in Washington on August 27 with Jim Wallis and Joyce Hollyday and laid the groundwork for a more permanent organization: an advisory committee, staff, fund-raising, local support groups, and a committee to recruit the first Nicaragua volunteers. By September 15 the group had grown to ten members and had its first conference call under its new name, the national steering committee.

ACTS OF THE APOSTLES

At this point the story begins to sound like the Acts of the Apostles. Word started getting around. Returned members of the July vigil wrote, sang, preached, marched, and picketed all over the country, finding new recruits as they went. A natural following existed among organizations and individuals involved with Latin American or third-world causes, the civil rights movements, and the struggle to end U.S. involvement in Vietnam.

The Fellowship of Reconciliation, which had formed a task force on Latin America, was a natural ally, as was CALC. The Catholic Worker, which, like Sojourners, had a national publication, was another. The Quakers and their action arm, the American Friends Service Committee (AFSC), were drawn to Witness as a natural extension of their long years of opposition to U.S. wars abroad.

Support from the traditional Anabaptist peace churches was significant in those early days. A renewal was stirring in the peace churches, calling for a more activist approach to long-held stands in opposition to war.

More surprisingly, the response from the mainstream churches was encouraging. On second look, the churches' reactions should not surprise us so much. It had been a long time coming. U.S. churches had been taking up the challenge of solidarity offered by their Latin American colleagues, and in the concrete political realm of Central America policy, they had stood firmly for the very position that the Witnesses were advocating.

Even as the Action for Peace vigilers flew to Managua, the July 3, 1983, edition of the *Washington Post* described the flourishing sanctuary movement and church lobbying efforts to change Central American policy, and noted that "the Reagan administration is on a collision course with the mainstream of Christianity in the United States . . . over its policies in Central America."

By 1983, every major Protestant and Catholic body had gone on record questioning U.S. Central America policy. The churches came to these positions as a result of their evolving relationships with partner churches and communities in the region and through the work of missionaries who had been working in Central America for decades.

Since the turn of the century, missionaries from the United States had been working in Central America. Since the late 1950s, the meaning of the word *missionary* had been undergoing a metamorphosis. Over the years some of those missionaries shifted from ecclesiastical and charitable works to social and development work. Instead of building churches and pulling teeth they were helping build dams and schools. Seeing the failure of such efforts to improve the lot of the poor, many church workers throughout Latin America became critical of social structures that keep people poor. Missionaries began to realize that they were not only bringing their message to the "mission lands," but that they must listen to the message that the people had for them. That message was sharply critical of the U.S. role in supporting structures that oppress the poor.

The Presbyterian Church (U.S.A.) adopted its stand on Central America in June 1983, just about the time that Witness was being formed. A position paper entitled "Adventure and Hope: Christians and the Crisis in Central America" urged that "a special churchwide effort be made to help Presbyterians become familiar with the situation in Central America." The authors went beyond politics to proclaim that "a new reformation . . . in Central America is at the heart of the political and social turmoil." Whereas the Reagan administration blamed the Soviets for the crisis, the church blamed the Bible:

> The Bible is being read in a new way [in Central America] and with a fresh vision. . . . This new vision of liberation, as seen through the eyes of the poor and oppressed, calls for nothing less than a conversion experience. The old political and

economic structures are being threatened by a new theological vision of the Kingdom of God. Much as the feudal institutions of Europe could not withstand the challenges of Luther, Calvin, and Wesley, so *all existing political and economic systems are threatened by the historical consequences of this new reformation* [emphasis added].

Hundreds of congregations studied the report, which insisted that believers grapple with the moral dimension of the Central American crisis. The call from the Central American churches was no less than "a call to faithfulness."

"Adventure and Hope" directly confronted the Reagan administration's characterization of that crisis as the product of Soviet/Cuban expansionism, warning instead that "the specter of communism is being used to justify terrible acts of brutality and inhumanity." It challenged pastors to preach about this radical change and the laity to do something about it.

The problem, they said, was of internal inequality and external domination by economic interests. The president proposed military solutions, but they were no solution at all. Part of the solution was for people to go see for themselves. The church-to-church relationship, said the report, "provides a communications link that is quite distinctive from that of the state."

The Presbyterians were by no means unique. The American Baptist Convention had always been extremely supportive of CEPAD and held a special affection for Gustavo Parajon, who had studied medicine and theology in the United States. The United Methodist Church had set its public policy office to work on changing U.S. policy and beefed up its missionary corps in Nicaragua to respond to the challenge of living the gospel in revolutionary times.

The U.S. Catholic church was straightforward in opposing military solutions in spite of mixed messages from the Nicaraguan bishops. The Maryknoll order had played a key role in educating grassroots Catholics. Like missionaries of other denominations, they felt a responsibility to serve as "reverse missionaries," bringing the message from Central America back home.

Congregations, religious communities, committees, and local ecumenical caucuses concerned with Central America had been popping up since at least 1980, when four U.S. missionary women, Archbishop Oscar Romero, and twelve thousand others were murdered in El Salvador.

National solidarity networks had been organizing support

among secular groups for the struggles in El Salvador, Guatemala, and Nicaragua. The InterReligious Task Force, based in New York, and the Religious Task Force, in Washington, D.C., served as resource centers for faith-based groups. When Jeff Boyer and Gail Phares began to call people for the July vigil, they could rely on an IRTF listing of more than one hundred Central America task forces among religious groups.

By the time it came along, most people could hear of a venture like Witness for Peace from a familiar forum: the pulpit. This combination of fertile ground in the churches, the call from the Nicaraguans, the presence of inspired leadership and seasoned organizers, and, by all accounts, a smattering of grace transformed Witness from an idea into an organization.

Nicaragua had already become a mecca of sorts, a repository of the hopes of freedom-minded peoples of many nations, akin to Spain in the 1930s. The image of a budding socialist democracy seeking its own destiny, ambushed at every turn by the lumbering colossus of the north, invited the solidarity of the world. Its youthful, enthusiastic leaders excited individuals of many generations looking for a third-world model of a new society. Its poets enjoyed a worldwide audience, its priests became theologians of a nascent international fellowship that challenged centuries of church doctrine, its coffee was marketed to first-world consumers like liberty bonds.

Nicaragua was a different kind of revolution, a revolution in a bubble, open to all the world. Language institutes sprang up in Managua and Esteli, flooding neighborhoods with eager foreign students of Spanish and revolutionary politics. Coffee brigades from Europe and the United States, patterned after the Veneceremos brigades that helped harvest Cuban sugar a generation earlier, worked side by side with Nicaraguans in the mountains picking the precious red beans that made up 30 percent of Nicaragua's export income.*

Witness for Peace was not the first group to have the idea of sending U.S. citizens to Central America. Solidarity groups had long been organizing brigades to assist Nicaragua. Hundreds of committed individuals were giving their lives and their talents in volunteer work all over Central America. Dozens of U.S. citizens had formed part of a rotating international presence in Salvadoran refugee camps in Honduras. Religious delegations had been coming to Nicaragua since before the revolution.

*Tom Barry, *Roots of Rebellion* (Boston: South End Press, 1987), p. 24.

A year before the Jalapa vigil a Hollywood actor named Drew Katzman organized a delegation that traveled to Bismuna, in the Nicaraguan province of Zelaya, to hold a vigil in the aftermath of a contra attack. The trip generated some publicity, a few photos, and then was forgotten. A sporadic vigil now and again wasn't enough to confront very determined U.S. policymakers. It would require a long-range view, organizational skill, and a ready constituency. Among the 153 people on those four buses that bounced up to Jalapa and back, the ingredients were present for putting together something lasting.

Sideshow

While the Witnesses were still getting organized, a "sideshow," to use David Sweet's term, developed on the West Coast. Sweet spoke to a San Francisco meeting of Peace Brigades International, with his usual eloquence and sense of urgency. PBI is an international activist group in the Gandhian tradition, which places brigades in conflict situations to facilitate peacemaking. Formed in 1981, PBI is a descendant of the World Peace Brigades that were involved in peacemaking gestures in support of African independence struggles in the 1960s.

PBI had been exploring possible action in Central America for two years. Several members present in San Francisco felt that the scenario in Jalapa, as explained by Sweet, was ideally suited to the placement of a brigade. As they understood it, the Sandinistas were predicting a contra offensive or a U.S. invasion by October 1, and a presence by that date was essential.

Jack Schultz, a Quaker engineer and airplane pilot from Santa Cruz, offered to organize the group. Schultz, described by Sweet as "the Peace Buccaneer of Santa Cruz," performed an organizational and logistical miracle and had a ten-person brigade in place by mid-September. "I felt it was a patriotic duty," he said in an interview five years later. "In five weeks, from a standing start . . . we got fourteen thousand dollars, ten people, equipment, and a ham operator. Only two people spoke Spanish. We got to Managua two days before the supposed invasion date."

On September 17 the Brigade arrived in Jalapa. They were the best outfitted peace activists in history. They conducted two peace vigils a day, broadcast radio updates, planted a community garden, picked coffee, and performed other community-service work as requested. The group consisted of two ship captains, two deep-sea divers, two rape counselors, two jazz musicians, a long time antidraft activist, and Schultz.

Problems that had surfaced during their training at the Resource Center in Santa Cruz and in Tegucigalpa (where they met with a delegation from the contras) exploded once they got to Jalapa. Schultz's authoritative style went against the grain of the free-spirited group, which included a number of strong feminists. Group dynamics almost sunk the project, and Schultz was sent into exile in Costa Rica after a week.

Language and cultural barriers compounded the difficulties. On the second day in Jalapa, two soldiers knocked on their door warning of an imminent invasion. They advised the group to leave town within the hour. Their driver, Sixto Ulloa's brother Franklin, was anxious to pull out. The group decided to send one member with him while the rest stayed to await the invasion. The hours ticked by and the attack never came. The alarm was either a product of the language barrier or a test by people uncertain as to the meaning of their presence. While they waited, they broadcast radio reports of the threatened invasion, which turned out to be merely rumors. The Nicaraguan Army was not pleased to be picking up English-language broadcasts of troop movements from the war zone.

After ten days the Brigade returned to Managua and headed back to the United States on October 1. The legacy they left behind is a friendly one, a testament to their pluckiness and the graciousness of their Nicaraguan neighbors. Jalapans still remember Mary Duffield, a 67-year-old woman who lives on a boat off Santa Cruz, putting Jalapa's children in touch with youngsters all over the world by ham radio. And the garden they planted in the church grounds still sports an occasional bloom.

Jack Schultz believes that they did a lot more than make friends. "I still think, to this day, that we stopped an invasion," he says. He attributes the fact that Jalapa was not overrun to the presence of the Peace Brigade. More serious students of the war attribute that to the buildup of the Nicaraguan army in the region and to internal problems in the contra ranks. The worst threat to Jalapa had occurred earlier in the year, and by September the town was well fortified.

But Schultz wasn't there primarily for the Nicaraguans. "I was going there to protect my country," he says. "I was so ashamed of what this country had done in Vietnam, and I thought we would . . . destroy ourselves . . . if we went into Nicaragua. I had to do something." His spirit was 100 percent American "can do." It was precisely this type of impulsive movement that had gotten Witness off the ground, and that, if not tempered, could bring it crashing down. Dan Clark, an attorney working with PBI who was involved in the decision to have Schultz organize the Brigade, says that in spite of the many problems, "if Jack Schultz hadn't agreed to do it, it never would have happened." David Sweet, who denies paternity for the venture, shakes his head when he speaks of it, but allows that it takes wild people to get wild ideas off the ground. Phil McManus of the Resource Center, who helped train the group, calls it "an example of the spirit of reckless abandonment and deep commitment with which [Witness] got started."

The Santa Cruz Brigade dissolved, but Peace Brigades International continued to develop a Central America program. Today PBI volunteers are performing human-rights monitoring and protection of individuals and communities under threat in Guatemala and El Salvador. Witness for Peace survived the sideshow and continued its planning to be on the ground by October. Both Witness and PBI learned important lessons about the importance of careful training and selection of participants, about cultural sensitivity, and about careful analysis of the political and military situation that Witnesses were to enter.

Sixto Ulloa tore out more than a few hairs over the episode, yet recognized the importance of their gesture, telling them on their departure that all of Nicaragua was deeply in their debt. He tempered his own eagerness to start the permanent presence as soon as possible with a realization of the need to lay the groundwork carefully for the long term.

3

LAYING THE FOUNDATION

To develop an ever-broadening, prayerful, biblically based community of United States citizens who stand with the Nicaraguan people by acting in continuous nonviolent resistance to U.S. covert or other intervention in their country. To mobilize public opinion and help change U.S. foreign policy to one which fosters justice, peace, and friendship. To welcome others in this endeavor who may vary in spiritual approach but are one with us in purpose.
—Original statement of purpose, Witness for Peace

The mail at the Resource Center in Santa Cruz made for some interesting reading once applications for the first Witness team of long-term volunteers started to arrive. It was one thing to ask people to give up a week and travel to a war zone; quite another to ask them to give up their job, their family, maybe their life, and go live there. But applications poured in, and their pages told the stories of challenging lives salted with a willingness to risk.

Four applicants were ready, willing, and able to go by October 1. Among them they had more than thirty years of experience living in Latin America.*

Russ Christensen, a burly, bearded lawyer from Maine, had served in the army as a paratrooping medic during the Korean War. Since then he had worked with the development agency CARE in Central America and Chile, married and had two children in Costa Rica, and run for state office in Maine.

*A fifth candidate, a Catholic priest named Jim Conroy, dropped out at the end of training.

Rose Dalle Tezze was a no-nonsense Sister of Mercy from Pittsburgh. As a community organizer and administrator, she had worked in Peru and in Puerto Rico.

South Dakotan Dan Anderson had worked as a Peace Corps adviser to the Honduran Boy Scouts during the 1970s. From that vantage point he watched Nicaraguan refugees fleeing the war and learned of the brutality of the Somoza regime.

Janet Wenholz was a middle-aged housewife in Corpus Christi, mother of three grown children, and formerly a partner in a family insurance business. In 1968 she had moved her family to Colombia when her draft-age son decided he would not go to Vietnam.

In their pre-trip planning the Witnesses tried to anticipate every possibility they might face in Nicaragua. During endless hours of training in a Quaker Peace Center in the Redwoods, volunteers from the Resource Center tried to help them recreate the tenor of life in a remote Central American town like Jalapa. They rehearsed dozens of scenarios they might face. The preparations took on the atmosphere of protracted frenzy usually associated with Apollo moon launches. After the Santa Cruz training, they were ready to fly to Managua when word came that the steering committee had put them on hold until after an organizational meeting planned for October 8 in Philadelphia. The delay meant that David Sweet's promise of having a team on the ground in Jalapa by October 1 would not be met.

Christensen and Anderson packed into a driveaway car and, like a pair of peace pilgrims, headed east. (A driveaway car is one that is driven to a given destination free of charge for someone who needs the car transported.) They took advantage of their delayed launch to stop in and speak to peace groups and churches along the route. They were given blessings and support all the way across the country by people who had no way of knowing whether they would ever return alive.

PHILADELPHIA

The Philadelphia meeting proved to be the time of definition for Witness for Peace. In one long weekend, disparate concepts of the organization's goals and purpose were discussed and debated by twenty people. In a marathon session at the Convent of the Good Shepherd a statement of purpose and plan of action were distilled, a national coordinator hired, and the principles that would guide the organization into the '90s—faith basis, nonviolence, and political independence—were set out in a covenant.

The steering committee contained members from a variety of political and religious cultures, who were veterans of struggles as old as pre–World War II pacifism and as current as the nuclear freeze. Each brought the culture and the issues of the struggles that had been central to their lives over decades. Middle-aged Presbyterians concerned with structure and order had to learn to work with New Age Westerners who worried that such concerns threatened to imprison the very spirit they sought to set free in Witness. Modern evangelicals and activist Catholics found themselves at home together as they looked for ways to focus attention on Nicaragua and to channel that attention into creating a movement to change U.S. policy.

The most important person at the meeting was a woman who hadn't planned to go, whom few of the participants knew, and who slept through many of the sessions. Yvonne Dilling, from Fort Wayne, Indiana, had been working until recently with Salvadoran refugees in Honduras. She was in the United States for treatment of a recently diagnosed case of Hodgkin's disease. In Washington between chemotherapy treatments, she wanted to visit friends in Philadelphia and hitched a ride with Jim Wallis and Joyce Hollyday, who told her on the way about Witness for Peace.

"My hair was one-fourth of an inch long," remembers Dilling. "I had to take a nap every two hours. All I wanted was to see some friends and relax. Jim said, 'Why don't you stick around?' So I stayed for a couple of hours. After the first night I called my friends to tell them I wouldn't be there until tomorrow. For the rest of the weekend all I did was listen, sleep, and call my friends every half hour to tell them I was still busy. And then at the end of the weekend they asked me to be the national coordinator."

Dilling accepted, despite worries about the strain on her health. "It was just that kind of thing. You knew you had to do it," she said later. Her presence on the staff helped give the project the credibility it needed to make the leap from wild idea to viable undertaking.

The group had just enough experience to know that there were philosophical issues that had to be faced, and enough impatience to get things moving. They tackled three key philosophical issues that were to undergird Witness for the rest of the decade.

Faith Basis

One of the thorniest questions was religious identity. The April CITCA delegation and the July Action for Peace had been explicitly and exclusively Christian in their language, style of worship, and public image. Sojourners felt strongly that the Witness, born of an ecumenical delegation and married to Christian agencies in overwhelmingly Christian Nicaragua, should be "Christian and welcoming to others." In a memo prior to the meeting, Jim Wallis wrote:

> The stronger the religious identity, the stronger will be the Witness. The concern for a "prayerful, biblical approach" and . . . a strong Christian character is, I think, critical . . . If the identity were more liberal and secular, or, even more problematic, left or Marxist in character, it would be easily written off by the U.S. government and press and would not attract the numbers and kind of people whom we need. . . . And [the] risk factors of the vigil require a strong spiritual rootage, as well as keen political perspective.*

John Collins, a Methodist, disagreed, arguing from his experience of coalition work in the struggle against the war in Vietnam. He cited two elements of the issue: (a) to identify the organization as religious would alienate secular activists; (b) to identify it strongly with Christian churches would alienate Jews, Buddhists, Unitarians, and other non-Christians or "post-Christians."

Collins and others felt that the use of specifically Christian language and symbolism was wrong in principle because it would exclude people who were important to the social justice community and foolish in practice because it unnecessarily limited the support base. They suggested an alternative statement noting that participants derived strength from a number of sources, including Rabbi Abraham Heschel, King, Gandhi, and Christ. Wallis countered that the core of the Reagan administration's arguments against Nicaragua was its appeal to fundamentalist Christian values and an attempt to equate Sandinismo with an "evil empire." Only from a position as credible church people, he argued, could they muster the public attention and moral authority to combat such charges. It was pointed out that the adminis-

---

*This was not the first time that the issue of affiliation with Marxists came up. Henry Atkins, the campus minister who was on the first trip to El Porvenir, claims that he suggested to Gail Phares early on in that trip that some sort of permanent vigil be organized, but that she rejected his idea. He contends that Phares was uncomfortable with his Marxist outlook and preferred the more centrist politics of the church people. Even as the debate in Philadelphia proceeded, Russ Christensen, the lawyer from Maine, was waiting outside as part of the first long-term team. Russ, who had run for office in Maine as a Marxist candidate and had a high political profile as such, felt that one of the main reasons the official launching of Witness was not announced at the time the long-termers went to Nicaragua was the fear of allowing a Marxist to hold such a visible position.

tration also labeled the Sandinistas as anti-Semitic, a charge best answered by groups with a strong Jewish identity. The administration also pointed out Sandinista mistreatment of the Miskito people, a charge that might best be answered by Native Americans, who might be reluctant to work with a Christian group.

Based on her work in Honduras, Dilling believed that the team in Nicaragua would need a common language and resources for prayer and reflection, and that a fuzzy identity might inhibit the vital spiritual life essential to the project. "The last thing you want to be doing when people you love are getting killed is worrying about whether your prayer is going to offend someone," she offered. That sentiment carried the day.

After much debate, a statement of purpose drafted by Bob Bonthius was adopted. It described Witness for Peace as a "prayerful, biblically based community." Witness delegations to Nicaragua accepted people who were "comfortable" with a prayerful, biblical approach, even if they were not identified with any particular faith.

The final sentence of the statement of purpose committed Witness for Peace "to welcome others in this endeavor who vary in spiritual approach but are one with us in purpose." In practice, however, the profile of the organization remained decidedly Christian for several years. Every newsletter for the first year carried New Testament scripture readings or a reference to Witness participants as Christians on its front page. The press release for the first delegation was titled "U.S. Christians Launch Witness for Peace in Nicaragua." The internal correspondence, the prayers that began each conference call, and reflections at the various gatherings, both in the United States and in Nicaragua, had an almost unanimously Christian flavor.

Phyllis Taylor, the only Jew at the Philadelphia meeting, did not oppose the decision, but she and others constantly challenged the organization to convert its stated welcoming attitude into active outreach. At times, she appreciated the fact that the organization had clearly stated its identity at the outset, rather than calling itself "interfaith" and struggling to include Jewish participants as an afterthought. At other times, she and others found the Christian majority insensitive to the concerns of non-Christians. Taylor later organized three Jewish delegations to Nicaragua.

Nonviolence

Witness for Peace embraced just-war theorists, crusading absolute pacifists, and a collection of struggling souls somewhere in between. Gail Phares was concerned that the Witnesses not go to Nicaragua "preaching" nonviolence. She worried that "first-world pacifists" might impart a judgmental or holier-than-thou attitude toward the Sandinistas, which she found particularly enraging given that the United States was making war on them. There was consensus that Witness was to focus its peacemaking efforts on silencing the U.S. guns.

Everyone agreed that participants, at a minimum, had to agree to practice nonviolence while involved in Witness for Peace activities. This "lowest common denominator" approach allowed room for people who viewed nonviolence as a way of life and for those who saw it as just a tactic. While they resolved the issue in the negative sense, by making it clear what could not be done (e.g., pick up a gun in case of attack), the discussion did not get far on the positive side. The covenant committed each participant "to nonviolence in word and deed as *the essential operating principle* of Witness for Peace." The question remained open as to how actively nonviolence was to be employed as a means to achieve the organization's goals.

Dick Taylor felt that risky nonviolent actions, including interposition, should be at the core of the Witness experience. Gail Phares took the opposite tack, arguing that risking the lives of Witnesses was foolish; it would only scare people away and deprive the movement of valuable activists. This difference in conception had been visible behind the scenes at the July vigil. Before going to Nicaragua in July, Dick Taylor had talked over the idea of interposition in Jalapa with Mennonite author Ron Sider, who has a keen interest in the subject. In June the *National Catholic Reporter* referred to the upcoming Action for Peace as a "human shield." Meanwhile Joe Moran, associate director of CITCA, was telling the press that he would make absolutely sure that the road was safe before he let the group travel to Jalapa.

The conferees got down to more practical matters, such as the length and number of trips to Nicaragua. David Sweet had envisioned a long-term team living in Jalapa for months at a time as the essence of Witness. Paddy Lane and Scott Kennedy of the Fellowship of Reconciliation tended to agree. Gail Phares pressed for an avalanche of short-term visits, some as brief as seven days, "to tear open people's hearts, open their eyes, and blow their minds." She wanted to start organizing these visits right away.

The question of risk arose again. Dick Taylor, Jim Wallis, and

Buddy Summers stressed that willingness to risk was essential to the experience, and that the prayerful vigil in a war zone was what made Witness different from the many other groups already sending study or work groups to Central America. Phares felt that risking was irrelevant. "Expose people to the reality," she said, "and they'll come back rarin' to go. That road is too dangerous to be out driving on unless we absolutely have to." Buddy Summers felt that delegates absolutely had to share the risk in order to understand and faithfully convey what the Nicaraguans lived through every day. Dick Taylor went further and expressed his hope that, if a Witness bus were blown up by a mine one day, "we would be willing to be back on the road again the next day."

Long-time Latin America activists had suspicions about nonviolent activists. Phares felt the urgency of getting people to Nicaragua and back again and had little time or patience for the idea of a nonviolent crusade. She saw the key to changing U.S. policy as being in the careful selection of delegates who would bring pressure on Congress to cut off the contras. "Some people had this romantic idea," said Phares, "that we'll go to Jalapa, and just sort of be there at the border—crazy! We didn't see ourselves as martyrs. We needed organizers, not dead people."

Phares and others like her in movements in solidarity with Latin America had not looked at nonviolence seriously, particularly after the mortal failure of Salvador Allende's Peaceful Way to Socialism in Chile when the military overthrew his government in 1973. When the U.S.-backed coup brought General Augusto Pinochet to power, thousands were killed or disappeared, and the progressive movements were decapitated. It was taken as a lesson by the left throughout Latin America that state power equaled military power—liberation movements were not interested in hearing about nonviolent means.

To a generation of Latin America activists who had come of age in the '60s and '70s, pacifism was a weapon used against the poor, a means of maintaining the status quo. The political culture of pacifists seem to them ill-suited to the rigors of a struggle where torture and disappearance could happen at any time. "We had problems," Phares recalled years later, "with people being soft, being nice all the time. Then I heard about Gandhi saying that violence was better than doing nothing," she says, "and that didn't sound so bad." Just-warrior Phares heard that from Dick Taylor, of whom she once said,

"Dick taught us that true nonviolence is not preaching . . . I learned that it meant creativity."

Dick Taylor helped to open ears. A white haired, six-foot-two-inch teddy bear of a man, Taylor had spent part of the 1950s as a development worker in El Salvador and most of his time since then as an organizer for nonviolent projects or as an author writing about them. An avid canoer and champion body surfer, Taylor was particularly fond of actions on the high seas. He had written a book about the efforts—similar to Greenpeace actions—of a group of his friends to stop the shipment of U.S. arms to Pakistan by using canoes to blockade the arms vessels in the Philadelphia harbor back in 1971. In the early 1970s he miraculously escaped death when a train carrying arms bound for Vietnam passed over him as he knelt and prayed on railroad tracks at a New Jersey arms depot.

In a 1984 memo he defined nonviolence as

> a way of fighting for human liberation which involves the
> following elements:
> 1. Faith and trust in God.
> 2. Active struggle against evil, injustice, or oppression.
> 3. Removal of support or cooperation from unjust
>   structures.
> 4. Refusal to use violence or killing to achieve ends.
> 5. Willingness to suffer personally, rather than to inflict
>   suffering on others.
> 6. An effort to express goodwill toward all, including op-
>   ponents, as persons made in the image of God.
> 7. Openness and truthfulness, guided by love.
> 8. Constructive program of concrete work to create and
>   point to a new social order.

Words like these were food for thought to people who tended to associate nonviolence with passivity. To hear of nonviolence as a form of fighting for something and not just a personal life-style choice was a revelation. There was movement in both secular and religious circles to develop the use of nonviolence as a means of conflict resolution. Almost simultaneously with the founding of Witness, the Mennonite and Brethren churches began to work on selecting and training recruits for Christian Peacemaking Teams, ready to move to areas of conflict to serve as a nonviolent witness against war, even positioning themselves in harm's way if need be. No group had ever been able to sustain such a presence in a war zone in a foreign country, though the World Peace Brigades had tried in East Africa during the Zambian and Namibian independence struggles of the 1960s. Witness was seen by some as a continuation of that tradition.

Bob Bonthius was still concerned with making Witness a witness for pacifism rather than a witness to the need to change U.S. policy. A former pacifist, he took pains to elucidate his own vision of nonviolence and to insist that the organization not assume that all who partook at the table were absolute pacifists. He wrote that "vocational pacifism has an important role in societal change but . . . is not an option for nation states." He worried that the organization might focus more on means than ends, or that it would exclude people other than absolute pacifists.

The group agreed that the long-term team would be supplemented by short-term visits on a rotating basis. The long-term team would maintain a permanent vigil and would host the short-termers, referred to as "rotating vigilers." There were to be two types of short-term delegations: a one-week, fact-finding trip for those whose time was short and propensity for risk low, and a two-week trip for people ready and willing to share the perils of riding to Jalapa and standing with the people.

The week-long delegations were soon discontinued. More people signed up for the "risky" two-week delegations than anyone had expected. Their willingness to risk traveling to the heart of the war and accompanying the people most at risk came to distinguish Witness from other groups. As it turned out, the greatest risk was not facing death but facing conversion, as they encountered what Henri Nouwen called "the most heartrending suffering and at the same time an incredible hope."

Political Independence

Feelings at the Philadelphia meeting regarding the Sandinistas ranged from enthusiasm to skeptical support. The July experience had generated such good feelings about Nicaragua and such awful feelings about the contra war that it seemed obvious who wore the white hats. Nonetheless, the founding few found the wisdom to make a distinction between opposing U.S. policy and supporting the Sandinistas.

While most had high hopes for the Sandinista program, and some had played prominent roles in solidarity activism, the group agreed that Witness for Peace would attract more people and ultimately have a greater impact if it were careful to preserve its independence from the Sandinista government.*

Gustavo Parajon had reminded the July group that his loyalty was not to the Sandinistas but to their *actions* on behalf of the poor. "Put not your trust in princes," he had said, quoting from Psalm 146.

Jim Wallis warned in a memo that "the U.S. government . . . will attempt to dismiss the vigil simply as a group of Sandinista sympathizers. . . . The project must be independent enough to include those who are very sympathetic with what the government in Managua is trying to do, as well as those who have legitimate concerns about its present direction, and of course those who feel both these things." This bothered some, particularly John Collins, who felt that what Nicaragua most needed was people willing to clearly state their support for all that the revolutionaries were trying to do—land reform, state control of vital resources, literacy, health care, and so on. Merely opposing U.S. policy did not go far enough; he, like many in the Central America movement, felt that defending the intrinsic value of the revolution in Nicaragua was one way to highlight the need for such changes here in the United States.

Collins thought it was useless to fight the label "pro-Sandinista." "Just by going to Nicaragua, we are going to be called Sandinista," he argued, "so we might as well call ourselves supportive and go from there."

Dick Taylor countered that if the organization were to call itself pro-Sandinista, "we would spend all our time defending the government in Managua rather than focusing on what our government is doing." Meetings with Miskito leaders and *La Prensa* had made him feel that the Sandinistas, while their program contained many positive points, should not be placed above criticism.

In the end, the group recognized that even among those in the room, there was no shared impression about the Sandinistas. This, as much as the force of any argument, pushed the group to affirm an independent course. Witness for Peace became an anti-intervention organization, quite distinct from a solidarity group.

Among those who most supported this approach, ironically, were important Sandinistas. Leana Nuñez later called the organization "the ones who have done the most" to stop the U.S. war, and she credited much of that success to the public perception of Witness as

---

*Implicit in the concept of political independence was an understanding that Witness would also not make alliances with U.S. political parties.

independent. The Sandinista leadership, as David Sweet recounted from his visit in August, recognized that Witness would be credible to the extent that it was independent of the government.

This principle required constant refinement in practice over the years, as journalists came to bait Witness and ask for condemnations of the Sandinistas as proof of independence, and people in the United States and Nicaragua regularly confused independence with being apolitical. The founders never intended to be apolitical—from the start the intent was to become deeply involved in what Henri Nouwen called "the messy deal" of politics, on the side of justice and peace. What they hoped to avoid was turning the debate on the U.S. war policy into a debate on Sandinista behavior. In such a debate, the administration tended to act as judge, jury, and executioner. By not allying itself with the Nicaraguan government but instead challenging U.S. behavior, Witness hoped to refocus the debate.

Three days of debate produced a statement of purpose that remained unchanged for more than five years. The ethos and manner of working was expressed in a covenant based on Jim Wallis's draft.*

For many, the sense of community that grew within delegations, among the long-term team, and within local support groups back at home was the most attractive feature of the organization. Activists who had burned out during the movement against the war in Vietnam found that the commitment to working as community, with all its difficulties, was enough to make the difference between sticking with it or jumping ship when the going got rough.

That community had limitations that would have been striking to anyone who peered in the window of the convent in Philadelphia. First, like many peace groups, the founding group was all white and highly educated. The programs they devised, the culture, and the image that began to evolve made Witness appeal to white, educated people. In later years Witness struggled to overcome this limitation by conscious outreach and inclusion efforts, which produced mixed results.

Second, no one from Nicaragua was present. This omission made it very difficult to get a reading from the Nicaraguans about the appropriateness of the group's actions. Since a basic value held by all was that Nicaraguans should have a say in what happens to them, this omission now seems all the more glaring. Failure to incorporate

---

*See the appendix for the text of the covenant. The text of the statement of purpose is at the opening of this chapter.

Nicaraguans into decision-making roles left Witness for Peace permanently exposed to the dangerous virus of paternalism.

After the Philadelphia meeting, Witness for Peace was here to stay. A six-member executive committee (Bonthius, Hollyday, Phares, Summers, Sweet, and Dick Taylor) agreed to meet each week by telephone. Wallis agreed to organize an advisory committee of religious leaders.* National offices were established in Washington, D.C., Durham, North Carolina, and Santa Cruz, California. Buddy Summers became the first executive secretary. Within a month, seventeen delegations were on the schedule, extending into mid-1984, and the names of nineteen advisory committee members adorned the letterhead.

By mid-November Witness had $25,000 in hand, $13,000 in grants expected, and four regional pledges totaling $1,100 per month. CITCA also donated $2,000 for the Durham office. Twenty-seven local support groups were functioning around the country, and seven regional Witness for Peace offices soon opened to support the local work, recruit volunteers to go to Nicaragua, publicize the Witness, and carry out public policy work.

The Philadelphia meeting demonstrated that the organization was able to tolerate diversity of opinions. Individuals who differed could find ways, in their local or regional activities, to carry on in a way consistent with their own priorities, keeping the main purpose in mind. Geography may have been their saving grace. If everyone who came together for the founding conference had lived and worked in the same town, Witness might never have gotten off the ground. Distance and the cumbersome memos and conference calls that became standard fare in Witness caused their share of miscommunication, but they had their up side. There was too much leadership experience and too much history, but when those leaders were given specific functions to perform and spread around the country, they found they could work together and stimulate one another. Without decentralized operations, Witness for Peace might never have survived its birth.

Time was running out. As they gathered in Philadelphia, the *New York Times* reported that the CIA was using Salvadoran pilots

*The steering committee by this time had expanded to include, in addition to the executive committee, Grace Gyori, Fran Truitt, Bill Webber, Phyllis Taylor, Jim McLeod, and Betty Wolcott. Yvonne Dilling, as staff, had voice but no vote, although voting was very rare, since the organization made decisions by consensus whenever possible.

flying from Salvadoran air bases to supply the contras, and the Kissinger Commission, escorted by an unknown Marine named Oliver North, was touring Central America. Two days later, three of the five fuel storage tanks exploded at Nicaragua's main port, Corinto. Though the contras took credit, the job was in fact carried out by the CIA.*

*Scott Armstrong et al., and the National Security Archive, *The Chronology: The Documented Day-by-Day Account of the Secret Military Assistance to Iran and the Contras* (New York: Warner Books, 1987), p. 40.

4

JALAPA'S OPEN HEART

If they come for the innocent and do not have to step over our
bodies, then cursed be our religion.

—Dorothy Day

On October 18, 1983, Sixto Ulloa drove to the Managua airport
and picked up the first team of long-term volunteers. He steered Dan
Anderson, Russ Christensen, Rose Dalle Tezze, and Janet Wenholz
through the maze of customs and immigration, helped them change
money and find their luggage, and then lodged them with his in-laws,
a prominent Baptist couple, Eugenio and Candelaria Zamora.

Just as the team got to Nicaragua, the war ended. Or so the U.S.
public was led to believe. On October 20, Congress voted for the second time to cut all aid to paramilitary groups fighting in Nicaragua. In
practice, aid shipments to the contras barely skipped a beat, as the
administration took its war underground. The vote didn't make any
difference in the countryside, where the attacks continued and the
death toll was rising every day.

The new arrivals spent a week finding their way around Managua, one of the world's most confusing cities, and getting acquainted
with government agencies, the U.S. Embassy, opposition political
parties, and the Catholic church hierarchy. They would later be taking many short-term delegates to visit these same organizations.

Ulloa and CEPAD were the lifeline for the team, supporting them
emotionally as well as logistically. Ulloa fervently believed that the
U.S. churches had the potential to prevent a U.S. invasion and to
turn the war around, and he worked feverishly to get Witness off the
ground.

At the end of the team's first week they were jolted by news of the U.S. invasion of Grenada. Managua was gripped with a sense of fear and defiance—the government believed Nicaragua was next on the Reagan hit list. The new team went to a rally of tens of thousands of Nicaraguans protesting the invasion. Activists around the United States reacted with rage. More than anything else, the Grenada invasion brought people active on other peace issues to the recognition that the Nicaraguan revolution was in mortal peril as long as Ronald Reagan occupied the White House.

On October 27, Witness for Peace arrived in Jalapa. As the group rode through the Segovia mountains, two Spanish nuns, Sister Marimer and Sister Esperanza, narrated the history of each bend in the road, a chronology of the triumphs and travails of four years of revolution. Their stories of ambushes and mine explosions, accompanied by the visual evidence of rusting hulks of vehicles, were grim reminders of how precarious life in Jalapa could be.

The sisters, along with a Basque priest, Father Lucinio, and a Sacred Heart sister from Boston, Lisa Fitzgerald, quickly became guides and soul mates for the new team. The team was impressed by their pastoral work, which was rooted in an evolving liberation theology that identified closely with the revolution. Though the Catholic church in Latin America had shed some of its reflexive conservatism in recent decades, the Nicaraguan bishops, who had opposed Somoza, viewed the Sandinistas with suspicion and did not look kindly on pastoral workers mixing religion with revolutionary politics. From the start, Witness for Peace was identified with the base communities and the progressive sectors of the Catholic church.

Years later in Nicaragua, the word Jalapa came to symbolize courage, resistance, and progress in spite of obstacles. In 1983, it was a name associated with terror and death. Yet driving into town, anyone who had heard the horror stories of the war couldn't help but feel the contrast between such tales and the beauty of the place. Bright red hibiscus flowers, orchids, and poinsettias filled the yards of almost every home in town. Pigs lounged in the backyards and horses stood in the muddy streets. A large wooden cross, erected by Capuchin missionaries in 1920 while the U.S. Marines were occupying Nicaragua, overlooked the town from a hillside to the north.

Tobacco barns dotted the green valley. Tranquil, aging mountains wrapped around the village and give a deceptive feeling of protection. In times that people called normal, the valley's rivers drew bathers from all over the country, especially during Holy Week.

The soil is some of the richest in Central America. By 1983, the

Sandinistas had formed thirty agricultural cooperatives in the Jalapa valley, giving land, including parcels held by the Somoza family and associates, to hundreds of families. But that land jutted dangerously into Honduran territory that was occupied by a contra force growing in size and brutality.

Jalapa's farmers spent as much time carrying guns as they did picking coffee and tending tobacco plants and cornfields. Dark green German trucks filled with boyish recruits rumbled past wooden ox carts as they raced northward along the dirt roads leading out of town. The same trucks lumbered back through town carrying stacks of corpses southward.

The Witnesses' "job description" was still a bit vague: to witness and document the impact of the war and to share the life of the people. The threesome quickly put flesh on those words. At dawn the next day Dalle Tezze and Anderson went with the nuns to pick corn at the community of Santa Cruz while Christensen traveled to another cooperative to pick coffee.*

For the next month, except when their intestines or immigration paperwork dictated otherwise, they were on the trucks at dawn, riding out to Escambray, Santa Cruz, or another of the refugee resettlement communities that had begun to form as the war forced people in from the surrounding mountains. They learned to pick red coffee beans from the thin, six-foot coffee trees and drop them in a can tied around their waist, and to pick corn by hand, toss it into a pile at the center of the field, then snap the corn stalk and bend it over—all with one eye on the horizon looking for contras.

It was hard work, but coffee trees at least provide a bit of shade, which makes the chore tolerable once you get used to having people twice your age running circles around you doing three times the work without breaking into a sweat. Anderson and Christensen often worked with a coffee brigade organized by the evangelical churches, and they began a friendship with the pastor of the Assembly of God church, Nicaragua's most conservative.

They worshiped with that church, one of four evangelical congregations in Jalapa. The pastors were key figures in the rural areas and good sources of information because they often ventured into areas where they had contact with both contras and local farmers. Winning the trust of conservative evangelicals, many of whom had

*Janet Wenholz decided to stay in Managua due to personal problems and disagreements with the other three teammates. She returned to Texas shortly thereafter.

family and fellow church members in the contras, was no easy task, but by working and worshiping with them, they were making headway.

Dalle Tezze worked with the nuns tending to the needs of the many refugees pouring into town. They held classes for the children and helped distribute food and medicine within the six refugee communities forming outside of town. She soon began to feel as if she never wanted to leave.

Christensen began to organize an exchange of children's drawings between Nicaraguan and U.S. kids. Anderson made plans for a photo essay documenting the work in the tobacco fields. The team went about trying to fit themselves into everyday life as best three gringos can in a small, rural Central American town. They learned to eat ice cream and sip Coke from plastic bags—bottles and cups were in short supply. They came to know where and when the best fruits showed up in the marketplace, they spent hours chatting with people at the local eating place run by a woman named Reina, and they attended church, school graduations, parties, and, increasingly, the wakes of young men killed in the mountains.

On the one hand, they wanted to be as inconspicuous as possible, to fade into the woodwork and become part of the town, to share the trials and joys of everyday life. On the other hand they were supposed to make their presence as visible as could be, both to publicize the impact of the U.S.-backed war and to deter attacks.

Each morning the team met for biblical reflection and, during most of December, they held a nightly vigil in the town square. Russ Christensen, who was reacquainting himself with Christian rituals and was learning about nonviolence for the first time, remembers those nights looking out into the darkened mountains where the contras were moving about as a time of personal transformation and healing. "We held candles. We were always surrounded by Nicaraguans. There was a sense of solidarity, of standing up to an immense power that was wrong. And you did it by love, not shaking a fist. It was a message of love. That was very good for me."

And always they carried a question with them. Did the fact that these few people were there, holding candles and writing letters home, actually stop contra attacks? Honduran jets and helicopters were flying over Teotecacinte every day. At night strange, shiny, silver, lighter-than-air balloons floated over the valley from the north. Their purpose was never determined, but they spooked the population. Reagan had invaded Grenada just days earlier. That same week a contra force devastated the town of Pantasma, killing thirty-seven people and scrawling "for God and country" on the walls with the blood of their victims.

"I came to believe that [our presence] was [a deterrent]," says Russ Christensen. "Most of our friends in Jalapa, in the trucks on the way to the fields, with us living in Jalapa, they felt safer . . . "

"Some of them came with the idea that their presence alone would be enough to stop the war," recalled Francisco Machado, a soldier stationed in Jalapa who later became a government leader in town. "But they quickly learned," he adds with a smile. Like many Nicaraguans, he saw their support as more symbol than substance.

Sixto Ulloa says without hesitation that the presence of Witness for Peace kept the contras from mounting another assault on Jalapa. "Witness for Peace . . . made the counterrevolution move away [from Jalapa]," he said. By visiting the resettlement communities, Witness extended a certain amount of protection to those areas as well. On the chance that visitors from the United States might be in the community, he believes, the contras had to avoid attacking. Dr. Parajon, too, found the idea of the Witness being a deterrent "very logical."

Most Witnesses saw their role as being somewhere in between. "I don't think anyone came down looking to be a martyr," remembers Doug Spence. "The idea of standing up and taking a bullet never appealed to me. I never thought it was a smart idea. We perceived ourselves as a presence that would make the U.S. government think twice before attacking. If it didn't stop them, they would at least have to take responsibility for whatever happened."

Arturo Cruz, who served for a time as one of the directors of the FDN, said in an interview six years after Witness took up its role in Jalapa that he would not expect the presence of North Americans to make a difference in the plans of the contras. By his analysis, some field commanders cared nothing about civilian casualties of any nationality and others were very careful to avoid endangering civilians.*

The presence of U.S. citizens may have been more of a deterrent against a direct U.S. invasion than in deterring hostilities from any particular contra group. Contra troops typically owed their loyalty only to a single field commander. The field commander would not know precisely just who was or was not in a town they planned to hit. Pentagon planners, on the other hand, had to consider long and hard

---

*Interview with author, February 20, 1990.

the implications of invading a country so thoroughly overrun with North American civilians.

After the Grenada invasion, the Committee of U.S. Citizens Living in Nicaragua began weekly protests at the U.S. Embassy to say that they did not want to be rescued by Marines. Francisco Granados, who succeeded the Ulloa brothers as bus driver for the delegations, said in 1988, "I think that this Witness has been fifty percent of the reason that this señor [Reagan] has not invaded us." It is hard to calculate the impact of this kind of deterrent action. Claims of triumph are easy to discount; the reality that the U.S. Marines never landed is not.

Thoughtful members of the long-term team, like Peg Scherer of the New York Catholic Worker, suggested cutting short the debate and testing deterrence by expanding the placement of long- and short-termers. "We cannot say if our presence here in Jalapa," she wrote to friends, "has thwarted one military action, saved one life. We can't say it hasn't done that either. Yet from my experience and belief, it strikes me as very important that we keep trying—and that we extend that effort. To do so requires a certain kind of people . . . Mary Dutcher and I were talking yesterday, wishing there were a hundred of us. The Pentagon has managed to get 35,000 or so, why not?"

At the end of the first week, Anderson wrote in the team's journal:

> As I sign off now at 9:30 P.M. we have heard shots of automatic rifle fire . . . in the distance as well as close to the edges of Jalapa. The shots are always sporadic. We never know if these shots represent a release of tension by a soldier having a few drinks and shooting into the night sky, or perhaps anxious night patrols shooting at sounds in the dark, or if they may represent people shooting at people. We pray that Nicaragua may be liberated soon from this anxiety and ever present threat.

SHORT-TERM DELEGATES

The long-term team fulfilled David Sweet's idea of a small community of U.S. citizens living at the open end of the barrel of U.S. militarism. But that was just part of the Witness idea. Gail Phares's proposal for a perpetual, rotating presence of U.S. citizens to go to Nicaragua and come back to tell what they had seen and heard was the other half. Over the next seven years nearly four thousand people traveled to Nicaraguan war zones as part of what became the biggest exchange of church people between the United States and Latin America since the Catholic church launched the Papal Volunteers program in the 1960s.

The first short-term delegation arrived on December 2, 1983, the third anniversary of the murder of the four U.S. churchwomen in El Salvador and the beginning of Advent. They had left Washington, D.C., after an emotional commissioning service at which family and community members bid farewell to their loved ones and prayed for God's blessing upon them.

Vincent Harding, a veteran in the black freedom struggle, referred to the delegation as joining the "cloud of witnesses" that the apostle Paul refers to in Hebrews 12. Harding sounded a theme of faithful defiance. "The message," he said, "to the people of Nicaragua, is that there are men and women of love and compassion who refuse to give consent to our government's intervention. Regardless of what our government does, we are filled with the spirit of another authority and we will act on that authority as long as we are able."

The Washington service marked Witness for Peace's debut in the national media. Dennis Marker and Sojourners carefully cultivated an image counterposing the mainstream background of the participants with the risky nature of what they were doing. "These were U.S. Christians going into a war zone—ordinary people motivated by conscience to do a radical thing," said Marker. "That's the image we wanted to get across."

Ordinary people—extraordinary risk: that is exactly what the media conveyed. *Newsweek* referred to them as "Christian soldiers" in a full-page article. The *Washington Post* said that the "team of Church members will leave tomorrow for Nicaragua's war-torn northern province where they plan to form a 'human shield' along the border. They hope their presence in the area will discourage attacks by U.S.-backed counterrevolutionaries."

The initial press release, controversial within the steering committee because of the emphasis on interposition, read as follows:

> The aim of the witness is to provide . . . a 'protective shield' between the Nicaraguan people and the U.S.-sponsored contras. . . . The group hopes that the constant presence of

North American church people in the war zone will hamper
the operations of the contras.*

It was the clearest statement before or since of Witness as a
shield. It was also widely successful and drew the media like flies to
honey. An NBC camera crew made the whole trip with the delegation,
and at one point three TV crews were covering their time in Jalapa.
Most of the coverage focused on the risk and the hope of preventing
attacks.

Some Witnesses resented the implication that instead of
"standing with" the Nicaraguan people they were standing between
them and the attacking contras. "That phrase 'shield of love' drove
me right up the wall," recalls John Collins. "We would be just silly if
we didn't recognize that the real shield for the Nicaraguan people was
the Nicaraguan army. The army had strengthened its position in Jalapa, and no one could seriously assert that attacks had dropped off
due to the visits of delegations or the presence of a few long-termers."

To some, the idea of standing between Nicaraguans and the contras smacked of paternalism and superiority, precisely the attitudes
that had justified so many instances of U.S. government and corpo-
rate intervention in Latin America. Douglas Schirch, a Mennonite
biochemist who came to work on the long-term team, was attracted
to Witness because of the shield idea but later rejected the idea as
"condescending, first world-ish." "Anything that is done has to be
done with the Nicaraguans, not for them," was his conclusion.

Others, including the first Witness staff person, Paddy Lane,
had been drawn to, even "fixated" by, to use her own term, the idea
of a nonviolent presence that would force the war to a halt.

The delegation leader was Phyllis Taylor, a Jewish nurse with
strong ties to the Quakers. She and her husband Dick had involved

*Joyce Hollyday, who wrote the press release, took the term "shield" from a
funding proposal written by Jim McLeod. On a November 27 conference call, Bob
Bonthius challenged the use of the term, arguing that the concept had been to
"stand with" the Nicaraguan people, not in front of them, and that the press
release had not been approved by the full committee. As it happened, Yvonne
Dilling was to have run the draft by the committee but had taken ill and so was
unable to make the needed calls. Hollyday, working along with Dennis Marker
under deadline pressure, was in search of "an easily assimilated image." By the
time Bonthius raised his objection, the release was already out and had really
grabbed the attention of the press. So the shield of love idea got off the ground in
part by accident. Had the steering committee's process been followed to a T, the
resulting NBC and *Newsweek* coverage that was so crucial to the launching of
Witness might never have happened.

themselves in radical acts of civil disobedience since their first date in 1962. They first visited Central America in 1967, at the height of the bloody counterinsurgency war in Guatemala. In the '70s, their home became a sanctuary for Chilean refugees.

Taylor's life had been dominated by a question about the Holocaust and passivity. "How could I avoid," she asked herself, "being a 'good German'?" Going to Nicaragua scared her but the choice was simple. "Good people in the '30s and '40s," she believes, "should have been on the railroad tracks. . . . For me [Witness] was the train tracks in Germany . . . we were a peace shield, [trying] in some way by our presence to protect people."

Joyce Hollyday and Jim Wallis also felt they were on a mission to save lives. "We had been going around asking people all over the country, in person and through the magazine, to take this step, to go to the border, and we felt that we had to be first in line." Hollyday and Wallis had been to Nicaragua the previous year and established strong ties with CEPAD.

"Dick Taylor came to me after the July trip," remembers Wallis. "The more he talked, the more I felt it stir things in my own heart. As crazy as that sounded," says Wallis, "it was simply to save lives in response to the cries of these [Nicaraguan] people. Faith and risk were at the heart of it."

In Hollyday's words, "We wanted to make it clear to the U.S. government that in order to kill Nicaraguans they would have to come through us."

Bob Simpson, a retired businessman and long-time activist from Philadelphia, and David Gracie, a chaplain from Temple University, each dropped what they were doing to make the trip. Mary Dutcher, a Catholic Worker and lawyer from St. Louis, came along and ended up spending most of the next six years in Nicaragua. Anita Bender, a Mennonite student from Philadelphia who had heard Henri Nouwen speak about the July vigil, was the youngest in the group. She had spent ten months in Nicaragua the previous year.

Four veterans of the July vigil made the return trip: Sister Kathleen Breen of Manhasset, New York, a minister to Spanish-speaking prisoners; Grace Gyori; Father Bill Brisotti, a Catholic priest from Long Island; and CALC member Hogan Yancey, a Presbyterian minister from Tennessee. Art Schmidt, a professor of Latin American studies at Temple, Tom Butler, a twenty-nine-year-old Southern Baptist seminary graduate, and Shirley Dodson, another seminary graduate, rounded out the crew.

When the group got to Ocotal, they found the road to Jalapa closed and the contras ten miles out of town. With the leaders of Catholic base communities and the Maryknoll sisters, they organized a procession through three neighborhoods. An NBC crew broadcast the procession live to the "Today" show from Ocotal.

In the streets of Ocotal they found what Phyllis Taylor called "an amazing mix of war and normalcy." "During our procession," she wrote, "we passed an open movie theater, a bingo game in a church, and people in a restaurant—[I] came away feeling how life goes on on the surface but wondering what [the war] is really doing to people deep down."

The next day, with the road still closed and fighting audible up ahead, the group grew more and more anxious. They wanted to be closer to what was happening. The local authorities were firm—the only way they could go up the road was in a military vehicle.

The Witnesses were in a quandary. They had come to be a non-violent witness. The war was going on right under their noses but they couldn't get to it. Some argued that under no circumstances could they accept a ride with the military. Others felt that to stay in Ocotal would be tantamount to failure.

Mary Dutcher felt particularly strongly that nonviolence meant, among other things, absolutely no armed accompaniment. To travel with a Nicaraguan army escort would send the wrong signal to the contras and to the civilian population and would make a mockery of the project's proclaimed goal of sharing the risk. The group agreed to hold off until they could manage the trip in their own unarmed bus. Still the army sent a patrol ahead to scout the road. This collision between theory and practice surfaced again a few days later when the bus driver reflexively stopped on the way to Teotecacinte to pick up five hitchhiking soldiers, to the consternation of some of the Witnesses.

They did make it to Jalapa at last on December 7 and inaugurated their stay with a press conference that filled the tiny living room of the house where the long-term volunteers were living with reporters, equipment, and curious townspeople. This put a quick end to the era of the low profile for the long-term Witnesses.

"A WAR AGAINST THE CHILDREN"

The next day the delegation visited La Estancia, a community of war refugees that had swollen in recent months from 80 to 400 people. The people, just getting on their feet after suffering attacks, kidnappings, and relocation, gave them a huge welcome. They prayed together at a mass celebrating Purisima, the feast of the Immaculate Conception, the most raucous holy day of the year. Women, children, and soldiers with rifles slung over their backs all joined to celebrate the Eucharist.

Of the 400 people who lived in the tiny settlement, 230 were children. The few family-age men were all in the fields or out on patrol. None of the children had the bloated bellies caused by malnutrition so common in rural Central America. The innocent, deep brown eyes in the photos taken by this delegation made one simple point that somehow escaped the U.S. media—this was a war against the children.

Even a dedicated pacifist like Phyllis Taylor wrote in her journal that night that "it is so clear that the arming of Nicaragua is for their protection. The U.S. is like the gun on the back of the 13-year-old, weighing him down, keeping him from getting where he needs to go."

The short-term delegation experience has been described by many participants as a time of "falling in love" with Nicaragua. They fell in love with the graciousness of the Nicaraguan people, whose everyday lives seemed to be acts of heroism. Dan Anderson described a day one delegation spent picking coffee as "an experience of opening [ourselves] to the beauty of Nicaragua, of Escambray, and the love and charm of the 'Nicas' amidst the realities of violence which they live."

Community leaders, young and articulate, captivated their guests with vivid testimonies of a faith that led them into the struggle against the dictatorship and now motivated them to promote social programs and defend the revolution. There was a natural inclination among the type of people drawn to Witness, many of them on their own search for a simpler life-style and upset by the consumerism of U.S. society, to appreciate, and at times to idealize, the back-to-basics way of life lived by poor Nicaraguans.

Denis Leder, a Jesuit who traveled on one of the earliest delegations, wrote in his diary:

> I met a people whose warmth is disarming, and whose power to forgive exceeds the normally expected. I found a young and struggling nation with great lengths to go in developing programs for health care, and literacy, as well as a shared economy, but who have experienced a beginning in these areas, perhaps for the first time in their history. I found an

idealism that gives arms to the people for the protection of their land, and honors the parents of the dead as Mothers of Heroes and Martyrs.

The delegates also fell in love with one another. At least two couples met on Witness delegations and later married. Two couples actually held their wedding ceremonies in Nicaragua—one in a resettlement community, the other at the Managua airport.

Most delegations, through the sharing of their feelings and intense experiences, become a tightly knit group. The training sessions were designed to promote this sense of community. One delegate, Maria Judge of Somerville, Massachusetts, described it this way: "By the end of the first night I really liked the twenty people I had just met. By the end of the second night, I felt I could trust them with my life."

In fact, group dynamics were as important as the contact with Nicaragua as far as motivating witnesses to keep on working.

John McCormally, a reporter from Iowa, regarded the group he traveled with in May 1984 this way: "What a rollicking, robust, good-humored, ready-for-anything bunch they were. And how remarkable I find it that we've been able to share our feelings as freely as our canteens of boiled water—and become even closer friends."[*]

Back in Jalapa, they joined the long-termers in their nightly vigil in the plaza. One night a fourteen-year-old named Isac spoke out in his squeaky boy's voice and asked the group to set up an exchange of children to promote peace. "Ask Reagan," he implored, "to trade in the eagle of war for the dove of peace, and to convert the arms into food for our people." He was just one in what seemed an endless stream of enthusiastic, articulate young people with a simple message—we want to live in peace.

Isac's message did not carry to the White House. That same day President Reagan signed legislation authorizing $24 million in aid to the contras. Simultaneously, the CIA was going ahead with "Operation Elephant Herd," a joint Agency/Pentagon project to circumvent Congress by declaring war materiel left in Honduras as surplus and then turning it over to the contras.

EL COCO: STAND BY ME

Sixty-nine-year-old Aciscia Mattei Polanco was pinned down by heavy gunfire. As she lay on the dirt floor of her home, she helplessly

*John McCormally, "Witness for Peace: John McCormally's Journey to the Nicaraguan War Zones," in The Hutchinson News, June 20, 1984.

watched as her twelve-year-old granddaughter bled to death of a bullet wound. When a mortar shell hit the house, killing another, still younger, granddaughter, and breaking the old woman's arm, she gathered an infant in her good arm and fled into the hills. Her husband, Julian Ramirez, stayed behind and was killed in the attack, and a third granddaughter, Maria Santos, sixteen, was raped and then shot with a pistol stuck in her mouth.*

It was December 19, 1983, when the contras attacked El Coco, a refugee resettlement community, killing fourteen people. The second Witness for Peace short-term delegation was in Jalapa, and villagers asked them to accompany the survivors to a protest at the U.S. Embassy in Managua. In just a few hours half the group was on its way. The remainder continued the Jalapa vigil.

Those who went to accompany the survivors found blank faces on women who had just buried their husbands and their children. Jean Walsh, who along with Betsy Crites had organized the delegation, wrote later, "I have never seen people look so traumatized. Two days before these people had been living their lives as usual. Their husbands and children were alive. Now their lives consisted of nothing more than the clothes on their backs."

Over the course of the next day and night the women told them their stories of months of devastating attacks. For Julie Knop, another short-term delegate, it was all the more heartbreaking. "We could see," she said, "the benefits that the government was bringing to the people, and see how that was being destroyed by the United States." The injustice of that situation so moved her that Knop decided to spend the next two years in Nicaragua building houses with Habitat for Humanity and then joined the Witness long-term team for two years.

The delegation went with the mothers not to protect but simply to accompany them. The word accompaniment gradually crept into the Witness vocabulary and self-definition. North Americans typically go to Latin America with the idea that they have to do something concrete to justify their presence. But the concept and the practice of accompanying the people, simply being at their side, apart from whatever concrete assistance or political support might be marshaled, distinguished Witness from other organizations working in solidarity and development and in defense of the Nicaraguan people.

*David Sweet, *Bitter Witness* (Santa Cruz, Calif.: WFP Documentation Project, 1984).

It harks back to the moment when Jeff Boyer tore himself away from the woman at El Porvenir, telling her to take care but wanting more than anything to simply remain with her. The question was not whether or not he could do any good there. The impulse was simply to be there. The covenant committed Witness to undertake effective political action but also to do much more. It committed them to stand with, to accompany, and to listen to the Nicaraguans.

Nicaraguans understood intuitively and appreciated these gestures. While many North American activists both within Witness and outside protested that they should "do something," most Nicaraguans attached great importance to the simple fact that people came to "accompany" them. This was natural in a society where doing things alone is rare. In a Nicaraguan family, it is common for someone to take off from work just to go along with a family member to the doctor or to run errands. No one ever spends the night alone in a hospital, and routine tasks like going to the market are usually group expeditions. Nicaraguans don't like feeling lonely. You never let anyone spend a night in a house alone. Wakes last all night long, and people would never consider leaving the body of a loved one alone before burial.

When asked what Witness meant to them, years later the most common answer among Jalapans who remembered their international visitors was "It made us feel like we weren't alone." In hundreds of conversations with Nicaraguans touched by Witness for Peace, they most frequently came back to the mere fact that people cared enough to visit them, to sacrifice their own comfort and perhaps their safety to stay with poor people in the midst of hard times. Secondarily they mentioned the importance of getting the truth back to the United States so that the war would end. The idea of Witness being a shield was a distant third.

Witnesses accompanied the Nicaraguans in times of celebration and joy as well as trauma, in work, and in worship. While Jean Walsh and part of the delegation was in Managua with the women, Betsy Crites and the rest of the group harvested rice and beans in a field near Jalapa, within earshot of a gun battle.

Julie Garner of Seattle remembers squatting in a bean field, sweat streaming down her forehead, when a campesino next to her asked, "Do you hear that helicopter? It's a contra helicopter coming from Honduras."

Seeing no place to take cover, she asked excitedly, "What shall we do?"

He looked surprised and answered calmly, "Keep picking beans." Later that day they attended the wakes of two boys, thirteen and fifteen years old, killed in the fighting.

Julie Knop remembers standing at the U.S. Embassy in silent vigil with the women and children of El Coco. At one point they walked up to the castlelike steel gates and laid blood-stained clothing and spent shells on the pavement. The letters *U.S.* and *NATO* were visible on the shells.

After the trip to Managua, the delegation was reunited in Jalapa, spending three more days there before returning to Managua on Christmas Day. Sharon Hostetler, recently brought on to help run the program from Managua, was with them. The long-termers stayed in Jalapa and enjoyed a turkey dinner at Reina's diner, which was becoming their regular place to eat. That night, Rose Dalle Tezze described the sumptuous dinner and partylike atmosphere in the team's log book, then wrote "Merry Xmas," followed by "P.S.—funeral for a militia man in A.M.—he was killed in a battle near Ocotal." The Witnesses themselves were already becoming one more part of that strange mixture of war and normalcy.

PERMANENT PRESENCE

A delegation from St. Louis came on New Year's Eve and spent a week in Jalapa. The next group, organized by Carl Kline, a campus minister from Brookings, South Dakota, arrived in early January accompanied by two reporters from the *Rapid City Journal*. They drove to Jalapa just hours before a jeep was destroyed by a land mine on the same road. While they vigiled in Jalapa, a Sandinista border patrol shot down a U.S. helicopter in Nicaraguan airspace, killing the pilot, U.S. Army Chief Warrant Officer Jeffrey Schwab. Schwab was the first known U.S. casualty in the war. The incident renewed tensions and fear that the U.S. would intervene directly, on the pretext of coming to the aid of Honduras in a Nicaragua-Honduras war.

A group from New York organized by Bill Webber quickly followed and spent a day picking coffee near the border post at Las Manos. That night they learned that two young men had been kidnapped from the same hill where they were working that afternoon. Like every delegation, they sought to find some outlet for creative nonviolent action. The New York group held a blood drive outside the U.S. Embassy in Managua, donating their blood to save Nicaraguans wounded by U.S. bullets.

They were followed by a Chicago group that spent five days in Ocotal. There they heard from Alfonso Desalles, a leader of the base communities and the local Sandinista Defense Communities. His message was simple: "Please don't send your sons down here to attack us." In later years, the rotation of U.S. citizens in and out of Nicaraguan communities became routine, as three or four delegations came and went each month. "Don Alfonso," as Desalles was known to everyone, described the visits of delegations from all over the United States as "sustenance much greater than the kind that fills the stomach. These people understand us."

Don Alfonso told Witness that he would like everyone in the United States to come visit Ocotal. But in 1983, each person who signed up was regarded as something of a miracle. Jim Wallis, when he began his evangelizing tour for Witness in late autumn, wondered if there were twenty, maybe fifty, or perhaps a hundred people willing to put themselves on the line in a war zone. By the end of January 1984, the long-term team had grown to six, and people were lining up all around the United States to be part of the short-term delegations. They wanted to come because, as Frank Dorman of Harvard Divinity School, a long-time opponent of the war, put it, "We're beyond the hand-wringing stage and we're willing to put our bodies on the line."

Betsy Crites, who had just completed a master's program in public health when Gail Phares asked her to organize the second delegation, set up an office in her home in Durham, North Carolina, and began organizing more delegations from across the country. Josefina Teriyakan, a history professor at North Carolina State University who had made the July trip, took time off to work on recruiting, screening, and training long-termers.

Enduring changes were taking place in the dozens of people who were coming face to face with Nicaragua at war. Each delegation, as well as the long-term volunteers, prayed and reflected on what they saw and felt in the light of their many faiths. That process had consequences going beyond Nicaragua. "Anyone," said Jean Walsh, "who comes on a delegation and sees what U.S. policies are doing here in Nicaragua, can't go back without questioning everything we were ever taught in the United States. The experience brought [us] face to face with the mirror image of what our government was doing. It challenged us, not just about Nicaragua but about everything we are as North Americans."

Peter Olson, a delightful and energetic dancer and musician, was studying Spanish in Esteli in preparation for joining the long-term team. He went along that day with the mothers of El Coco. He wrote a long poem that night. As he readied his mat to sleep on the floor in Managua, he held off exhaustion a moment more to write in his diary. He concluded with a question that all of Witness for Peace was asking itself: "What do I have to do to realize that the eighteen-day-old baby and Maria Santos [killed in the attack] are my brother and sister?"

Such was the unpredictable power of the face-to-face contact between people of conscience and the victims of oppression. Peggy Cohee, a young theology student from New England, wrote after two weeks with one of the early delegations:

> The people of Jalapa . . . have ripped me open. I feel so vulnerable and yet empowered somehow, to return to the U.S. and let these people speak through me. When I left Massachusetts I wished for eyes and ears ten times larger than my own. Returning I wish for a voice that can reflect the voices of all those who have confided in me with the hope that I might change their fate. Their hope is so large—I feel afraid, yet it is a fear that does not paralyze, but charges.

The challenge of Witness had just begun.

5

COMING HOME

What are you going to do, when you get home, to save our lives?

—Gloria, a day-care nurse in Ocotal,
speaking to a delegation from Chicago,
in January 1984

In a matter of months there were hundreds of Peggy Cohees giving voice to the simple, profound, unassuming but vital testimony of the Nicaraguan people they had come to know and love. Their energies and their commitment were like leaven in the bread of a growing movement.

Like an invasion in reverse, in Louisville, Albuquerque, Syracuse, Chicago, and Boston they were barely off the plane before they were in front of the TV lights telling what they had seen. In St. Louis, Des Moines, and Dallas, Witnesses deployed themselves in the pulpits of their own and neighboring churches and preached their good news of the hope they had seen in Nicaragua and the tragedy of the contra war that threatened to extinguish it.

The U.S. people were waking up to the fact that there was a war going on in Central America and that their government was involved, but there was still tremendous confusion about the issues and which side we were on. The Witnesses took to the air, speaking on talk shows and news programs. They went to the halls of power, sometimes politely, sometimes angrily, firmly challenging their elected representatives to stand up against the war policy.

Going to Nicaragua was a Pentecost experience, a realization that fear must give way to action. Having conquered language and cultural barriers to communicate with Nicaraguan campesinos, people who had never written a letter to the editor were speaking eloquently before TV cameras. Having conquered their fear of contra bullets, people who had never spoken at school board meetings found themselves toe to toe with congressmen in front of hundreds—and holding their ground. In places where no one had ever heard a word about Nicaragua, returnees from the front forced the issue into public debate.

Standing alongside Nicaraguans whose lives were on the line every day gave them strength and conviction. The memory of days and nights shared with families in the war zones stuck with them. For months after their return, Witnesses gave talks and showed their slide shows at Sunday Schools, Wednesday night church suppers, Kiwanis clubs, and civics classes. They became the local experts consulted by their hometown papers and the focus of conversation at family gatherings and parties. They challenged their pastors and rabbis to speak out and their congregations to act. Mostly they told the stories of the Nicaraguan people who had shared so much with them, and they invited their friends to join in trying to save those people's lives.

Virtually every returnee visited his or her congressional representative and gave interviews to the local media. To command such attention in the days before Oliver North made Nicaragua a household word was no small feat. It took more than words. In March 1984, Vermonters, including Witness for Peace members, occupied the offices of Senator Robert Stafford, a Republican favoring the contras, and turned it into a peace center. The occupation lasted until police arrived and carted forty-four people off to jail.

A song often sung at church services in Nicaragua echoed in the hearts of returning Witnesses:

> I have to shout, I have to speak,
>   Woe to me if I do not;
> How can I not speak of you,
>   How can I not speak—
>   if your voice is burning inside me?

Nicaragua burned in their hearts for a long time to come. Fran Nye of Vermont wrote upon her return in early 1984: "After experiencing the Nicaraguan revolution I will not be the same again. It was the fullest, most complicated, exhilarating, and heartrending time of my 60 years of living."

They took their message directly to the public. Reverend Betsy

Sowers, an airline flight attendant turned denominational executive for the American Baptist Church in Massachusetts, met with her representatives, wrote and called her senators twice, gave five media interviews, wrote three articles, and spoke at seventeen churches and church-sponsored forums in the first six weeks after her trip in February 1984. Her message was simple: "It's violence that my tax dollars are paying for."

They brought the war to their hometown media. Richard Deats and Jack Copas, two ministers from Rockland County in New York, took a fragment from a bazooka they had found near the border to their local newspaper to show them the "Made in USA" markings on it.

They challenged their faith communities. Four Nebraskans who returned from Nicaragua in March 1984 mailed a letter to 150 pastors pleading for an end to business as usual while Central Americans were dying. Among the signers was Ruth Thone, a writer and long-time activist married to former Republican Governor Charles Thone, the first governor to endorse Ronald Reagan for President in 1980.

Capital letters across the top of the page spelled out the theme: PLEASE, NO ORDINARY EASTER SERMON.

> Palm and Easter Sundays have been changed for us because of our experiences during . . . the past two weeks [in Nicaragua]. . . .
>
> We invite the Pastors of Lincoln to call us to repentance for the violence and insensitivity of our nation and speak with the passion of God. . . . We share from . . . our own spiritual journeys . . . in the hope that you will openly challenge the American policies which are bringing such sufferings to people. As prophets of old, would you continue to speak boldly and lead your congregation in repentance to direct action?

Each of the four shared some memories of their trip in the letter, and recalled the challenging words of a base community leader:

> "Aren't there any Christians left in America?
> "Then why are they not stopping this evil?"
> We have no answer. But we are determined to "Stop It."
> . . . Will you join with us and lead us by arousing your congregation to STOP IT this Palm and Easter Sunday?

The people going to Nicaragua with Witness for Peace were good copy for local papers. Try as some might to dismiss them as "vaguely reminiscent of the '60s," the photos of upstanding citizens who made up the Witness contingent spoke louder than the slanders spoken against them.

Dan Anderson may have been just one more gringo in Nicaragua, but in Rapid City, South Dakota, he was seen as a hometown boy in the middle of a war—big news. Fran Truitt taking a delegation to Nicaragua might not be enough to get Dan Rather out of bed, but in Ellsworth, Maine, it might be the biggest news since last year's Thanksgiving dinner at the Methodist church.

Most Witnesses found their local press intensely curious about their mission. Delegations collected thick scrapbooks of articles about their preparation, their time in Nicaragua, and activities upon their return. They were given phenomenal amounts of local press coverage. Each time a delegation went to Nicaragua they kept the issue alive in places where Latin America was seldom, if ever, covered.

Delegates were interviewed on the radio before they went, filmed by news crews as they boarded planes, sometimes interviewed live from Nicaragua, and were often given both news coverage and a chance to write editorial columns when they came home. Most returnees found that having gone and seen for themselves, at some risk and sacrifice, gave them a credibility that was hard to refute.

Once they made themselves known to the local reporters and editors, a local Witness for Peace person could usually count on hearing from his or her local paper, thanks to Ronald Reagan, whose dogged insistence on promoting the contra cause kept Nicaragua stories on the wire and on network news. Rather than run just a wire story, editors sought a local reaction from someone who had been there and in so doing opened up space for local opponents of the policy to voice their views.

Armed with first-hand reports from the countryside, Witnesses learned how to dialogue with editors, prepare press releases, orchestrate letters to the editor, and conduct radio call-in campaigns. Some took pride in making nuisances of themselves. A reporter from the *Philadelphia Inquirer*, upon meeting a Witness for Peace volunteer in Nicaragua, recoiled and said, "So—you're the people always calling up my editor and complaining every time I write something they don't like about Nicaragua."

Tens of thousands of letters to the editor ran in the most widely read section of daily and weekly newspapers. One returned Witness, Bob Barns of Nevada City, California, wrote three letters to the *Grass*

Valley Union after he came home from a two-week delegation in October 1984.

All three letters were printed. Angry missives appeared in response, followed by rebuttals from Barns. In the course of nine months he filled the column with thirteen letters and generated twenty in response—thirteen opposing him and seven coming to his defense.

At one point a reader wrote to complain that Bob Barns was getting too much space. "I have begun to wonder if he has been hired as a regular *columnist*."*

The editor ran the complaining letter under the headline "Hired as Regular *Communist*." The next day the editor printed the following correction:

> A headline on a letter from Jim Higgins to the editor of the *Union*, published Tuesday on the editorial page, was incorrect and should have read: "Hired as regular columnist." The *Union* regrets the error.

The following week, after another exchange of letters, the editor of the *Union* tried to call a truce. She wrote to Barns asking if he could be more selective and limit the number of letters he wrote. "I believe," she wrote, "the letter-writing situation may be getting out of hand. . . . The letters to the editor are intended to give our readers an opportunity and space to voice their opinions. . . . not for an ongoing debate between readers."

Her pleas were to no avail, and the letters continued to pour into the *Grass Valley Union*.

Returned Witnesses garnered press and air time by making the national controversy over contra aid into a local story as they held meetings, vigils, prayer services, and other events aimed at changing the votes of pro-contra legislators. Instead of being an issue in far away Central America or Washington, it became a hometown issue. Activists turned legislators' town meetings into debates on Central America. At one such town meeting, in Syracuse, New York, in 1985, the first four questioners called on by Republican George Wortley asked him about Central America.

A few delegations went even further and took their local reporters with them to Nicaragua. Some of the most human and in-depth reporting on Nicaragua came from journalists traveling with Witness

---

*The *Grass Valley Union*, July 2, 1985. Letter by Jim Higgins.

for Peace from small and mid-sized newspapers. The *Akron Beacon Journal* sent a reporter on the April 1984 delegation. A film crew traveled with the Vermont delegation in February 1984 and produced the video "American Journey." The *Rapid City Journal*, which sent a reporter and photographer to cover the January 1984 South Dakota delegation, did a sensitive, insightful, seven-part series combining the delegation experience with essays on political and social life and profiles of everyday people in the city and countryside.

John McCormally, a writer for the Harris newspapers in Kansas and former editor of the *Hawk Eye* (circulation twenty thousand) in Burlington, Iowa, visited Jalapa and Ocotal in May 1984 with the first Iowa delegation. When he returned, he wrote some of the best first-person articles ever dedicated to Nicaragua and to Witness for Peace.

The credibility and effectiveness of Witness for Peace hinged on these ordinary citizens, respected members of their communities. They were ordinary people being called to do extraordinary things. Beth Stock, a twenty-six-year-old social worker and a Catholic, was one of them. "I really don't know what to be afraid of," she said before her trip to Ocotal in April 1984. "I've never even heard a gun go off in my life."

They were ordinary people in some ways, but in the society of their day, their very willingness to stand up and be counted made them unusual.

They were swimming against a powerful tide. It was "morning in America." Ronald Reagan was conducting the most thorough revision of the nation's self-definition since the New Deal. America's military might was back, as the bullying of tiny Grenada made clear. The film *Rambo* was breaking box office records as effortlessly as its main character mowed down scores of Asians who stood in his path to glory. Televangelists in tandem with the White House preached the good news of prosperity and twentieth-century manifest destiny. "America" put on its white hat and pointed the finger at the "Evil Empire." A theology of the greater good—and constant celluloid reminders, like *Red Dawn* and *Amerika*, of a hell that awaited if we dropped our guard—propelled a race to build weapons and a willingness to use them.

It was also the season of *The Big Chill* with its message of despair and its implied invitation to activists to come in from the cold, forsake the idealism of youth, and recognize that the '60s are over. The currency of the '80s was not struggle but comfort. People who insisted on challenging the status quo were in danger of obsolescence.

In this climate the options posed by the dominant culture were apathy or acquiescent self-congratulation. It took a strong measure of faith even to raise a question about U.S. government policy. To actually travel into the heart of a country defined as "enemy" was risky, not just because of the dangers of a war zone but because the fires of self-righteousness were burning so hotly at home, and people got angry when Witnesses waved in front of them evidence that all was not well in the soul of this newly proud "America."

Miraculously, the voice of the Central American poor was heard. Thousands of Witnesses rejected the emphasis on the decade's most odious idiom—the bottom line—and opted not just to go to Nicaragua but, in most cases, to pay their own way and to risk their lives and their reputations. At least two ministers, Baptist James Gamble of Texas, and Lutheran Glenn Remer Thamert of New Mexico, were fired for going to Nicaragua. Many more were harassed, received threatening phone calls, and had their patriotism challenged in public.

What kind of people were they? They tended to be people for whom faith is not so much an answer but a decision to live the question, people willing to struggle with ethical and moral implications of issues, people willing to look beyond their own situation to a broader world picture, people willing to make connections and to speak out, even if that means going against the grain. Long-term volunteer Joe Gorin explained why he chose to go to Nicaragua: "Maybe it's that I . . . am allergic to exploitation and domination."

While many in the rank and file were newcomers to social and political action, the leaders of Witness were people with decades of experience in social action. They came from many streams of the movement for social justice: the civil rights and women's movements, work to end apartheid, protests against the Vietnam war, urban ministry. Contrary to popular stereotyping, many activists were not scratching their heads wondering where the '60s went wrong but were continuing a struggle that predated Moses and would go on till kingdom come.

Leaders of social movements have been compared to tornadoes, huge tumultuous churning cones of energy drawing everything in their path toward them, altering setting and composition, and leaving a revised landscape in their path. Witness for Peace had no single charismatic leader, no tornado, but instead a pack of dust demons.

The combined impact of so many people spinning and churning and moving tiny bits of earth began to make a difference over time.

The impact of these mini-tornadoes was tough to predict and even tougher to coordinate.

GETTING ORGANIZED

Witness's great strength was the burning moral outrage of its returnees. Its most frustrating weakness was an inability to focus those energies. From the latter part of 1983 through 1985, Witness sent more than a thousand people off into the most important experience of their life, but it had no national organization or strategy to involve them in upon their return.

Stateside organizing went on, but support from the national and regional organizations was spotty. The lion's share of the steering committee's efforts in 1984 and 1985 focused on setting up the Nicaragua portion of the Witness. In fact, it would be an exaggeration to call Witness for Peace in the United States a "movement" before 1985.

After the Philadelphia conference in October 1983, the steering committee did not meet again in person until February 1985, in Santa Cruz. Monthly meetings of the full committee and more frequent meetings of subcommittees were held on the telephone. Membership on the national steering committee was serious business. The term lasted three years, and the job required a commitment to dedicate substantial time, energy, and resources. It was a working body, and anyone who didn't put in their time was asked to leave. A number of members were full-time volunteers.

While Witness was getting organized, other Central America organizations, both religious and secular, gladly put the returned Witnesses to work. A Central America movement had been growing for years before Witness for Peace.

The Central America Resource Center in Texas listed more than five hundred U.S. groups dealing with Central America in 1985 and more than twice as many two years later. These groups maintained audiovisual resources, speakers' bureaus, telephone trees, and information hotlines; held regular vigils and leafletting; visited editorial boards of newspapers; set up tables on street corners and at community events; and conducted teach-ins, sit-ins, and campaigns of civil disobedience.

What Witness did in its early years was energize people, providing a ready supply of activists for other organizations concerned with Central America. It also redirected toward Nicaragua the energies of many groups that had been focused on El Salvador. Returnees sometimes formed their own Witness chapters, but more typically they worked with an existing local group. In North Carolina it was CITCA; in Nebraska, Nebraskans for Peace. In northern California, the Resource Center for Nonviolence was the focus. In Texas and Oklahoma the American Friends Service Committee (AFSC) played a major role, as it did in New England. In St. Louis the Catholic Worker community became the focus of Witness for Peace activity; in Cincinnati the New Jerusalem Community offered its support. Activists in the Midwest came to rely on the Chicago Religious Task Force and Detroit's MICAH (Michigan Interfaith Task Force on Central American Human Rights).

Washington-based organizations like the Washington Office on Latin America, the Coalition for a New Foreign and Military Policy, and the public policy offices of religious denominations provided information on legislative developments. As the war escalated, dozens more national organizations formed or dedicated their ongoing efforts to the Central America struggle.

The decentralization of Witness, which some participants advocated and others accepted reluctantly, created its share of confusion. Returned Witnesses received mail from Santa Cruz, from Durham, from Washington, D.C., and in some cases from regional offices as well. In addition, national Witness for Peace eventually opened a development office in Syracuse, New York, mailed its newsletter from Ellsworth, Maine, and later from Berkeley, California, and asked that contributions be sent to 198 Broadway in New York City or to any one of eleven regional offices.

A satellite photo of Witness for Peace in the United States in 1984 would probably have shown something resembling what TV meteorologists refer to as "scattered storm activity." The number of local Witness groups grew from twenty-seven in November 1983 to ninety in April 1984. Responding to the call of the spirit and the pleas of the Nicaraguans, veteran organizers and social-action novices worked together with every last ounce of energy to expand their base of supporters, to recruit more volunteers for delegations and the long-term team, to gain access to the media, and to protest an endless series of aggressions against Nicaragua.

No one knew how long the war would go on, but already Witness was committed to staying on the border as long as the war continued.

As time passed and it became clear that the struggle would be a long one, the process of recruiting, training, and sending a delegation to Nicaragua became more routine and organizers were able to dedicate more time to the war at home.

A real spirit was moving, a rebel spirit battling the complacency, the materialism, the militarism of the times. In churches and religious communities across the country, small voices were questioning the right of a mighty nation to bully its smaller neighbor, and more people began to listen.

They tugged at the edge of the nation's conscience while powerful forces sought to put conscience to sleep. But individual witness was not enough. Witness for Peace faced a challenge in the United States as daunting as facing the contra threat. Could they organize the necessary political pressure to change the policy? Would the same people who were drawn to such risky witness be capable of and willing to build the type of organization to sustain what was clearly going to be a prolonged struggle? Translating moral outrage into effective political pressure is one of the most difficult areas faced by religious groups. This section examines some of the issues that Witness faced, in one way or another, throughout its life.

EFFECTIVENESS VERSUS FAITHFULNESS

Activist participants promoted organizing for direct political action right from the start; they faced uneasy resistance from those who stressed the primacy of prayer, out of which would grow witness and symbolic action. Some believers from Catholic Worker, evangelical, or charismatic backgrounds insisted that planning actions solely on the basis of immediate impact was inappropriate. They felt that symbolic actions had a great potential to inspire even if the immediate consequences could not be measured, and that to focus only on strategic goals placed the soul of the organization at risk. "God gives the increase," or, as the Nicaraguans would say, "Uno pone, y Dios dispone" (You do your part, and God decides how it turns out).

Radical Christians are easily motivated to symbolic witness, but often ambivalence about power makes organization building and strategic planning tough going. The cloud of witnesses referred to in Hebrews 12, and which Vince Harding referred to at the first commissioning service, was also a cloud of losers by earthly standards. The New Testament is a story in which the good usually come up on the short end of the stick, and their ancestors in Israel did not fare much better. Consciously or not, many Christian groups feel ambivalent about power and about winning. The religious wing of the Central America movement often seemed more comfortable commemorating martyrs like Archbishop Romero than standing with victors like the Sandinistas.

From a very different perspective, long-time leftists like David Sweet wanted Witness to explicitly reject attempts to influence either Congress or the media and to let the message from the border work its way into the hearts of the people and effect change at the grass roots. The results, he agreed, were unpredictable, but the results of traditional political organizing, while predictable, were unsatisfying.

Such attitudes often led to a reluctance to jump into the "messy deal" of politics. As political organizers pointed out, the religious right suffered no such reluctance.

Nothing trains people as well as experience. The difficulty of working with the power structure in the United States on a foreign policy issue was drummed into Witness for Peace by hard experience. From the *Cleveland Plain Dealer* of Tuesday, June 12, 1984:

> WASHINGTON—When a group of Ohioans went to Nicaragua this year they risked their lives in territory contested by U.S.-funded rebels.
>
> When the Ohioans, part of the non-denominational Witness for Peace program, returned to Cleveland they were met by 200 people carrying palm branches and praying for peace.
>
> But when the Ohioans took their story to Capitol Hill yesterday they were seen by only a handful of congressional staff members. One meeting to which 135 staffers were invited was attended by a half dozen.
>
> "Congress seems a much harder nut to crack than the average American," said Doug Van Auken of Cleveland.

Confronting this hard reality convinced many that to be faithful they must learn also to be effective, and it led to some of the most spirit-filled and effective campaigns that Witness conducted.

BASE COMMUNITY OR
POLITICAL ACTION COMMITTEE?

The statement of purpose defined Witness for Peace as an "ever-broadening, prayerful, biblically based community."

Community had several dimensions. Returnees from such an intense, cross-cultural experience in Nicaragua often felt like aliens in their own homes, and they longed for a supportive community to help them make the transition. Many Witnesses found their concepts of faith challenged so thoroughly in Nicaragua that they needed to continue to share prayer and reflection with people who had been through a similar experience.

Others viewed the commitment to community as an opening to deeper analysis and reflection on U.S. society. In the early years, newsletters, papers, and memos discussed the philosophical, moral, and theological implications of the revolution in Nicaragua, the war, and the work of Witness. As time went on and the organization grew, the ethos, particularly at the national level, changed. The size of the organization and the costly telephone communication meant that proposals usually had to consider immediate political gain and cost implications in order to merit consideration. Over time, the importance of community faded, and it became more like an agency committed to social change, modeled in some respects on the social-action offices of mainstream Protestant churches.

Reflection and prayer remained a crucial component for most delegations and the long-term team. The team customarily concluded each day's reflection by mentioning the names of their companions spread throughout the countryside.

Some saw the base Christian communities in Nicaragua as a model for organizational structure. Stuart Taylor outlined this line of thinking in a newsletter: "The example of the Base Communities and their role in the Nicaraguan Revolution has left many North Americans with the conviction that it is not simply the reform of U.S. policy which is our goal but the basic transformation of our social, political, and economic structures."

In 1985, a long-term team for the United States was formed. It was a conscious attempt to emulate the lifestyle of the base communities while carrying out the Witness work of nonviolent direct action and public education. The idea was to have a roving crew of long-termers who would live, pray, and work together and travel the country to support local organizers. Taylor envisioned communities organized to act as "leaven in the bread" and to infuse the stateside work with the same sense of community, sacrifice, and risk taking that had formed such bonds among the long-term team in Nicaragua.

The group, never more than five in number, settled in Denver, where they aided a drive to get the CIA off the Boulder campus of the University of Colorado and organized protests against the Coors corporation, a major private supporter of the contras.

The team, led by Stuart Taylor, had a somewhat romantic image of the base communities. The model was a tough fit for U.S. organizing; in fact the LTT-USA was modeled more on the long-term team in Nicaragua than on the base communities. The base communities were typically formed by poor people struggling for their own rights; the Witness constituency, primarily middle class, was always people supporting the struggle of others. Nicaragua's base communities were following a political movement, the FSLN; the U.S. long-term team was working with no such vanguard to give a broader political significance to their work.

REFORM VERSUS REVOLUTION

Jean Walsh's statement that anyone who had seen Nicaragua could not help but question all their assumptions about U.S. society reflected a widely held sentiment within Witness. Greg Hessel, a long-term volunteer from a Catholic Worker background, expressed it this way. "The problem is not how we think about Nicaragua," he said. "The problem is how we think."

Individuals involved in Witness worked on a variety of issues, and local Witness groups worked in coalitions against apartheid, in support of striking coal miners and the nuclear freeze, and more. There was never a stated consensus on an analysis of structural injustices in U.S. foreign policy or society. During the contra war, national Witness did not have a program to link issues of injustice at home with injustice in the third world abroad. While there was sentiment in favor of taking on other struggles, Witness remained essentially a single-issue organization throughout the 1980s.

Some Witnesses worried that a narrow focus on contra aid would expend energy on seemingly endless legislative battles and exhaust the movement and restrict its vision. Ultimately the more radical but nebulous visions of social change took a back seat to the concrete work of changing U.S. policy toward Nicaragua. Building for the long term, making connections, dreaming and preparing for a new society was important work, but Witness kept its feet firmly on the ground, choosing to accept rather than challenge the nature of the current power structure in the United States. The task orientation of key individuals anxious not to dissipate the enormous power and energy being generated by contact with the Nicaraguan reality ordained that the strategies followed were short term, concrete, and focused on stopping contra aid.

The issue of contra aid, they reasoned, was one in which the middle-class churches could form a core constituency and make a difference. Witness decided they needed to organize people who would never consider going to Nicaragua and would never involve themselves in street protests, but who would write letters and checks. Ordinary Americans who would walk out of church or synagogue if a sermon attacked "U.S. imperialism" listened and responded when the issues were framed as respect for life and international law, and opposition to terrorism and secret wars. People who liked to believe in their country and were willing to concede that it could be wrong on this one count formed the core constituency that Witness tried to reach. Activists young and old organized and preached a more radical line, but the organization stuck to a very simple position: friendship, peace, and justice toward Nicaragua.

It was a practical decision, made with a thousand tiny steps. There was reason to believe that the churches could weigh in heavily on the legislative front. Many congregations had grown used to writing Congress and visiting their legislators through their association with groups like Bread for the World, Network, or Impact. These and similar organizations, which had a larger social agenda but focused their action requests on very specific legislative issues, had brought social issues into services of worship over the past two decades and made discussing them and doing something about them acceptable. It might be argued that the legislative clout carried by such people eventually made the difference when contra military aid was finally defeated by a very slim margin.

"Witness for Peace," says Bob Bonthius, "is as reformist as you can get. That may not be a good thing, but it's about the best thing we [progressive movements] have going for us."

The focus on legislation, effectiveness, and "respectability" had important long-range implications for Witness. It won acceptance and cost a bit of prophetic zeal. Witness gained a spot in the national debate about contra aid but had no chance to challenge the assumptions underlying foreign policy. It gained adherents in the East and lost them in the West. It truncated the nature of the dialogue occurring between U.S. and Nicaraguan people of faith by reducing many issues to a question of how they affected votes on contra aid. As the need to dialogue with and curry favor with legislators became more prominent, Witnesses found that they had to be on top of the legislators' agenda (U.S. national security), which was a world away from the agenda they heard expressed by the Nicaraguan campesinos (peace and life for them and their children).

It also kept Witness primarily within a middle-class constituency and may have been an important reason why Witness "won" the battle against contra aid and the most important reason they "lost" the struggle to change U.S. policy at its core. As it entered the nineties, Witness for Peace began to work more and more with third world communities in the United States.

The more radical members bemoaned the fact that Witness, as it grew, came to focus on short-term goals. Father D'Escoto, while not proposing to change Witness strategy, concurred that the problem went far beyond the contra war. "The question," he said, "is not what is the future of Nicaragua, but where is the United States going, and what is the future of the world with this monstrosity developing in the U.S.? Someone has to stand up for the sake of world peace and for the sake of your very nation itself. You find so many good people in the United States talking about helping to save Nicaragua, and I say, 'My God, please save your own country.' "

But was there ever another realistic option? The Nicaraguan government as well as CEPAD and the other partner agencies were encouraging U.S. groups to work to defeat contra aid as a first priority.

The challenge was to harness the energy without cooling the fire of Witnesses who returned from Nicaragua like burning embers of moral outrage, to convert that outrage into effective political pressure without diluting the message. The future will tell how many Witnesses transfer their insights gained in Nicaragua to other struggles.

MEANS VERSUS ENDS—
THE EXPERIMENT IN NONVIOLENCE

Witness for Peace struggled to develop more effective use of nonviolence. Some believed that the experiment in nonviolence was an end in itself and an important part of the organization's identity. They pushed for ever more risky and visible forms of direct action, in the tradition of King and Gandhi.

Others advocated more traditional forms of political action, which were seen as appropriate to the predominantly middle-class constituency that they hoped to attract. They felt that people who would cringe at throwing blood on the Pentagon wall but who would be glad to write a letter to Congress should still be able to feel comfortable within Witness. No one disputed the value of the letters, but many within Witness felt that it had the potential to be more than one more generator of mail to politicians and editors, to be a moving force at the edge of the resistance movement.

As it happened, Witness held together both nonviolent activists and traditionalists. A synthesis of political strategies began to emerge as the organization started to gel. The May 1984 newsletter gave a hint of the synthesis of organizing styles that Witness was to become:

> WFP is beginning to build on our nonviolent strategy in Nicaragua for nonviolent actions in the U.S. But we are not forgetting the wide range of traditional political actions needed to convince candidates that U.S. foreign policy in Central America is an issue that they cannot ignore. Support for candidates who propose change in U.S. policy, opposition to those who support the present policy, petitions, door-to-door contacts, public debate, media exposure, rallies, demonstrations, local congressional office sit-ins; these are some of the many nonviolent political means available.

The effectiveness of this combination of nonviolent direct action with more traditional political tactics may be one of the lasting lessons of Witness. Many people were arrested or otherwise risked themselves in nonviolent action as a result of Witness, and many nonviolent activists took a second look at the value of traditional reform tactics. This combination was not invented by Witness. Martin Luther King worked relentlessly on behalf of civil rights legislation as he was jailed dozens of times for civil disobedience. The environmental group Greenpeace has used this combination consistently and effectively on issues for a long time.

The movement, like a train, needed both an engine and tracks to get where it wanted to go. The nonviolent direct actions, both in Nicaragua and in the United States, provided the steam and the fire, while the legislative strategies served to assure that the train got somewhere instead of just spinning its wheels and generating smoke.

CITIZENS' HEARINGS— UNCOVERING THE WAR

In May 1984, the newsletter stated the greatest achievement of Witness to date and its greatest challenge all at once: "U.S. policy in Central America has gone public. What will the people do with it?"

As election time approached, there was hope that an end to Reagan's reign would enhance prospects for peace, and fear that a second Reagan administration, unfettered by reelection worries, would invade Nicaragua. If Reagan were to win, positive outcomes in congressional races could limit his ability to carry out his plans. "We have more leverage in the next six months," said the March 1984 newsletter, "than we may have again in the next four years to change U.S. policy toward Nicaragua."

A short-term delegate asked Moravian Bishop John Wilson about the future of Nicaragua. He replied simply by asking, "Who are you going to vote for?"

Though Witness did not play a leadership role in the electoral efforts of the Central America movement, it contributed what it knew best—the firsthand Nicaragua experience of nearly a thousand people. In October, forty-eight Citizens Hearings on Nicaragua were held in thirty states. Five Nicaraguan church workers toured the United States, and David Sweet prepared a book-length report, *Bitter Witness*, on the war. People gathered to hear testimony, watch slides and films, share information, and express their feelings of outrage. Bolstered by a summer in which hundreds of Witnesses traveled to Nicaragua, the network attained wide publicity through the hearings.

Rebecca Gordon, writing from Jalapa in the aftermath of a contra attack on Ocotal, offered these words to participants in the hearings: "I don't know what you can do, but I am asking you: sit in your congressman's office, clog the streets of your city, send a hundred telegrams, talk to a hundred new people. The people here don't want to be burned in their offices by the contra. They don't want to be raped, dismembered, decapitated. They don't want to be bombed. And neither, for that matter, do I."

This kind of testimony made the voice of Witness unique, caused people to sit up and listen, and sowed doubt in the minds of many who wanted to believe in their government. Such efforts helped prevent the development of a solid "patriotic" consensus behind the war effort. The administration was never able to garner a stable majority willing to support the contras or the regional military buildup in Central America.

Even as the Witnesses became more politically sophisticated and organized, it was the powerful elegance, the spirit-filled quality, of their words and gestures that allowed them to touch hearts at the same time they made sure that Congress felt the heat of their passion.

CONTINGENCY PLAN

One goal of the Citizens Hearings was to build the "Contingency Network," a plan of action in case of a U.S. invasion of Nicaragua. This commitment had been foreshadowed by "A Promise of Resistance," adopted at a November 1983 peacemakers retreat at the Kirkridge Center in Pennsylvania. Meeting for prayer and reflection in the aftermath of the Grenada invasion, the authors condemned the invasion and warned that it "raises the real possibility of a similar scenario for Nicaragua."

In the event of an invasion, they committed themselves to "assemble as many North American Christians as we can to join us and go immediately to Nicaragua to stand unarmed as a loving barrier in the path of any attempted invasion, sharing the danger posed to the Nicaraguan people." They also called on U.S. Christians to surround or occupy congressional offices in a nonviolent, prayerful presence until the invasion ended.

The idea of a massive presence in Nicaragua at the time of an invasion was dramatic. It was also wildly impractical and would scarcely have been permitted by the Nicaraguan government in time of full-scale war. No one knew this better than its organizers, who hoped and prayed that the mere threat of such actions would be enough of a deterrent to force the policy planners to take them into account.

Over the coming months, the Contingency Plan was refined through discussions with the Witness Philosophy and Strategy Committee, Nuclear Freeze, the IRTF, Fellowship of Reconciliation, and others. In August, "A Pledge of Resistance,"* was launched with an article in *Sojourners* magazine.

The Contingency Plan, and its later incarnation, the Pledge of Resistance, was signed by over seventy thousand people and attracted national attention. It captured the imagination of people all over the country and provided an outlet for many who fiercely opposed the U.S. policy, wanted to do more than write letters, but could not travel to the war zones themselves. With the founding of Witness for Peace, the religious community had made it clear that by attacking Nicaraguan border villages the Reagan administration risked killing its own citizens. "Now," said Jim Wallis when the Pledge was announced, "if Reagan invades Nicaragua, he's going to have to put thousands of U.S. Christians in jail around the country."

*The full text is printed in the Appendix.

Witness for Peace was part of the original "signal committee" charged with deciding when and what the Pledge signers should be called on to do. Pledge signers were called on many times to commit civil disobedience or to hold other protest activities throughout the years of wrangling over contra aid votes. With the implementation of the Contingency Plan, Witness could rightly claim that the two pillars of its strategy—nonviolent direct action and traditional political action—were in place.

6

THE WAR EXPANDS: WITNESSING FROM COAST TO COAST

Ideally we would wish to be able to assure the Contra that any attack on the Nicaraguan people would also be a simultaneous attack on U.S. citizens.

—Arnold Snyder,
writing to Nicaraguan church partners

By early 1984 the contras had already received upwards of $30 million in legal U.S. aid and untold millions more under the table. They no longer resembled the tiny bands that began to form in 1981 and 1982 nor the scraggly hoodlums under Suicida who laid siege to Jalapa in mid-1983.

The Witnesses saw the results of these cash infusions. Development projects in rural areas were being slowed and stopped by the danger and by the shift of resources from civilian projects to military uses. Government workers, including teachers and nurses, could no longer travel freely in remote areas. The roads were littered with the carcasses of vehicles ambushed and burned. Conscription for all boys over age sixteen, begun in December 1983, was making the government unpopular with farmers who needed their sons to harvest their crops. The economy began the slow and draining process of shifting from reconstruction and development to a wartime footing.

On the Atlantic coast the Miskito people were increasingly being drawn into the conflict. The Miskito conflict, which began as an indigenous claim for long-denied rights, soon became an enormous problem for the Sandinistas both at home and in the United States, where the Reagan administration seized upon it as evidence of Sandinista totalitarianism.

The contras shifted their strategy away from Jalapa. Faced with the impossibility of taking the town, they spread themselves up and down the mountain ranges that led to the Honduran border, and by early 1985, their high-water mark, they had the potential to commit deadly harassing attacks in all provinces save those closest to Managua.

Meanwhile, the long-term team was getting the hang of life in Jalapa. They learned their way around the market, learned not to throw toilet paper into the latrine, learned the Nicaraguan custom of pointing with pursed lips instead of hands. They learned the names of the numerous varieties of orchids that grew in the countryside, the taste and smell of a dozen different fruit and cereal drinks, and the pleasing rhythm of northern Nicaraguan campesino conversation.

They learned that everything that went bump in the night did not mean an invasion was under way. Doug Spence, who joined the team in January, tells of his first night under Jalapa's clear skies:

> I was just getting down to sleep, settling into my room, which was just off the street. . . . Just as I fell asleep, I heard a full clip of machine-gun fire go off, right outside my door. I jumped up and ran, thinking "Oh my God, this must be it!"
>
> Of course I really didn't have anywhere to run so I just kind of moved around the house and then ventured into the courtyard, listening the whole time. And since I didn't hear any return fire, I just went back to my room and went to bed. It turns out that it was just a drunken compa [soldier] letting off a little steam.

Jalapa in turn grew accustomed to the Witnesses. Even those with early reservations and fears that the vigils were a cover for the CIA had gotten the word that these gringos were OK. The regular vigils in the plaza and the open-door policy at the Witness house hastened the process of getting acquainted.*

*In almost every town or rural area where they worked, Witnesses, whether they were aware of it or not, had to overcome suspicion that they were either CIA agents, Sandinista spies, or, in some cases, East German military advisers. One pastor in Quilali who later became very friendly with Witness for Peace initially would have nothing to do with them beyond polite chatter. He made a special trip to Managua to speak to the head of his denomination, who knew of Witness and explained the purpose. After that, he accepted them, assisted them in finding lodging, spoke to delegations, and was as helpful as he could be. But as the years went on it became ever more difficult for Witness to avoid being cast as partisan in the Nicaraguan countryside, by virtue of simple things such as where one stayed or with whom you were seen walking down the street.

The children were among the first to greet them. In Nicaragua, however, children grow up very quickly. Isac Gahona, a fourteen-year-old veteran of the war against Somoza became a fixture at the vigils in the park. He took on a crusade to spread the word to the townspeople, becoming the first ambassador for Witness. Next came the mothers of those killed or kidnapped in the war, urged by the parish priest or sisters to share their experiences with visiting delegations.

Not everyone understood what the gringos were all about, or how their work differed from the other foreigners who had come to live in Jalapa, but most townspeople remember the Witness house as a friendly place full of helpful people. They remember being entertained and uplifted by the groups marching through town carrying banners and singing. Saidi Andara, who lived a block away from the Witness house, said years later that she remembers the Witnesses parading around town with banners that said Peace Corps. "It was very beautiful," she adds.

Others remember concrete gestures like the blood donated by three long-termers when the hospital blood bank was dry, or the six milking cows that Moses and Ada Beachy, a Mennonite couple who joined the team in January, brought to La Estancia to provide milk for the children.

The volunteers took on many community tasks—teaching English, carrying late night coffee to residents on guard duty, participating in drills to shelter children in case of attack, pastoral work with the church. In addition, they had the urgent task of documenting what they were seeing and hearing.

"We had to give echo to the voice of those suffering the aggression," said Doug Spence. Communication problems were a nightmare, but they managed to bang out newsletters on an old portable typewriter and send them back with returning short-term delegates for reproducing and distribution stateside, where a growing membership waited eagerly for news from the border.

The shield of love held a venerated place in Witness folklore for years and was an important part of the self-concept of many who participated. Many participants later recalled that the danger was one compelling reason they felt they had to go. In training sessions prior to going to the war zones, all delegation members were encouraged to share their fears with one another. Many took care to write their wills and settle personal and family matters before making the trek.

Very few of them ultimately thought they were there to field bullets. Many did feel and continue to feel that they were a deterrent to contra attacks. Still more saw the large presence of U.S. citizens as forcing policymakers to think twice if they entertained ideas of a U.S. invasion.

The training encouraged delegates to seek ways to practice nonviolence in a public way every day. Often this took the form of vigils in Jalapa. The daily gatherings of yellow-shirted gringos hand in hand with Nicaraguans were tame by comparison with the derring-do of the training exercises, in which they role-played ambushes, kidnappings, and worse. One Nicaraguan observer reportedly said to a friend, "I don't know what they're doing, but they do it every time they come."

STANDING WITH THE PEOPLE

The long-term team was seen by some as a peacemaking force available to confront the contras at a moment's notice. It was also immersed in the spirit of nonviolence, the spirit that calls for creativity, "making the road as we walk."

This was the vision that Paddy Lane had changed her life to help create and that had inspired hundreds who met David Sweet as he ambled across the country. It was the vision that Jeff Boyer, though he never used the term *interposition*, had glimpsed in the throes of his own anger at El Porvenir, and the vision that many of the July vigilers had sensed as they stood hand in hand with the people of Jalapa. It was also the vision that had led to the unhappy experience with the Santa Cruz Peace Brigade.

Witness was able to work out any sustained nonviolent tactic, but its very presence in the war zones over a sustained period was an experiment in the uses of nonviolence. At least two delegations of people trained in and committed to nonviolent methods came in and out of Nicaragua each month. The question of whether Witness offered protection was still a matter of debate, but as the nature of the war changed, it mattered less all the time.

Witness was pioneering the idea of consistent, specific challenges to covert action or guerrilla warfare.The main contribution of the devotees of nonviolence was more spiritual than tactical. The reality of Witnesses for Peace putting themselves on the line broke down barriers in people's minds, opened up new possibilities for peacemaking, and led people to explore audacious and creative ways to oppose war.

When the war pulled Witness away from Jalapa, the tactic of interposition became less important, but the team kept challenging themselves and the entire movement to seek new and creative ways to live nonviolently in the war zones and back in the United States.

BEYOND JALAPA

It was the contras who gave the practical coup de grace to the shield of love. The war spread to other areas as the contras saw their chances of taking Jalapa diminish and then disappear. As the randomness of contra attacks slimmed the chances of being in the "right" place at the "right" time, all but the most devoted proponents of interposition rejected the idea of providing safety by fielding bullets or hampering contra operations. Devotees were reluctant to let the idea die, especially since ordinary Nicaraguans continued to tell them that they felt safer having them around.

Even when the months of peak tension had passed, Jalapans still wanted the long-termers to accompany them. In January 1984, the long-term team went to Managua to meet and train new members. That night a helicopter flew over Jalapa and threatened the town. When the team returned, the people were in shock. The team felt that they should have been there to share such a crucial moment, whether or not they served as direct protection.

The team agreed that they would not leave Jalapa alone. Nonetheless, the war itself was drawing them away. They had to figure out how to best accompany and be witness to the suffering of people in communities most directly affected by the war—and over time Jalapa was not one of them.

Doug Spence expressed the challenge facing the new organization almost as soon as it began when he said, "We had to be where the war was happening, but we also had a commitment to the people of Jalapa." Strategists also regarded a presence in Jalapa as crucial if U.S. or Honduran troops should invade from the north.

By February 1984, the contras were operating on a number of fronts, discarding the frontal assault on Jalapa for a more conventional guerrilla strategy. In March, speedboats attacked the Pacific port of San Juan del Sur. A delegation from Massachusetts received a letter from survivors of the attack and decided on the spot to go and hold a vigil on the sands of San Juan del Sur. Kate Stevens, the coordinator of the delegation, went with Doug Spence as an advance team and set up a very moving procession followed by an ecumenical service and an all-night vigil on the beach.*

One participant gave this eloquent personal account, which also reflected the growing Jewish role in Witness:

> . . . arm in arm, under the moonlit sky, we prayed and sang and were silent together. And then, as the town slept, we went to the waterfront, and positioning ourselves between the people and the harbor, stood together through the night as a shield of love. It was a shield of love that had not been there when my uncles and aunts and great-grandparents were herded into boxcars; a shield of love that had not been there when they were taken to Auschwitz. Standing there it struck me that this was the most important single act that I may have occasion to do in this lifetime. It was a shield of love which said very simply, "No, we cannot look the other way; we cannot remain silent."

The team met after the San Juan experience to reflect on how to respond to the attacks in Chinandega, on the Atlantic coast, in Matagalpa, and elsewhere, all the while not abandoning Jalapa. They decided to send exploratory teams to other parts of the country. This meant physically following the pattern of contra attacks, usually at the expense of putting down roots in one community.

This was to be a continuing issue as the war expanded and Witness grew, never quite large enough to cover both "fronts": permanent presence and immediate response. The long-term team grew from three people in January, to five in February, to fourteen in May, and eighteen by August, 1984. In the first six months of the year, 260 delegates came to Nicaragua in thirteen separate delegations from sixteen states. They chased after the contras with notepads and cameras; they visited the victims carrying prayers, sympathy, and promises; and they almost always left the country aching to put an end to the war.

The delegations were recognizable on country roads by the blue-and-white Toyota microbus that took them around. Many groups hung a banner on the bus with peace messages in Spanish and English, both to send greetings and encouragement to the people they passed and to let any contra lookouts know who they were. If the

---

*Ironically, at the time they believed that the culprits were Nicaraguan contras backed by the United States, but later it was revealed that the contras themselves knew little or nothing of the attack, which was carried out directly by the CIA's Unilaterally Controlled Latino Assets—UCLAs.

banner, the bus, and the sunburned faces weren't enough of a bill-board, they also wore bright yellow T-shirts.

The typical actions of the team and the delegations did not in-volve risking death so much as dealing with the grief it leaves in its wake. All too often the Witnesses found themselves at gravesides with weeping family members, watching the burial of innocent peo-ple killed by guns supplied by the U.S. government. Long-term Wit-nesses regularly visited hospitals and refugee resettlement areas to comfort the wounded and the homeless as well as to gather informa-tion about the war.

A TRAVELING WITNESS

Somotillo, tucked between Honduras and the Gulf of Fonseca in Chinandega, was an area under siege. Peter Olson and Mary Chatlos went there in late March to begin setting up contacts with the base Christian communities, many of whose members were involved in land reform and other revolutionary activities and so had become targets of the contras. Contra bands were coming across the border every day, attacking agricultural cooperatives and burning crops and new machinery. Olson and Chatlos's contacts were to assist with bringing delegations or documenting contra attacks.

With a similar purpose in mind, Peg Scherer went with Doug Spence to Potosi and Chinandega. Most of the people of Potosi, a beautiful beach community, had been forced to flee to refugee reset-tlement areas inland because of three days of air and sea bombard-ment in early January. In the settlements, these "fishermen now having to farm," as Peg called them, were suffering from lack of wa-ter and food and were living on dry dusty land in makeshift shacks. Several delegations visited these hard-hit communities, literally standing on the border and looking into Honduras, where the contra bases were.

After Holy Week, Doug Spence and Jean Abbott went to Was-lala, up the road from Matagalpa, where the mountains give way to the jungles of Zelaya. Two Brazilian nuns working there wanted them to report on a recent contra attack and ongoing abuse of the campesi-nos in those mountains, already considered a "no-man's-land," where neither contras nor Sandinistas governed. Abbott and Spence hitched into town on an army truck and were taken in by Sister Rosiana, one of the pastoral workers. (The practice of traveling on army vehicles was later banned as contrary to both political independence and nonviolence, but the scarcity of transportation on the rural roads at times made this a difficult rule to observe.)

The sisters asked Abbott and Spence to take the testimonies of the contras' victims. Spence later described what happened:

> Word had gotten around town that we were taking testimonies. In the morning there was a line outside the door—people were just pouring their guts out. The campesinos desperately wanted someone on the outside to know what they were suffering as a result of the war. Jean was talking to the people as they waited and as they spoke, offering consolation and moral support. I realized that this was more than taking notes—this was a form of standing with the people.

The team acquired a new understanding that accompanying the victims and documenting the impact of the war were part of the same process. When they returned to Managua and sent their information about Waslala to Washington, Witness for Peace published it and mailed it out in a format that was to be used for years, a one-page publication called Newsbrief.

Once the break with the "Jalapa model" became a reality, Witness entered its most dynamic phase. It was a time of active reflection, questioning, groping, and experimenting while working very hard under extremely trying and at times risky conditions. Volunteers had to become even more sensitive to the culture and the political situation, as they sought out the meaning of standing with the people in numerous settings.

And it was a time of traveling, both for the long-termers and for the delegations that continued to arrive, at times as many as three per month, including as many as sixty new people, most of them experiencing Nicaragua for the first time.

As 1984 wore on, Witnesses were standing in more and more places, and this nonviolent presence took on a variety of meanings. Long-termers joked that they were literally "standing with" the Nicaraguan people on the buses traveling over the dirt roads because a seat on the crowded, overworked monsters was an impossible dream.

The town of Cardenas, on the southern shore of Lake Nicaragua, had been attacked six times by the contras. Cardenas was accessible only by boat, and the boat wasn't in great shape. Short-term delegate Bill Stuart-Whistler wrote about a trip to visit Cardenas:

Pentecost in Nicaragua, 1984

We started Pentecost morning waking in a small village by the side of Lake Nicaragua. . . . It was raining gently and the skies were dark as we thought of our boat trip back to Peñas Blancas.

The moment came for us to embark on our journey. We looked at the thirty-foot boat with the outboard motor we would entrust our lives to: it was bobbing a distance offshore. To reach the boat, we took off our shoes, put our shoes and our packs on our heads and waded waist-deep to the boat's side.

The boat started its voyage across the lake. The water was choppy, the clouds were a dark curtain on the horizon. The boat bobbed and twisted on the turbulent water.

As we got out on the lake, I sat near the bow looking back at our group of pilgrims and our guides, crew, and protectors. I had the strongest image that we were moved back in time: we were in Galilee, bobbing on another sea passing through another fearful, unknown time. And we had the same Protector and the same faith and confidence that we were safe in the palm of God's hand.

God's hand proved a bit unsteady in this case. Visits to Cardenas ended abruptly in late 1984, when the boat finally gave up the ghost and went to the bottom of Lake Nicaragua in the midst of a storm.

Short-term delegates visiting southern Nicaragua were most moved by the people's experience of religion combined with social activism. A strong base community movement had grown up during the time of Somoza. The parish priest in San Juan, Gaspar Garcia Laviana, eventually went off to join the Sandinistas and died fighting in the mountains before the triumph. These communities, which suffered heavily under Somoza's repression, were still strong years later. Their reflections inspired both long-term volunteers and short-term delegates, many of whom had only read of such communities in works such as Ernesto Cardenal's Gospel of Solentiname.

ATLANTIC NICARAGUA

In their zeal to cover the entire war, the team assigned Rebecca Gordon, a poet from San Francisco, and Doug Spence to traverse the country reporting on the war and making new contacts for future delegation visits. They headed out on a journey that would take them through a firefight in Siuna and on to the Atlantic coastal town of Puerto Cabezas. Gordon chronicled those trips in her book *Letters from Nicaragua.**

Kaki McTigue, Stuart Taylor, and Doug Insch traveled by boat up the Rio Escondido to Bluefields and around the southern Atlantic coast to make the first of many attempts to establish a presence there. They traveled in the Pearl Lagoon area and interviewed Creole and Garifuno victims of contra attacks.

They found a many-sided conflict. The long-termers arrived in Bluefields in the wake of protests against the draft, which had torn the town apart. They spoke to Rama Indians forced off their small island by the Sandinistas after the contras overran it and to black and Miskito people from Pearl Lagoon, who told stories of imprisonment and harsh treatment by the Sandinistas.

The Atlantic coast reality was a tough one to digest for the generally prorevolution long-term volunteers and short-term delegates. Few people exhibited the enthusiasm for the revolution that the team was used to finding on the Pacific. Instead of the lived experience of liberation theology that one found in the base communities of Cardenas and Jalapa, the *Costeños* by and large practiced a lively but otherworldly form of Protestantism inherited from British missionaries.

The Witnesses in Bluefields, a Caribbean town of one- and two-story wooden homes, easy-going people, sea breezes, and torrential rains, were invited by Moravian church leaders and government officials to play several roles that recognized the unique nature of nonviolent witness. After the protests against the draft, which had erupted into fighting between progovernment and antigovernment students, Stuart Taylor was asked to address an assembly of students at the Moravian high school about the role of nonviolence as a means of seeking redress.

A few months later, on October 15, Doug Insch and Stuart Taylor accompanied the first Rama Indians to return home to their island after being forced to leave by the war. The Ramas, who number fewer than one thousand, have all traditionally lived on one island, Rama Cay, and their displacement had threatened their survival as a people. Taylor later wrote:

> We docked in a small harbor and . . . everybody split up in different directions looking to see what damage had been done in

---

*Rebecca Gordon, *Letters from Nicaragua* (San Francisco: Spinsters/aunt lute, 1987).

three months since the battle. Five houses had been burned.
The roof of the church had been shot up. Many other houses
were damaged and all were in disarray. . . .

I try to imagine what it was and as it soon will be with
houses all tended to, and the men fishing and the children
playing and the women calling out to one another from their
huts, almost side by side. I watched as the boat returned with
another load of Ramas. I watched their smiles and wide open
eyes as they set foot on their island for the first time in three
months. I pray that Rama people will be able to stay on the
island and live in peace.

Taylor's prayer was not answered. The Rama people spent the
next three years being evacuated again and again, and many of them
ended up heading back into the bush on the mainland or living an
impoverished existence in Bluefields. Witness was twice involved in
discussions about joining an unarmed international presence to
guarantee the safety of the island, if the residents were allowed to
return. Witness was willing to participate in such a force despite mis-
givings at getting so heavily involved in internal political matters.
The Nicaraguan government vetoed both plans.

In 1985, a church medical team asked Witness to accompany
the first medical trip in three years up the contra-held Kukra River.
Dr. Ed Myer and Terry Toma made the trip. Ann Dohrmann, a long-
serving Atlantic coast volunteer, believes that such requests were
evidence that Costeños had a greater experience of and understanding of the possibilities of nonviolent action than their counterparts in
the Pacific area. The coast, where people were less politicized and
less willing to bear arms for either the government or the contras,
offered possibilities for nonviolent action.

When the contras twice attacked the main river boat carrying
civilian traffic to Bluefields, the team thought once again of interposition. Herb Gunn and Ann Dohrmann raised the idea of mounting a
"Peace Guard," a presence of clearly identified yellow-shirted Witnesses riding the boat on its daily eight-hour round-trips between
Rama and Bluefields. The Anglican, Moravian, and Catholic pastors
and the Catholic bishop of Bluefields, Paul Schmidt, all endorsed the
idea, and their congregations voiced approval of the Peace Guard.

Initial reaction from the government was positive. They were
willing to pull their troops off the boat and have unarmed, nonviolent
Witnesses provide protection. While the logistics were being worked

out, Bluefields pastors read a letter in all the churches in town announcing the project. Hours before it was to be announced publicly, Lumberto Campbell, the head of government in Bluefields, nixed the project.

Campbell's reasons were twofold. First, he felt that the contra group that had attacked the boat was an out-of-control group that would neither understand nor respect an unarmed guard. It was his judgment that the boat would be as susceptible or perhaps more susceptible to attack if the Peace Guards were substituted for soldiers.

His second reason surprised everyone. Campbell said that the worldwide movement for nonviolence was too important to risk taking a false step in a situation where it might fail. These words, carefully chosen, coming from a Sandinista military commander, once again confirmed that this revolution was and would remain anything but orthodox. Commander Campbell's comments were interesting and heartening, but his decision was final.

The complexities of the Atlantic coast situation demanded years of presence, study, and listening before any such activity could bear fruit. Witness was simply not experienced enough to undertake more than sporadic efforts at building the necessary contacts and knowledge base to carry out an effective program.

CEPAD, Moravian pastor Norman Bent, and other partners encouraged Witness to have a program on the coast, but it was never easy to figure out just what such a presence should be. Church leaders on the coast were not happy with the high turnover and inconsistent presence. A Moravian church leader said in early 1985, "So many foreigners come here, no one knows just what they do, then they go away. It takes a long time to get to know our people, and to have them get to know you. If you want to work here, be prepared to come here to live for a long time."

Witness tried to station people on the coast for a long time, but the nature of the program always pulled people away. Mike Hamer, an easy-going former resident of a monastery, resumed the presence in 1985 and made many friends and contacts through his guitar and song. Ann Dohrmann maintained a low-key but effective presence by living in Bluefield's Miskito neighborhood and performing community service for more than a year. She was followed by Sue Severin, who taught childbirth classes and accompanied health workers.

Wherever long-termers went, delegations soon followed. By mid-year, delegations had visited Matagalpa, Chinandega, San Juan del

Sur, Somotillo, and Ocotal. The first delegation to visit the Atlantic coast, a third-world delegation led by Vincent and Rosemarie Harding, traveled to Puerto Cabezas in June 1984.

A third-world caucus developed, which pressed the organization to deal with, among other things, the concerns of Nicaragua's non-Mestizo ethnic groups. But in the heat of the contra war, an effective strategy for keeping a presence on the coast was never developed. As late as August 1990, Witness was still sending exploratory missions to the coast to see what its role might be.

The most serious effort began in 1987 when Witness initiated a program of African-Americans from the United States working with the primarily black communities in the Pearl Lagoon. An African-American couple from Atlanta, Birdis and Mildred Coleman, took on the leadership of the project after a trip to the Pearl Lagoon region with a delegation in August 1986. It was to involve accompanying the communities of the Lagoon as hostilities ceased and they returned back home, and receiving visiting delegations from communities of color in the United States. Witness for Peace saw the effort as important for its own sake as well as a way to broaden its outreach beyond its predominantly white constituency.

Early Witness efforts on the Atlantic coast had suffered from excessive timidity—without a clear strategy, little beyond direct service was achieved. For all of its many problems, the Coleman period was never timid. Problems began to surface and Birdis Coleman and two other volunteers were expelled from the coast by the Sandinistas in August 1988. The people in the Lagoon area had come to regard Coleman as a leader and a source of development aid rather than as someone who accompanied them. When he involved himself in a shipment of goods, the ensuing rivalries caused the government to put a stop to the project. The many issues raised by the Colemans and by Witness for Peace's attempts to become a more inclusive organization did not stop with his departure.

OCOTAL

Just as the focus of the war appeared to be moving south and east, the contras attacked Ocotal. A city of twenty thousand, Ocotal had become a frequent stopping place for delegations en route to Jalapa. Long-term witnesses, especially Peter Olson, had cemented friendships with the base communities there and the Maryknoll sisters who worked with them.

It was not the first time Ocotal had been attacked with U.S. weaponry. On July 16, 1928, U.S. planes carried out what many believe to be the first air raid in history—against Ocotal, during the war against Sandino.

On June 1, 1984, the battle between the contras and the defenders of Ocotal raged through the morning. The road to Jalapa was closed and reports reaching there were inconclusive. Jalapa went on alert.

By the time the contras were driven back, more than thirty civilians and defenders had been killed and a great deal of damage done to the town's facilities. A coffee processing plant, a sawmill, and the radio station were severely damaged. The grain silos at the edge of town were destroyed—corn, beans, and rice lay strewn about in piles, mixed in with charred embers and exposed to rain.

The team was in the midst of a planning session when the news came. Seven long-termers went to Ocotal as soon as the road reopened and joined the cleanup efforts, helping rebag the grain before the rains came and ruined it. Peter Olson wrote: "I spent hours inside what remained of a crumpled bean silo helping in the effort to salvage whatever possible of that vital food supply. Standing before the demolished silos, I was disgusted and angry, especially considering how the president of my country would champion such crimes as the work of 'freedom fighters' and that many good people in the U.S. would believe him."

When word of the Ocotal attack reached the United States, protest calls flooded the State Department almost immediately. All around the country people heard news of the attack and understood it not just as cold words coming over an AP wire but as something happening to real live people who had opened their homes and their lives to them. Jim Wallis spent that night with a group of Ohioans who had visited Ocotal and remembers the depth of feeling in the room as they began to pray for people in Ocotal by name.

Olson's letters, like many from the long-term team, inspired hearts as well as informed minds.

> The spirit of the local people working inside the silo was amazing. There was a sense of unity and strength and even, incredibly, laughter. A couple of times the inside of the silo erupted into a small bean war, laughing as we attempted to cover each other with buckets and shovels full of the red beans . . . just another example of the deep spirit of hope I

sense from people here, a hope that I suspect comes only out of deep suffering.

Most times Witnesses found that they got much more from the Nicaraguans than they could ever give. Readers back home could not help but be moved to action.

In the aftermath of the Ocotal attack a campesino family showed Olson a ragged copy of a booklet that turned out to be a manual prepared by the CIA to train the contras in the tactics of terrorism. In both Washington and Managua, they showed the manual to the press and contributed to yet another embarrassment of the Reagan administration.

The week that Ocotal was attacked, the United States was conducting war exercises just across the border, and rumors of an impending invasion swirled throughout the north. Rebecca Gordon, in her first week as a long-term volunteer, was left in Jalapa when the rest of the team traveled to Ocotal. She described the scene:

> No one has slept here very much for the last week . . . for the last few days, we've lived on the edge of attack, never knowing when it might come. . . . Thursday night, our household was awake all night.
>
> I slept a couple of hours in the morning on Friday. At noon Miranda [Collet, another team member] came home saying "We have to meet right now." She'd just spent the last couple of hours getting the children into trenches and shelters at the school. The attack might come at any minute.
>
> . . . I'd been terrified all the night before, all the hairs on my spine raised, the back of my neck burning with fear. When Miranda came home with her news, her descriptions of twelve year old girls receiving last minute instructions in firing a weapon, I knew I was likely to die that day, and I was ashamed of my fear.

7

"NOBODY EVER CAME OUT HERE"

You don't have to agree with everything the Sandinistas are doing to disagree with everything our government is doing in Nicaragua.

—William Sloane Coffin

A month after the June 1984 attack on Ocotal, Jalapa was invaded by the largest Witness delegation ever. Nearly two hundred people from forty-two states descended on Managua in July for an anniversary reenactment of the founding vigil.

The delegation's experience mimicked in many ways the founding vigil one year before. In Ocotal, they held vigils at six sites that had been destroyed in the June attack. In Jalapa, the group broke up and stayed with families at resettlement communities and cooperatives and worked in the fields with their families. They came together to reenact the vigil in the cornfield, and they interviewed government and religious leaders.

In Managua, they followed what had become a routine for delegations. They visited sewing cooperatives, hospitals, clinics, and schools and attended meetings with political parties, religious leaders, and neighborhood groups. They requested a meeting with the new ambassador, Harry Berghold, who declined, sending an aide instead.

A bomb scare was telephoned to the Witness office just as the group was about to board buses for a meeting with Daniel Ortega and cabinet members. The premises and the buses were searched but no explosives were found.

The group of two hundred re-energized the organizing of the

stateside Witness. The vigil expanded the number of states in which Witness was represented from thirty-four to forty-six. The large delegation, affectionately nicknamed "Barnum and Bailey," was organized by geographic regions in the United States, so that those who shared the experience in Nicaragua could network with like-minded people in their area once they got home.

Among their ranks was Rabbi Balfour Brickner, who later joined the advisory committee. Glenn Remer-Thamert, a pastor and organizer who later was acquitted in a much-publicized sanctuary case, and Daniel Erdman, who joined the long-term team a year later and then became a coordinator of the team. Also along were Jane Cary Peck, a future vice president of the National Council of Churches and future national steering committee member of Witness, Angela Berryman of the AFSC, and Joe Lacy, who later became part of the long-term team on the Atlantic coast.

No sooner had they boarded the plane home than a controversy erupted. The issue was political independence. Many of the delegates were upset by favors done for the group by the FSLN and by what appeared to be special protection afforded them by the Nicaraguan army.

Some delegates complained that the long-term volunteers, who served as guides, gave them one-sided interpretations of issues. Others wondered why they were greeted by FSLN party leaders, rather than official government leaders, at each stop. At one point a soldier appeared in the Ocotal town square in a yellow Witness for Peace T-shirt—and his machine-gun slung over his shoulder! One participant wrote an article for *Chicago* magazine blasting Witness.

Daniel Erdman, a Presbyterian minister from New Mexico, recalled that "By the end of the delegation, . . . I came away with the impression that WFP was a pro-Sandinista organization." Erdman later joined the long-term team and was assigned to Nueva Guinea, a hotbed of antigovernment sentiment. There he came to understand the crucial importance of presenting his work as opposed to U.S. policy, rather than promoting the Nicaraguan government.

It was a tightrope act that many Witnesses, who tended to arrive in Nicaragua with prorevolution sentiments, learned to walk over time. The long-term team members often felt more at home with prorevolutionary people, free-spirited people like themselves. They were typically more willing to forgive government "mistakes" and look beyond economic hardships than the average campesino was. Peggy Healy had insisted from the very beginning that "the people of

Nicaragua need your questions and doubts and criticisms as well as your support," but many felt that they had no role critiquing or questioning Nicaraguans while their own government was pursuing a war against them.

As the war dragged on and the situation in the countryside became more polarized, walking that line became more critical. In some places, particularly cooperatives and refugee resettlement areas, the local residents assumed that Witnesses were progovernment, simply because the government allowed them to travel and work in such delicate areas.

Overcoming such perceptions was crucial for the team to gain the trust needed to conduct documentation and to arrange for delegation visits. Two factors were key—time and church ties. Where Witness had a presence for an extended period, their mission was usually understood; where they merely passed through, Nicaraguans found it more difficult to trust them. Where ties to the local churches were strong, as in Nueva Guinea, people opened up more easily. Erdman recalls that in the ambiguous environment there, "if a partnership with CEPAD had not existed, we would not have gotten to square one."

Opinions on the Sandinistas varied widely, as this sample of comments from Witnesses reflected: "Nicaragua is a Garden of Eden, and Nicaraguans can be counted among God's most beautiful children" (Jerry Genesio, Maine); "Either you are for Reagan or you are for the Sandinistas. I am for the Sandinistas" (Ruth Thone, Nebraska); "I have some real concerns about some . . . [Sandinista] policies and some of the ideology they are getting into. This trip is in no way to uncritically support the regime in power" (Betsy Sowers, Massachusetts); "Personally, I would not care to live under the Sandinista government, but that is not the question" (Warren Christianson, Alaska).

Such differences made it impossible for Witness to adopt any sort of policy statement on the Nicaraguan revolution, and opposition to U.S. policy remained their unifying issue. Some delegations made it a point to interview contra leaders in Miami or visit Nicaraguan refugee camps in Honduras to get the contra viewpoint. Most delegations, however, limited their contact to the civic, unarmed opposition working within Nicaragua.

Political independence was much more than an abstract concept—it became an absolute necessity, especially in areas where opinions about the revolution and the Sandinistas were sharply divided. In order to gain any acceptance by the community, whether for the purpose of documenting contra attacks or bringing a short-term delegation, the Witnesses had to be very careful to explain the difference between being opposed to U.S. policy of assisting the contras and being pro-Sandinista. Over time, it was a distinction that became less meaningful to the rural people who were suffering the impact of the war, and who were themselves being forced, by government policy and contra pressure, to choose sides.

CORINTO

People closely involved with Witness for Peace have a tough time explaining to the average person just what it is they actually do. Scott Kennedy used to joke that he would love a brochure that explained Witness in simple enough terms that his son could use it when kids in the school yard asked him the question, What does your Daddy do?

The problem was multiplied for long-term Witnesses who were constantly visiting new communities and having to explain their purpose. In addition to language and cultural barriers, they often found that people associated them with other foreigners who had been through the area, whether they were German engineers, French doctors, or Cuban teachers. Becoming known and understood in the countryside was not easy.

Actions, for the campesino, speak louder than words. It was a dramatic action that brought Witness for Peace wide recognition throughout the countryside. After November of 1984, the Witnesses would become known as "the ones on the boat."

The opportunity for action at Corinto came unexpectedly, when the Nicaraguan people had planned to be celebrating the results of their first open presidential elections in fifty years. Daniel Ortega and Ronald Reagan had just been elected and reelected presidents of their respective countries. (Ortega won 67 percent against six opponents, Reagan won 62 percent in a two-way race). Witness delegates and long-term volunteers served as official observers at polling places in Nicaragua and concurred with nearly six hundred other visiting delegations and comments by U.S. Embassy officials that the voting had been aboveboard and the process fair.

Suddenly a sonic boom exploded over Managua. Anonymous high-level administration sources, in their first postelection briefing, announced the advent of a foreign policy crisis severe enough to invite comparison with Cuba in October 1962. More sonic booms thundered, the product of U.S. spy planes crisscrossing Nicaragua.

"MiGs," the administration charged. The word had all the emotional wallop that another four-letter acronym, AIDS, was soon to acquire. "MiGs," the president reiterated, as he boarded his plane to return to Washington from California.

MiGs, the story went, were sitting in crates aboard a Soviet ship about to be unloaded at the Pacific port of Corinto.

Shovels and rifles were passed out. Bomb shelters were dug. Men and women mobilized to plan the defense of Managua. Several times a day, the sonic booms generated by the "Pajaro Negro" SR-71 Blackbird spy planes caused babies to cry, work on the trenches to stop momentarily, and reinforced a growing sense that the invasion that the Sandinistas had been warning about for so long was about to land. U.S. warships were sailing off Nicaragua's Pacific coast.

The long-term team met to pray and analyze their options. They decided to move the two delegations then in the country (one from New York, another from West Virginia) to Corinto and to camp out on the beach.

Then they went a step further. They rented a shrimp boat, loaded it with long- and short-termers, and steamed off to find a U.S. Navy destroyer that had been sighted in Nicaragua's territorial waters.

Stuart Taylor, the Presbyterian minister just weeks from completing his stint as a long-termer, was selected to speak for the group. His deep Southern baritone and ease with words made him a natural for addressing the press, the people on the boat, and, if contact were made, the crew of the destroyer. Taylor's eloquence knew no boundaries, either national or linguistic.

He was an easygoing but convinced believer. A friend once described him as "half theologian and half college sophomore." All the world was his pulpit. But when confronted with the destroyer, almost within earshot, with network cameras rolling, his seminary training failed him, and Stuart could only say in his best Southern rumble, "Y'all go home!" Over and over. "You're not wanted here! Go home."

Which was exactly the point. Simply and directly, this collection of U.S. citizens very concerned with a country they were coming to love, wanted to tell the military forces of their own country to go home. David Sweet could not have imagined a more direct confrontation with U.S. militarism. No elaborate policy prescriptions here, no room for debate. "Go home!" was the simple message.

That day on the high seas, the U.S. Navy did go home. Whether it was trying to avoid the TV cameras of an NBC crew that had come along, or Taylor's fire and brimstone, or it was time to head back out to sea, the ship turned tail and sailed away without responding.

There were no MiGs. There was no invasion. Three days later the administration admitted that there were no MiGs at Corinto. What role did Witness and the boat action play in stopping an invasion? Perhaps they were a factor. The State Department was calling the Witness office in Washington on an hourly basis to confirm and reconfirm that U.S. citizens were in fact on the beach at Corinto, leading some to conclude that a military action was planned. Most analysts felt that the administration had not laid the political groundwork for such military action. Nicaragua had just won much international support, albeit short-lived, by holding elections, and that support would translate into worldwide condemnation of the United States if it attacked Nicaragua.

Considerations of strategy aside, the Corinto action gave Witness a big boost in morale, gave it a very high profile both in the states and in Nicaragua, and re-energized those who saw the need for ever more aggressive pursuit of citizen peacemaking efforts in the war zone. From then on, the Witnesses were "those people out there on the boat."

Most times the impact of the Witness presence was much more subtle than the wallop of the delegation of two hundred or the headline-grabbing cruise at Corinto. What the long-termers and delegation members did with themselves each day varied with the area they were in and depended on the gifts of the individuals involved.

SANTA CLARA

Ed Myer, a doctor from Washington State, and Peter Olson were among the pallbearers at a funeral in Santa Clara, Nueva Segovia, in September 1984. The funeral was for three young girls and a twenty-eight-year-old campesino killed in an air raid the day before.

Helicopters and small planes had attacked a military school on an afternoon when families were visiting the troops. Among the attackers were two U.S. soldiers of fortune who were killed when their helicopter was shot down.

Two twelve-year-old cousins, Juanita Beltran and Elena Herrera, were selling fruit drinks when they were killed by a rocket fired from a plane. Thirteen-year-old Alba Luz Hernandez was torn apart by shrapnel as she committed the most childlike of acts—climbing a tree to pick fruit. Her remains were in the plain wooden box that Myer and Olson carried on their shoulders.

Myer later described the downed chopper and its cargo: "Burned boots with English printing on the insoles, danger signs inscribed on various parts of the helicopter in English, and English specifications on the main helicopter rotor. The three crew members had been removed . . . the one who had not been charred totally was noted to be of large physique, blue eyed, blond with 'blond body hair.'"

The Witnesses, from the same country as the attackers, were asked to be part of the victims' burial service, and they stood with the townspeople listening as local leaders condemned the attack and vowed to defend their communities.

Elena Herrera's father talked to Myer afterward as he stood grieving near the small container holding his daughter's remains. The box, covered with cut flowers, was small enough to sit on a three-foot-long table. "They scooped her up with a shovel," lamented the father. "This is what Yanqui imperialism brings to the underdeveloped and struggling nations of Central America—death to our little girls."

Myer later described his sadness and overwhelming shame. "I truly feel," he wrote in a letter about the girl's funeral, "that President Reagan would benefit tremendously from being present for these moments."

"Present" was a key word for Witness and for the Nicaraguans who wanted "internationalistas," their term for foreign helpers, to visit or live and work with them. Campesinos in some of the most forgotten villages, the most threatened rural cooperatives, the most primitive resettlement communities came to expect occasional visits from "los testigos" (the Witnesses) or "los cristianos por la paz" (Christians for Peace). In other places the organization wasn't even known by name; they were just the people who stopped by now and again, or the ones who brought the delegation, or "those who came after the attack to be with us." When Doug Schirch first arrived in Somotillo as a long-term volunteer, he tried explaining what Witness for Peace was and what work he planned to do, and gave up after a few days. "Now I just tell them I work with Marta [Martha Swan] and everybody knows who Marta is." "Marta" was Martha Swan of Syracuse, New York, the long-term volunteer who preceded Schirch in Somotillo. In the small-town environment, personal contact meant much more than organizational connections.

In the forgotten, threatened villages and communities, some of which had never seen or known anyone from the United States, individual Witnesses and delegations built up relationships that endure even today.

LIMAY

San Juan de Limay was one of the most forgotten places in Nicaragua. "Who ever heard of Limay?" said Maryknoll Sister Suzanne, who first came to the dusty town of three thousand in 1980. "Nobody ever came out here." Tucked into an arid valley in the mountain range west of Esteli, Limay might as well have been on the moon. Once the market hub of a vital agricultural region, deforestation and years of drought have damaged the ecosystem to such an extent that even cattle raising has become marginal. Dust swirls through the Old West–style streets and around the park in the center of town eight months out of the year.

As in every town in Central America, the Catholic church is located on the central park, or plaza, symbolizing its central role in many aspects of life. From the earliest days after the Sandinista triumph, Sister Suzanne and the whole parish pastoral team had jumped into the organizing work of the revolution with vigor, helping form sewing and farming cooperatives, educating the illiterate, preaching hope in places where it had been a subversive word in the past.

As contra bands began to appear and make scattered attacks on the farming communities near Limay, the sisters asked Witness to come to Limay. "We just had a sense of being abandoned," said Sister Suzanne. "The place was feeling the tension of war and no one was paying attention. And we also had some good things going on that we wanted to show off."

In December 1984, Julie Beutel, a twenty-seven-year-old teacher from Detroit with a golden voice, arrived in Limay with a duffel bag and a guitar on her back. Beutel, a peace activist who counted Jesus Christ Superstar as one of her peak religious experiences, moved right into the convent with the sisters.

One of the good things Limay wanted to show off was the new, more direct road to Esteli that the government had just built. Unpaved and tricky to navigate as it was, it was a godsend for the townspeople, cutting what had been a two-day trip to a journey of just a few hours.

Richard Boren, long-term volunteer with Witness for Peace,
in contra custody just before his release on March 9, 1988. © 1988
Paul Dix.

July, 1983: More than one hundred fifty U.S. Christians join with residents of the town of Jalapa for a peace vigil at the edge of town. The man in the hat is Bob Bonthius of Maine, who later became chair of the Witness for Peace steering committee. © 1983 Richard Taylor.

The first short-term delegation holds a nighttime vigil in Ocotal.
The road to Jalapa was closed for two days because of fighting.
© 1983 Phyllis B. Taylor.

Father Thomas Fenlon of Newburgh, New York, looks out at the Rio San Juan during captivity by the contra troops in August, 1985. Fenlon and twenty-eight others were held for twenty-nine hours before being released. © 1985 Virginia Druhe.

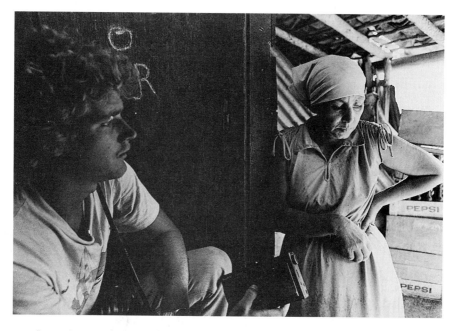

Long-term volunteer Larry Leaman interviews a survivor of a
contra attack in Jinotega. Such first-hand testimonies were critical
to Witness's work to bring the truth about the war home to the
United States. © 1985 Paul Dix.

Coffee harvesters at a cooperative near Condega. The coffee harvest, one of Nicaragua's principal sources of income, was a frequent target of the contras. Men and women living in areas under threat from the contras often carried arms to defend themselves while they worked. © 1985 Paul Dix.

To celebrate International Women's Day in 1985, a group of sixty women from all over the United States formed a special Witness for Peace delegation to Nicaragua. In the photo, a delegation member helps with the bean harvest in Jumuyca, a refugee resettlement community. © 1985 Paul Dix.

Rolando Mena (left) is greeted by his family as long-term team members greet Paul Fisher. Mena, an agronomy student, and Fisher, a long-term volunteer, were kidnapped from a bus by contras in October, 1987, and held for thirteen days. John Parnell, Witness for Peace radio operator, is at left rear. © 1987 Paul Dix.

Reina Isabel Ramos, the thirteen-year-old girl wounded in the attack on Mantocal, will always bear the scars of war. Witness for Peace volunteer Richard Boren helped stop the bleeding in her leg before he was marched off by the contra on the night of March 1, 1988. © 1988 Paul Dix.

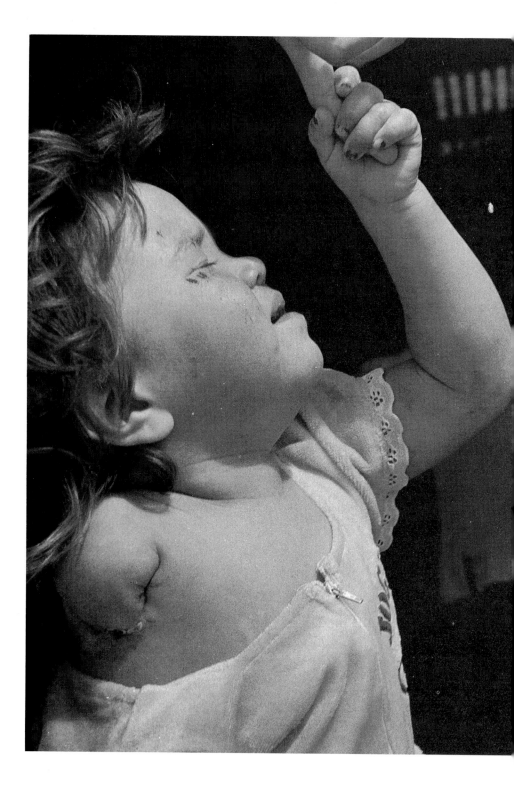

Luz Mabel Lumbi Rizo, twenty-two months old, lost her arm when
contras attacked her home December 8, 1986. Her father was
killed and her mother wounded in the same attack. © 1987
Paul Dix.

March, 1987: Two hundred religious leaders join Witness for Peace activists all over the United States in demonstrations demanding the end of contra aid. The crosses and markers bearing the names of people killed in the war were carried in marches and planted in public places nationwide. Left to right: Rev. Fran Truitt, New England regional coordinator; Rev. Norman Bent, Nicaraguan Moravian pastor; Gilberto Aguirre, CEPAD Executive Director; Charles Liteky, Congressional Medal of Honor recipient; Jim Wallis of *Sojourners* magazine. © 1990 Richard Reinhard.

Nicaraguans lining up to vote in national elections, February 25, 1990. One hundred twenty Witness for Peace delegates served as official election observers. © 1990 Paul Dix.

Before it was even completed, the road attracted the attention of the contras, who harassed road crews, placed mines, and set ambushes. It was a characteristic contra tactic to try to take away the benefits that the revolution produced.

On December 9, the contras ambushed and burned the town's only bus and kidnapped five people. The one phone line was cut and repaired and then cut again so many times that the telephone company workers had all but given up. Anyone trained in firing a weapon was on alert. Bomb shelters were being dug, refugees were pouring in, and an energetic, impulsive young woman from the United States was running about town making friends and making music.

The Witness community structure and the very open concept of being a presence encouraged each individual to make use of his or her own gifts. The "program" of the long-term team, such as it was, evolved according to those gifts. Among Beutel's gifts were an outgoing personality, a way with kids, and her music. She walked all over town almost every day, visiting the school, the children's dining hall, greeting and meeting people, playing guitar and singing.

"She came here every day, to visit us, to play the guitar," remembers Maxima Hernandez, the mother of three kidnapped boys. "She made us happy." Beutel had a way of communicating and reaching out past her own fear that allowed other people to share the burdens and the stress, and made it that much lighter on them. She provided a moment of laughter, a diversion for the children, and a promise that she and the delegations that came to visit would be the voice of the people of Limay to the outside world.

She wrote of her work in letters to friends in the Detroit peace community:

> How can I take my experience here and sing it to you to somehow make you *feel* it? . . . I've never seen so much death as I have in the past three weeks in my whole life. . . . The custom is to have an all night "wake" for the dead. When people are killed suddenly there isn't time to get coffins. The bodies get wrapped in sheets and lie there while people sit around looking at them or saying the rosary or crying or spacing out or thinking. By 11:00 or 12:00 the bodies start to stink. . . . The bodies more decapitated start to smell sooner of course.

She wrote an ode to a man whose two sons were taken by the contras, a man whose name sounds in cruel juxtaposition to the agony written on his face:

Tranquilino! You have suffered enough! May your son come back! . . . Tranquilino and his family and some neighbors went out and waited in the road going out of town for Marvin to come back. Waited . . . sure he was coming back. . . . (He hasn't.) Oh my heart aches.

In a later letter, she wondered:

How much more can this little town take? We hear combats regularly. Dead and wounded come in. People kidnapped, killed and wounded just a few miles away. Regular people. They have no bus now. . . . There has been no phone communication for over two weeks. The contra cut the line.

Tension. . . . Do they want to attack Limay? It would be so easy. [A few weeks ago] I interviewed . . . a 15 year old girl in the clinic. . . . She heard shots . . . threw herself to the floor . . . the contras shot into the window killing her brother and wounding her. . . . Today is December 31. On December 29 she died, in the hospital. . . .
That's the first person to die that I've spoken to myself.
They say it's all just beginning.
Beginning? Where does it end?

Such vivid, personal descriptions of the war were not reaching the public reading the *New York Times* or the AP wire releases in their hometown papers. The letters home from Witnesses would, over the coming years, reach tens and then hundreds of thousands with direct, personal testimonies. The live testimonies of returned delegates reached many many more, as they became the "living media" that Witness for Peace used to challenge the administration's attempts to monopolize coverage in the mass media.

On January 8, 1985, contras killed nine road workers and burned their truck. Another man from Limay was killed on his tractor. Beutel's roommate, Maryknoll Sister Nancy Donovan, and a seventeen-year-old named Freddy were kidnapped along the same road. Sister Nancy was held for part of a day and then released. A few days later Freddy's tortured and mutilated body was found.

A Witness for Peace delegation from Kansas and Missouri came over that same road on the day of Freddy's funeral. Two of the members were Catholic priests, and the people asked them to concelebrate the funeral mass.

Sister Suzanne remembers the priest struggling to learn the words of the consecration prayers in Spanish. His tutor was a little boy fascinated by meeting a grown-up who didn't know how to talk.

Beutel wrote:

Two of the priests together did the funeral mass . . . a few of
the men from the Witness for Peace team helped shovel dirt
into the grave (the custom here is for the friends and family
and community to bury their own dead, taking turns).

When I watched the first two North American men hum-
bly offer to take the shovels and start to shovel the dirt . . . I
cried for the first time here. Hard.

Oh God, it's the least we can do to show these people all
North Americans aren't murderers, that we're so sorry for
what our government (and CIA) is doing to them, that we love
them . . .

How can we make it up to them?

At least let me help you bury your dead that my own
country killed (indirectly but not secretly)

I don't know what else to do . . . to say . . .

Freddy Freddy Freddy

(gunshot in the night)

go to sleep.

Virginia Druhe, a strong, serene, contemplative woman from
the St. Louis Catholic Worker, arrived with that delegation and
stayed on to work with Witness and with the nuns. Druhe walked
slowly but always seemed to know where she was going. "The only
thing I know how to do is to live with the poor and to pray," she once
said. So Witness seemed the natural thing to do. She says in all sin-
cerity that the Holy Spirit taught her Spanish, and if that is the case
the Spirit is a good tutor.

Her gift was listening. She visited homes, spoke to women and
men in pain, listened to their stories. When campesinos were moved
closer to town from an area of conflict to a settlement called San
Lorenzo, Druhe made a practice of visiting them every day. Stopping
to talk to the families, eating with them, helping a sick child drink
oral rehydration fluid, or finding a ride for a pregnant woman, she
became part of a community experiencing one more trauma caused
by the war.

"Virginia," recalls Sister Suzanne, "was just there with them.
She went every day, and she would listen to their stories. The fact
that she was willing to go out and be with them, that just meant a lot
to people."

They called her the *grandota* (the giant) for her size. Others
referred to her as the quiet one. Her style could not have been more

different from Julie Beutel's extroversion. Yet she was received and appreciated by a community intimately feeling the violence perpetrated or at least aggravated by her own government. Her gift to them was to live with them, to pray with them, to be unafraid to feel with them—and at such a time, that was more than enough.

Witness provided the space for both Druhe and Beutel to do their part. Assignments of long-term Witnesses took into account the need to host delegations and to document the war, but also the need to accompany, to be present, in whatever way was appropriate to the needs of the community and the gifts of the volunteer. In Limay, the presence was witness, political action, documentation, prayer, and personal ministry all at once.

The relationships between the town and the long-term volunteers deepened the experience of short-term delegations. The delegations, though they spent only a few days at a given site, saw life in a place like Limay through a unique window—the relationship between the long-term volunteer and the town.

Five years later, both Beutel and Druhe are warmly remembered in Limay for being willing to share the risks and the lives, the daily joys and sorrows, of people who live at what can seem like the edge of the earth. Somehow they, like other Witnesses, managed to work their way into the hearts of the campesinos, transcending political and cultural barriers. Tranquilino's sad face glows as he shows photos and talks about Beutel's visits to his home. The walls of Maxima Hernandez's home are covered with pictures of Julie Beutel, her son Benjamin, and of delegation members who have stayed in her home.

In 1988, when Limeños had at last begun to hope that the war might finally be over for them, townspeople still remembered the two Witnesses who joined them when times were roughest, and who, each in her own authentic but very different way, touched their hearts.

When they pass the crosses on the road, they remember the delegation of women who marched from Esteli and planted those crosses on International Women's Day, May 8, 1985. They remember the priest who did his best to pray with them in Spanish, the Alaska delegation that helped with the tobacco harvest, and they even remember the woman who stayed back in town because she felt that joining in the tobacco harvest violated her principles.

And somewhere a continent away, she surely remembers them.

LAGARTILLO

A witness as defined by *Cruden's Complete Concordance** is someone who testifies to the truth at risk of his or her own life. Each Witness for Peace delegate who traveled down a road or stood in a cornfield in proximity to a contra unit was living in that tradition. Yet most Witnesses returned from Nicaragua humbled and less impressed by their own bravery than when they set out. If they thought they knew what witnessing was before they left, they usually came back with that vision altered or enriched by contact with Nicaraguan people of faith who were risking everything for what they believed.

Amancio and Florentina Perez, who met many long-term and short-term Witnesses, are campesinos who teach by example.

In the middle of a cloudless night, Amancio Perez lies on his stomach in a hole dug in the ground, his gun wedged between his arm and his right side. A cool wind, unusual for this region, is blowing. He is telling a story he has probably told a hundred times before, but he gives the impression of rethinking its painful meaning each time. He points to a tree silhouetted in the moonlight not far from the foxhole. Beneath that tree, on New Year's Eve of 1984, his niece died defending the cooperative from the contras. A few hundred yards away, where the road turns and begins its descent into town, is the place where his brother was killed that same night. Just over that little hill, he says, is the path that his sister-in-law, Florentina Perez, took as she scrambled in the darkness leading about seventy children to safety.

Amancio's khaki pants, green army jacket, fatigue hat, and gun are as much a part of him as the wispy, never-shaved Vandyke on his chin or the saucer-sized brown eyes that light up each time he speaks.

As he talks in the darkness it becomes apparent why he takes his turn every other night sitting in this hole scanning the horizon, and why he straps his wood-handled AK-47, a veteran of the Korean war, on his back anytime he leaves his house. "When they came the last time," he says, "there were maybe a hundred and fifty of them [contras], and we had ten AKs to defend ourselves."

In the light of day it becomes apparent why people from all over

---

*Grand Rapids, Mich.: Zondervan Publishing House, 1949.

the world have climbed this hill to see Amancio and his people. Florentina, his widowed sister-in-law, is a sturdy, thin woman in her mid-thirties. She has walked at least half a dozen Witness delegations through the farming cooperative, explaining where the contras attacked, how she escaped, and how six people, including her husband and her twenty-year-old daughter died. Her daughter insisted on staying to defend the cooperative, although she could hardly run due to childhood polio.

Every morning Florentina rises before the sun. She adds water to *masa* (corn meal), kneads it in a clay pot, then rolls the masa into balls that she flattens with her fist and fingers before patting them into perfectly circular tortillas. Tossing them on the earthen stove, she laughs, thinking about the dozens of women and men from other countries who've come through her kitchen and who she tried to teach, with mixed results, the ancient art of tortilla making, second nature to her.

"When the first delegation came," says Amancio, "I was still very affected by the death of our compañeros. I had my psychological problems, and talking to these groups—I just felt strange to speak to a group of North Americans. To think about our dead and to think that the principal one responsible was the North American government—I felt a bit strange."

In the back of his mind lurked another suspicion, which he voiced only after many months. "In such a big delegation, with their pretty T-shirts, it could be that among all those who come with much good will, that in among them are a few infiltrators." He discussed this with a long-termer, who explained the process that Witness used to select and screen people, but that undoubtedly if the CIA wanted to infiltrate, they would find a way. "But we already knew [before meeting the Witnesses]," he said, "that a part of the North American people were in favor of us, in favor of the poor, in favor of Nicaragua, in favor of our revolution." And so Amancio decided it was worth the risk.

The Perez family lives the kind of Christianity that Witnesses of many faiths were hungry for. The family had lived for generations in a valley just to the east of Lagartillo, where they owned a farm and nice homes along a stream next to a beautiful waterfall. The Perezes lived well, not extravagantly, but better than many families in the mountains around them.

In Somoza's time, through contact with one priest who came to visit and others they heard only on the radio, the Perez brothers began to, as Amancio puts it, "acquire some sort of commitment." They began to understand that their faith "wasn't just saying prayers when we got up in the morning and when we went to bed."

"When Somoza was in power, I as a Christian understood that things were bad. The gospel itself is enough to teach us that. Through the 'Bloque,' [an organization of base communities] and through the radio, we started to open our eyes and see where things stood, and to contribute a little and see if we could liberate ourselves. The Bible is sort of what woke me up."

The brothers began to help the Sandinistas, who at that time were just a band of students-turned-guerrillas in the mountains. Eventually the family had to flee to the mountains for fear of the National Guard.

After the triumph of the revolution they gave up living in their nice homes to try building up El Lagartillo, a desolate place high on a hill, barren, untilled, with very little water. The idea was that it would be a cooperative—a place where twenty-one landless families could have a piece of property, clean water, a school, a clinic, and a future to call their own. For Amancio, the rocky plot of land with a few broken-down houses was like a dream come true, a chance to build a new society, a more just society, from the ground up. The three Perez brothers became the cooperative leaders, and their full efforts for more than two years went into building the homes, the school, and the grain storage facility and creating a water supply system.

They moved up from the valley into their new homes. Two families were still living in the schoolhouse, awaiting completion of their home, when the attack came, in December, less than a month after they moved in.

In the year after the attack, Witness delegations helped rebuild the homes and brought tools and supplies. They listened to the stories and prayed with the survivors at the site of a monument to the dead. In the evenings the people of Lagartillo would explain to their guests about the faith and the community that kept them going. They enabled their guests to understand liberation theology and base communities from the ground up.

Peggy Cohee, the theology student from an earlier Massachusetts delegation, had come back to work as a long-term Witness and traveled with Tom Loudon, Mary Schoen, and Peter Olson to another cooperative near Lagartillo in mid-1985. She wrote:

Knowing that these people are a likely contra target and that they feel very vulnerable, we wanted to be with them. We volunteered our labor. They set us to work building a house from scratch.

We lay our rectangle, squared the corner, dug a trench all round for laying the foundation, then, wheelbarrow by wheelbarrow, mixed cement and lay the foundation. That's as far as we got in five days of work. . . . Everything had to be hauled a distance—sand, stone, and water (bucket by bucket from a water hole about an eighth of a mile from the construction [site]). My hands are just now developing the callouses they need to continue this kind of work.

In the Catholic eucharistic service there is a point where the bread is being blessed and is referred to as having been "made by human hands." This phrase came to mind often during the week as I worked and as I watched others work, pounding out tortillas, washing clothes at a water hole, collecting wood, whetting a machete . . .

The suffering, death, and rebirth of Lagartillo was a story that begged to be told. Witnesses passed through ground made sacred by the shedding of blood, then returned home and told their story over and over again, with a plea for an end to the killing. Before the Congress voted on contra aid in 1986, Witness for Peace flew Florentina to the United States to tell her story. In one month she covered twelve states and spoke to two thousand people. Film star Richard Gere traveled with long-term volunteer Tom Loudon and Dr. Charlie Clements out to see Amancio and the people of Lagartillo, and to take their message back.

8

RIO SAN JUAN: WAGING PEACE, OR FOLLY?

How many of you remember what you were doing on August 8, 1985?

—Ronald Reagan, answering a question
about the Iran-contra scandal

August 8, 1985, was a day Ronald Reagan couldn't remember. Sometime that afternoon, we now know, he authorized the first transfer of arms to Iran in exchange for U.S. hostages in Lebanon. That oft-denied and conveniently forgotten decision set in motion the events of the Iran-contra scandal that was eventually to stain his reputation as the Teflon president and seriously damage his ability to control foreign policy, including Central America policy.

While the president was meeting with his advisers, twenty-nine Witnesses for Peace were trudging through a muddy Costa Rican jungle as captives of the contra group ARDE. The Witnesses, along with a Nicaraguan crew of seven and more than a dozen journalists, had begun a three-day "Peace Flotilla" on the San Juan River between Costa Rica and Nicaragua the day before. After completing the trip downriver and spending the night on the river without incident, they were fired at and taken prisoner. By the time they were released the following day, worn out but uninjured, the kidnapping had become front-page news around the world.

The attention turned out to be a mixed blessing. Headlines in the sensationalist *New York Post* one day screamed "29 Yanks Held in Jungle." Overnight those headlines turned to "Yanks Duped by

Reds." Television commentators shifted their attention from the safety of the captives to unfounded suspicions that the whole event was a publicity ploy.

The Rio San Juan Peace Flotilla had three stated purposes: To pray for peace on the river, to commemorate those who died there, and to support any and all initiatives to bring peace to the border region.

Many people today will tell you that they have heard of Witness and of people being kidnapped on a river. Yet few among the general public remember or ever knew the stated purposes of the river trip. Most media accounts managed to turn the event into a circus.

KIDNAPPED ON THE RIO SAN JUAN

The San Juan River forms the border between Nicaragua and Costa Rica for more than one hundred miles, beginning just east of the picturesque riverside town of El Castillo. Before the contra war, the river had been a largely unguarded and peaceful home to smugglers and fishermen, owned by Nicaragua but open to transit by ships of both countries. At the end of May 1985, the border threatened to become a flash point when three Costa Rican Civil guardsmen were killed near the town of Las Crucitas. The Costa Ricans blamed the Sandinistas, the Sandinistas blamed the contras, and a special commission of the OAS couldn't tell who did it.

A presence of some sort on the San Juan had been inevitable once Witness made the decision to expand beyond Jalapa. The existence of contra camps in Costa Rica had been an open secret for years. Military strategists from the Pentagon to the Sandinista high command knew that for the contras to succeed militarily they would have to complement their forces in Honduras with an attack from Costa Rica. A southern front was, as General Richard Secord put it, the sine qua non of any serious contra strategy.

The conservative Costa Rican press used the deaths of the three Civil Guardsmen to whip up latent anti-Nicaraguan sentiment to a frenzy, and the United States stepped up military aid to neutrality-professing Costa Rica. Nicaragua offered to negotiate an internationally supervised demilitarized zone on the border. Witness wanted to support that initiative, since such a solution would block U.S. plans to use Costa Rica as a contra base. An international presence could also cut the risk that a border incident could become a pretext for direct military action.

No third country was willing to come forward to supply troops to supervise and verify such a zone unless Costa Rica also requested such a presence, and Costa Rican President Luis Alberto Monge was refusing to talk to Nicaragua until Nicaragua apologized for the Las Crucitas killings. Witness thought of a way that their presence could serve as a catalyst to break the impasse. In a meeting with Foreign Minister Miguel D'Escoto, representatives of the long-term team offered to place themselves on the river as observers, to serve as a peacekeeping force there.

D'Escoto was just about to embark on a month-long fast "in defense of life, peace, and against terrorism." Frustrated with the church for its failure as a peacemaker and impatient with the pace of diplomacy, he had decided to lay down his government portfolio for a time and open what he called a "new trench" in the struggle for peace.*

D'Escoto's fast inspired people in Nicaragua and around the world to consider what new steps they might take in nonviolent action for peace. His gesture sparked what was being called a "Gospel Uprising" (*Insurrecion Evangelica*), in which Nicaraguans took up the fast and other actions for peace. The same spirit that generated the fast gave rise to the idea of the Peace Flotilla.

D'Escoto took the Peace Flotilla idea to President Ortega. The president's first reaction was that it was too dangerous. As D'Escoto explained the mission and the importance of Witness being allowed to travel unarmed, Ortega came around. He hoped it might convince President Monge to work with him on a permanently supervised zone.

As Witness envisioned it, the Peace Flotilla was to be the first of many such trips as part of the verification of such a demilitarized zone. After a few trips they would establish a permanent presence, a series of tent villages, along the river. Witness hoped that individuals or governments of other nations, either Latin American or European, would come forward to support the idea, but was prepared to continue the presence on its own if need be. Peace and church groups in Costa Rica were approached but declined to participate.

A collection of peace activist boat owners from the San Francisco area offered to join the effort. Two of their number, Bob Heifetz and Tom Caufield, flew to Nicaragua on just a few days notice with nautical maps and captain's pipes and caps at the ready.

*D'Escoto was one of four priests to hold high positions in the Sandinista government. Their prominent roles were a source of tension between Managua and the Vatican.

Meanwhile the fifty-seventh Witness for Peace delegation, this one from New York State, was holed up in a church in Westchester County training and preparing for their visit. They were in many respects a typical Witness group: three nuns, three pastors, a Catholic priest, a peace activist and mother of six, one mild-mannered water engineer, a poet, two nurses, a sprinkling of students and social workers. They ranged in age from twenty-three to eighty-one years. They included Methodists, Roman Catholics, Jews, Episcopalians, Quakers, and Presbyterians. They had traveled varied roads to get there.

Judith McDaniel was a feminist activist and poet from Albany. Tom Fenlon, a Catholic priest, had worked in Harlem, in suburban Staten Island, and now served in Hispanic ministry in Newburgh. Lloyd Duren was a long-time activist and Methodist pastor. Kathy Maire, a Catholic sister, was a committed peace activist who later joined the long-term team. Kathleen Kennedy was a nurse and mother from Syracuse.

They ended up doing a lot of praying during their visit to Nicaragua, and they commemorated the dead Civil Guards, as well as Nicaraguan troops who had been killed by the contras on the river. Whether they advanced the cause of peace on the river is still an open question.

Pastora Threatens

The night before the flotilla set sail, contra leader Eden Pastora boasted on Costa Rican television that he had ordered his men to fire on the boat and the Witnesses. He described the Witnesses as wolves in sheep's clothing. His famous temper peaked when he learned that the boat planned to travel past the sites of some of his old bases, including La Penca, where he had been injured in a May 1984 bomb explosion.

That bombing, aimed at the charismatic but uncontrollable guerrilla leader, had left Pastora injured, three journalists dead, and his idea of launching an anti-Sandinista insurgency from Costa Rica in shambles. Pastora was angry at the CIA, the Sandinistas, and his partners in the contras. But for the moment his rage focused on a group of peacemakers from New York.

While Pastora raged, the participants prayed. In Managua and Washington, Witness issued a statement reminding the public that the U.S. government was ultimately responsible for anything that should happen to them. The night of August 5 was a time of soul searching for the ten long-termers as well as the nineteen members of the delegation, some of whom would not decide until the early morning hours to continue the journey downriver.

The next morning, as the delegates arrived in El Castillo, more than one hundred people lined the docks and cheered in an emotional greeting for the delegation. Shouts of "Viva la paz" filled the air. The tiny town, tired of war and eager to see their river safe once again, was in a mood to celebrate. After a church service and a rousing meeting, the group gathered on one long, flat barge and set off downriver. From El Castillo east, the southern bank is Costa Rican territory, and the contras could be anywhere along the steep-banked, thickly forested shores.

They sailed under the watchful eye of two network camera crews, more than a dozen photographers and print reporters, and at least one CIA agent.* They sang songs and hung a brightly colored banner on the side of the barge proclaiming their name and their mission.

Later, Witness was accused of making the trip as a publicity stunt. In reality, Pastora's threat made what would otherwise have been a barely noted cruise into a media spectacular. The day before the threat only two reporters of any significance had signed on. On the morning of August 5, as the Witnesses left Managua, their bus was besieged by network camera crews, photographers, and reporters. Having heard the threat, the press were now falling over one another to tag along. They appeared less interested in the story the Witnesses had to tell than in the possibility that the Witnesses might get their heads blown off trying to tell it.

On the River

Downriver from El Castillo, it was smooth sailing. Herons soared overhead and an occasional royal turkey flew across the flat bow of the barge. The captain, Enrique Reyes Gonzales, a hearty man of about sixty nicknamed "Chorrizo," told tales of his travels to New

---

*The Tower Commission Report on the Iran contra scandal contains an important detail that showed that the U.S. government was indeed very concerned about what those twenty-nine peace activists were doing on the river. In recounting his contacts with Pastora for the Commission, CIA station chief Joe Fernandez mentioned that he spoke with Pastora the day that the Witness boat was seized. Fernandez called Pastora to warn him that he shouldn't harm anyone on the boat, because the CIA had one of their people on the boat at the time. To this day it is unclear whether the person, most likely cloaked as a journalist, was there simply to observe or to provoke an incident.

Orleans and beyond in happier days. No more, he said. The last time he had gone this far downriver was in 1983 when he took a boatload of people from the Atlantic port of San Juan del Norte to Granada to see Pope John Paul II.

Long-term volunteer Julie Beutel played her guitar and everyone sang. The captains from the Peace Navy pumped the barge captain for information and made notes on their charts at every bend in the river. They were hoping to have a permanent mini-navy patrolling the river within a month or two. At Boca San Carlos, more reporters met the group on the Costa Rican shores, where Geralyn McDowell of Troy, New York, led a rousing bilingual chorus of Pete Seeger's "We Are the Boat" and overenthusiastically (and prematurely) announced, "We have come to claim this river for peace, and we have been triumphant!"

At La Penca, they sang their theme song, "We Are the Boat," to about twenty bemused Sandinista soldiers, who responded with a rendition of the hymn of the Sandinista People's Army. La Penca was as far downriver as they planned to go. The boat turned around and returned to Boca San Carlos, where they spent the night on the Nicaraguan side. Costa Rican authorities denied the group permission to tie up on their side of the river, forcing the crew to make a dangerous nighttime crossing. The group supped on rice and beans, then bedded down in good spirits. It was a restful night in mosquito paradise.

A Shot Across the Bow

The next day began like a river scene straight from the *African Queen.* Hollywood could not have created a more beautiful dawn— exotic birds chirping, the first shadows on the cloudy sky giving way to cracks of golden sunlight breaking through, mist rising off the river water, fish snapping at flies on the surface.

A toad or snake on the shore that morning would have stared in amazement or turned and fled in fright at the sight of over forty humans rising from mats on the deck or descending from hammocks strung three high, side to side, on the covered barge. It must have been the largest concentration of humanity in that spot before or since. Don Enrique's barge was the only civilian vessel to spend the night on the river in years—and would be the last for years to come.

Marta, the Nicaraguan cook who brought along her infant daughter because there was no one else to care for her, had coffee and beans and rice ready by the time they got under way at six. The group ate, prayed, and settled in for the ride back to El Castillo.

The boat didn't reach El Castillo until dark the following day. A single bullet fired by an ARDE soldier named Israel sent the group to the deck, put the trip onto page one of every paper in the United States, and began a long discussion within Witness about the future of such activities.

The group was seized by a band of contras on Costa Rican soil early on the morning of August 7, while heading back upriver toward San Carlos. One shot was fired over the bow, and the whole delegation hit the deck as Don Enrique cut the engine. Peeking up over the sides, the Witnesses saw four young men in camouflage carrying rifles moving along the grassy banks. The captain pulled over to the Costa Rican shore. By then eight armed men were visible. They gestured for everyone to get out of the boat.

The Witnesses explained who they were and the purpose of their mission. The soldiers, not knowing what to make of the trembling mass of pale-faced, English-whispering humanity standing before them, decided to take them to their leaders. It wasn't clear whether they had specific orders to seize this boat or standing orders to stop all traffic on the river. The latter was a likely possibility since there hadn't been a civilian boat on the river for almost three years.

The Witnesses and the boat crew clambered across the deck onto the shore, up a muddy embankment, and stood hand in hand awaiting the contras' next move. The delegates tried to keep a close watch on the Nicaraguan crew, those most likely to be in danger. The journalists scampered about, snapping pictures and trying to ask questions of the obviously poorly prepared contras.

The contras' immediate superior, a thin man with a wispy beard and eyes of steel, emerged from the rainforest. His name was William. William ordered the group to start walking uphill into the jungle. At first he insisted that the journalists leave their cameras and equipment behind in the muck but after a wail of protests allowed them to keep the equipment when they promised they would not use it. That promise was violated almost as soon as it was uttered.

The steep climb through the jungle was tough, especially for some older members of the group. Eighty-one-year-old Shubert Frye, a Presbyterian minister nicknamed "Sprye Frye" for his chipper attitude throughout, was assisted through the muck by Dr. Ed Myer. Others helped Geralyn McDowell, who was having trouble walking. Pat Hynds, a Maryknoll volunteer, found herself barefoot within five minutes when the sandals she was wearing broke under the pressure of the thick mud. (Hynds had come wearing heavier footgear but had decided to ditch them on the boat when she realized that the boots, borrowed from a friend in the Sandinista militia, were incriminating and dangerous).

The group had no way of knowing how long they would be walking. The soldiers indicated only that they were being taken to see their leader. Asked who their leader was, they said "Pastora." No one said a word.

The hike seemed endless. No one in the group knew if their destination was an hour or a day away, nor what awaited them upon arrival. William let it be known that the group's fate was not in his hands, and said—sounding not a bit friendly—that he would do whatever he was told with the group. His gaze was menacing. They stopped for a prayer and a song on a hillside, both to calm their fears and to take a measure of control of the situation.

At a small farmhouse the contras stopped and ordered the group to gather and wait under a porch roof. The contras seemed to have commandeered the home and its female occupants as a field kitchen and crew. The women were friendly but not talkative. William warned the group not to move from the site and warned the journalists not to take photographs.

The initial fear had subsided, but it was becoming clear that the hut might be home for a long time. The group gathered in prayer. Some lighthearted, others despairing, they remembered their loved ones left behind. A few minutes later they heard a news report on Sandinista radio describing their capture. The report mentioned the possibility that the group had been killed.

Managua

The news had gotten out quickly, albeit not too accurately, thanks to a ham radio on board. Warren Armstrong had managed to communicate one final message before being forced off the boat. The long-term volunteers in Managua had been taking turns monitoring the radio day and night and taping all transmissions. As it happened, two Ph.D. candidates, Pat Manning of Tucson and Terry Toma of North Carolina, were in the radio room at the time.

That message, as they heard it, was broadcast around the world that evening.

WARREN: There has been a shot fired over the boat.
PAT: Where did the shot come from, Warren?
WARREN: Costa Rican side, Costa Rican side. They are warning

everyone off the boat. We are on the Costa Rican side. They want everyone off the boat.

PAT: Who wants everyone off the boat, Warren?

WARREN: The enemy, the enemy.

PAT: You said the enemy, Warren? I didn't copy . . . Warren, who wants everyone off the boat?

WARREN: Armed people, armed people.

PAT: Armed people. How many armed people, Warren?

WARREN: One person, one person . . . two or more. . . . We can see three, we can see three. . . . We're getting off the boat.

PAT: You can see three armed people; Warren, is that correct? Please.

WARREN: That is correct. We are getting off the boat. That is correct. We're getting off the boat, we're getting off the boat.

PAT: Warren, is someone able to maintain radio communication throughout this?

WARREN: Negativo, negativo, negativo.

PAT: We'll keep in contact, just in case. You are in our prayers. Okay, we're standing by here with the radio on . . .

The break in communication was followed by the sound of ladders being dragged across the corrugated tin roof of the barge, which sounded, over the crackly radio, like automatic weapons fire. The sound was so convincing that when a tape recording of the broadcast was later played to reporters, many of them concurred that it was indeed gunfire.

Toma and Manning stared at the radio in horror. They called Sharon Hostetler and the rest of the team to the radio room. There was nothing they could do but listen. Before the transmission was over, Hostetler was on the phone trying to get a line to Yvonne Dilling in Washington. Next she called Nicaraguan government authorities to give them the news and to emphasize the importance of keeping any military presence at a distance from the boat or the captives. Two hours after getting the news, Hostetler informed the U.S. Embassy in Managua of the kidnapping. The Embassy sent an officer to the Witness for Peace office, who remained there all day long.

Stateside

It was the dead of summer in Washington, when everyone who can get out of town does so. Dilling got the call from Managua and immediately called down the hall at the Sojourners building, to whomever was listening. Dennis Marker came running, and listened in on the end of the phone conversation. The story as they unraveled it from the final radio broadcast from the jungle, relayed through Managua, was grim.

Dilling began to call members of the steering committee, the Nicaraguan and Costa Rican embassies in Washington, and the State Department. Marker got on the phone to Jim Wallis, who one day earlier had led a group of protesters in civil disobedience at the Nevada Nuclear Weapons Testing Site. It was 7:00 A.M. in Nevada. A sheriff had to pass the phone through the bars of a jail cell so that Marker could tell Wallis the news. "It sounds as if the worst has happened." The group of arrested peace activists began to pray, by name, for the safety, or for the souls, of the Witnesses; they weren't sure which.

A decision was made early on that the best way to save the lives of the captured Witnesses was by publicizing the kidnapping as widely as possible. The Witness for Peace network around the country began to mobilize. Plans were made for an afternoon press conference in Washington. All across the country, families and communities were reacting to the news about their loved ones with outrage, with anger, and, in many cases, with incomprehension and shock.

In a house just outside of Raleigh, North Carolina, Nancy Keppel, whose eldest son, Tim, was on the boat, was just saying goodbye to a luncheon guest when the phone rang. It was Betsy Crites from the Witness office in Durham. "Mrs. Keppel, I'm afraid we have bad news. The group has been attacked. We have a ham radio on board, and the last thing we heard were shots. We don't know if they're alive or not."

Nancy Keppel's luncheon guest, an old friend who had just been to Nicaragua on a Witness delegation, stayed with her. Keppel called Tim's wife, Lisa, with the news, and called Jane Golden, whose son Jake, a Methodist minister, was also on the boat. Jake and Tim had grown up for a time in the same town, Hickory, North Carolina; their fathers once sang together in a barbershop quartet.

Just as soon as Keppel hung up the phone, it jangled. For the next three days, it continued to ring. "That day I had at least eighty phone calls," she recalls. "The press, all the TV stations, the radio stations called, the AP called. People who knew me or Tim called. My minister called saying he'd called the State Department and they wouldn't give him any information. Then the State Department called me. They said they were trying to locate [Tim] but they weren't having any luck."

"The newspapers really wanted to play up the mother angle," she says. Keppel, a lifelong churchgoer who describes herself as a "radical liberal social activist from way back," had another angle. "They all wanted to know if I was worried or if I wanted him to come home. I just said that I was so glad that Tim and all these people were down there trying to get things straightened out, and that I hope they stay there until they realize that we need to solve this without use of arms. They all thought I should be worried, but I never worry about anything. I never once thought they were dead."

People in the Witness network around the country, already alerted to the danger by Pastora's threat, leapt into action. Within hours the switchboards at the State Department and in congressional offices lit up. Communities all across the country held vigils and prayer services and began petition drives, some comparing the contra's captives to the Middle East hostages.

On the River

Meanwhile Andy Mills, a water sanitation engineer from New Jersey, was taking care of business as usual deep in the Costa Rican jungle. He threw himself into the task of procuring safe water for the kidnappees. As he departed the boat he thought to carry one of the water jugs that had been treated for drinking. His quick thinking helped prevent dehydration in the early, stress-filled hours.

It also gave the group leaders a clue toward handling the contras. The group decided to ask the contras to allow some of them to return to the boat to get more water and to communicate by radio. They wanted to say two things: that they were OK, and that they didn't want any military intervention or "rescue." This appealed to the contras' self-interest in two ways—they certainly wouldn't want any of their captives to get ill from drinking unsafe water, and they didn't want the Nicaraguan military to come their way.

William allowed three people to go to the boat, but on his terms. The threesome went under armed guard, agreed to conduct the radio broadcast in Spanish, and agreed to include an appeal for all military forces to stay clear of the area.

Managua

When the radio in Managua crackled and came to life again, shrieks of joy filled the Witness for Peace office. Members of the team who for three hours had believed they had lost their friends, lovers, husbands, wives, and coworkers were like a congregation born again.

By this time, however, there was little time for celebration. The word of the kidnapping was spreading, and the international press corps soon came to camp out on the doorstep of the Witness house.

There were radio transcripts to transcribe, translate, and release, and communication had to be maintained with the United States, with the U.S. Embassy, and with the Nicaraguan government. A deluge of phone calls had to be answered once concerned parents, children, and friends of the kidnapped began to call Managua as well as the U.S. Witness offices.

Long-term volunteers who had been carrying out their normal activities in all corners of the country heard the news on the radio and headed for Managua. As the team assembled, a long vigil of prayer, waiting, and hard work began. Friends both Nicaraguan and North American began to show up with their arms open, willing to help. Meanwhile another delegation was on it way, and planning for the delegates had to go on as if nothing had happened and in the hope that nothing disastrous would.

Herb Gunn, a long-term Witness whose future wife, Julie Beutel, was one of the captives, later recalled the scene. "The Managua office instantly became a world media center, a task for which we had little experience and training. It was amateur radio operation and press work at its best (and worst). Long-term volunteers set out translating and typing each radio transmission and giving these to the press. But we lacked the savvy to control the message by playing into press deadlines, and as a result, were bested by the White House and State Department in those critical hours when the story was being interpreted for press consumption."

On the River

The silence of the jungle afternoon was pierced by the menacing buzz of helicopters overhead. The contras sprang to life, readied their weapons, and ordered everyone to get under cover of the house. They shouted and cursed at the pair of Sandinista choppers that appeared a mile or two away, running along the river.

An NBC cameraman nicknamed "Chicle" (chewing gum) tried to film the copters and quickly found himself surrounded by three angry contras, pointing AK machine guns with the safeties released. He put down the camera. ("Chicle" made good use of his idle time. He was planning to be married soon, and went to Father Fenlon to ask for pre-Cana counseling during the kidnapping. He was married a few months later.)

The helicopters put William in a foul mood. The incident temporarily put an end to conversations that a number of the captives were having with their captors. It made negotiating an early release that much more difficult. Photos of the tied-up boat, taken from the helicopters, appeared in *Barricada,* the Sandinista daily, the following day. The State Department later said the photos depicted the moment of the group's capture and used the photos to back their claim that the capture was orchestrated. The charge that the Sandinista helicopters were present at the time of the delegation's capture was simply untrue. The photos themselves reveal that there was no one on the boat or even near it at the time the pictures were taken. Yet the press repeated the charge again and again.

As many as twenty different contra troops guarded the captives at different times. They gave their captives the impression that a major camp with a large number of contras was right over the next hill, just out of sight.

Most of the foot soldiers were relatively friendly and even forthcoming with details of their lives before the war and life as a contra. One of them, a young man from Bluefields named Israel, told in great detail how Pastora's army functioned. He indicated that William had more than fifty contras under his command and that his superior, who went by the nom de guerre of Daniel, was one of eighteen of Pastora's commanders, each of whom was responsible for 300 troops. The captives had two strong reactions to the foot soldiers: they liked most of them as people, and they thought the soldiers seemed to be motivated primarily by fear.

One of the people the contras clearly feared was William. William was a breed apart from the men he commanded. His torn clothing and rumpled cap gave the impression of a man who knew how to survive in the wild. He was as comfortable in that jungle as a member of the New York delegation might feel in a New York subway car. Sitting on a rock smoking a cigarette, he said without looking up or changing his tone of voice that he would kill the whole delegation if he needed to or was ordered to. Nothing in his manner left any doubt that he meant it. The son of a former National Guardsman, he had joined Pastora almost three years ago, fearful that his farm, near Nueva Guinea, would be taken by the government.

In spite of his uncompromising demeanor, the group raised with William an issue that it had set as its goal for the day—to be allowed to go back down and sleep in the boat. This group of landlubbers from another part of the world had quickly become very attached to their boat. On the boat, in radio communication with the world, assured of a water supply, on their own "turf," the group agreed, they would not be as vulnerable. Taken aback by the suggestion, William grudgingly said he was willing to consider it.

As the day wore on, the mood of the group rose and fell with William's. They took to pressing him every hour or so about sleeping on the boat. He finally relented at about 3:00 P.M. and agreed to let them go down to the boat to spend the night. The group collected its belongings, assured one another that the Nicaraguan crew, many of them young and therefore prize "recruits" for the contras, was in their midst, and began the muddy march, or rather the slippery slide, back to the bank of the San Juan.

Lost in Space

As trailblazers go, the contras left something to be desired. The troops leading the group found themselves, within less than half an hour, hopelessly lost. As the group followed, members began to realize that they had made a wrong turn. William was nowhere to be found. For a while the group was wandering in the jungle on their own, out of sight of the guards, who had gotten themselves completely lost. The contras, who had made a point of explaining that they were unfamiliar with Costa Rican territory because they always operated in Nicaragua, seemed to be going to great lengths to prove the point.

The group reversed course and climbed back up to where they had turned off the path leading to the boat. After about half the group had gotten back on track, William came scampering by, furious, and ordered the group to climb back up to the house at once. Then he ran back down toward the river.

The group decided to keep on going down. No one wanted to face the prospect of spending the night on the ground outside the house, exposed to the elements and to William's foul temper. Several members of the delegation were suffering severe fatigue and stress at this point, and there was a real question as to whether one member could physically manage the long climb back up to the house. The group pressed on, sliding from tree to tree, some linked arm in arm, in the direction where they thought the river was. An hour of daylight remained.

Once he realized that his orders had been defied, William's rage grew. He had been embarrassed by his troops getting lost and now was doubly embarrassed to find that this group of gringos had disobeyed him. He was in no mood to talk. At the bottom of the hill, in a grove several hundred yards from the boat, three of his men blocked the group from moving any further. Geralyn McDowell lay on the ground, hardly able to continue walking.

Several contra foot soldiers, at the group's request, asked William to come and see her, hoping to convince him that it was futile to order the climb back up to the house. Each time one of his soldiers went into the brush carrying a message to William, the commander ranted and raved and hurled the man back out with the stern message that the delegation had better begin their retreat away from the shore. Yet none of his men moved to enforce the order.

The group had no thought of going back up. Yet asking William to change his mind was getting them nowhere. He had given an order and been disobeyed, thus losing face in front of his men. The only graceful exit for him would be to give another order and to have it obeyed. The challenge for this muddy and very weary group of non-violent activists was to get this machine-gun toting madman to order them to do exactly what they wanted to do. Successful negotiation in this setting meant avoiding escalation and allowing William to give the orders.

William came out of the brush, still blazing mad. His eyes squinted ever tighter and his stringy body snapped and recoiled as he screamed at the top of his lungs that he was in charge here, that they had disobeyed an order, and that under no circumstances would he reconsider. "Go back to the house!" he insisted. He waved his gun, he waved his finger, he threw down his hat.

The group was about one hundred yards away, gathered around McDowell.

To add to the tension, William's troops appeared to be trying to separate the Nicaraguans from the North Americans, but a group of Witnesses moved toward the crew and the contras backed off. They wanted the younger members of the crew, but apparently didn't want to take them in front of witnesses.

William refused several requests to go see McDowell and threatened violence if he didn't see people pick up their gear and start the march right away. He refused to budge. But by now it was obvious that the group was not about to move either. He finally walked over to her. McDowell tried to explain in a few words of Spanish that she could not walk back up the hill. She was in fact feeling very bad but had also been encouraged to ham it up. William looked down at her, looked back up and shouted, in the same tone as before.

This time the message was different. "How could you let one of your own people get into such a state? You people who call yourselves Christians!"

Rather than remind him that it was his men who had obliged them to leave their comfortable barge to march through Mudville, the Witnesses just waited. He finished his tirade and went on to give a new order: "You are going to go to the boat. I'm going to post my men on the boat. But we won't be responsible for your safety. You are to leave the lights off, and we are going to take your radio. If you try to move or any shooting starts, we are not responsible. Remember that, we are not responsible, and if anyone tries anything, it's all over."

It was the best deal they'd heard all day. They shouldered their gear, helped the infirm to their feet, and assisted one another along the final yards to the boat, which looked ever so good in the last rays of sunlight that evening. They radioed back to Managua, under armed guard, telling their colleagues that they were on the boat, tired but safe, and issued another call for military forces to stay out of the area.

Managua

The roller coaster of emotions that had marked the day peaked again when President Ortega paid a surprise, late-night visit to the house. He told the team of his efforts to secure the release of the captives, including phone conversations with Costa Rica's President Monge.

Ortega appeared a bit taken aback by the condition of the Witness for Peace office, which doubled as a dormitory for the long-term team. In normal times it was not an example of tidiness, and on this hectic day it was strewn with papers, books, sleeping gear, leftover food, and exhausted volunteers. "What is this?" asked the bemused guerrilla-turned-president. "A refugee camp?"

On the River

The group hoped to be on its way come daybreak. William said they would have to wait to see his commander, who would make a final determination. They waited all morning for the commander, who went by the name Daniel, and spent much of that time playing cards and conversing with the contras.

Daniel finally showed up, gave a brief speech in which he denied being a member of ARDE, then said goodbye. Consistent with the spirit in which the trip was undertaken, the group asked the contras to join hands and share in a prayer before parting. All but two of them let go their rifles for just a moment and joined hands to say the Lord's Prayer. The photographers, whispering their own plea for divine protection, snapped images unceasingly, using the sound of the prayers to cover the sounds of shutters clicking.

Daniel then approached each of the Nicaraguan crew, and for a moment, appeared as if he might try to take some of them. He finally turned away, leaving them to go with the Witnesses.

Just before noontime the captain cranked the motor and the boat was under way, heading back up the San Juan as if nothing had happened. They radioed Managua that they were under way, and passed on to them that Daniel had said he was not with ARDE, but rather part of an unnamed "independent, anti-Communist guerrilla force." No one present, reporters or Witnesses, believed him, but they were not about to say so on the radio while still in contra territory. Daniel's real name, they later learned, was Noel Boniche. He came from the island of Solentiname, where he fled three years earlier while under investigation for robbery. A photo of Boniche wearing an ARDE armband over his uniform had appeared in a German magazine.

The trip wasn't over yet. On its way upriver, the boat was stopped twice by the Costa Rican Civil Guard. The first time a Coronel Leimus inquired if everyone was OK. They told him they could make no comment while still in a potentially dangerous area. He was on Costa Rican radio within an hour saying that the group had been delayed by engine trouble.

The second time the Civil Guard stopped the boat, they held the crew and passengers against their will and claimed to be acting on orders from the U.S. consul, whom they claimed was on his way to see the Witnesses. The group believed, correctly, that if they did not get back to El Castillo that night, the network news would carry only Coronel Leimus's version of the story. Besides, their food and water supplies had run out. After a delay of more than an hour, and no appearance by the consul, the boat shoved off for the final leg of its river odyssey.

In El Castillo almost the entire town's population waited for the Peace Flotilla on the docks. Jubilant townspeople greeted each member as the Witnesses stepped from the boat like returning heroes. They escorted the group to the church for a rousing welcome ceremony and a prayer service to give thanks. The church was lit up with television lights as the group gave a report of the trip and issued a call for renewed international support for the plan to demilitarize the region.

Just hours after deliverance from their captors, they reaffirmed their commitment to nonviolence:

> We conversed with our captors. Our attitude with them was one of openness and dialogue. We called them "brothers" not because we felt it convenient but because our God teaches we are all one family, and because of the commitment that WFP has maintained since our beginning in 1983.
>
> Nonviolence as we try to live it is a belief in the power of love to open people's hearts. Our experience with these men confirmed this belief. They detained us against our will, and made us suffer . . . yet as individuals they treated us with respect. Tonight in freedom we can still call them brothers and we hold no ill feeling toward them. We pray that their treatment of their Nicaraguan brothers and sisters be guided by love and a desire for peace and be as respectful as their treatment of us.

They were not blind to the contrast between how they were treated and the horrors inflicted on so many Nicaraguans. "For example," said Virginia Druhe, "the captain of our boat, Don Enrique, has been ambushed three times while piloting his civilian transport on the Rio San Juan. . . . The tiny town of El Castillo, which received us so warmly on our mission of peace, has been attacked four times in the last two years."

A statement by the New York delegation read:

> The focus of the past two days has been on North Americans and their safety. Members of Witness for Peace and their families have felt the pain and uncertainty of separation . . . however we recognize that this pain is experienced by Nicaraguan families every day. It is unsafe for Nicaraguan people to ride along the roads and rivers because of the U.S. policy of funding the contras. Because we are North Americans, today we are free. But had we been Nicaraguans, we could have easily been killed and our deaths would have gone unnoticed.

"WITLESS FOR PEACE"

The people crowded into the church were among the few in the world that day who got an accurate report of what happened during the twenty-nine hours of captivity. The previous day, press coverage had turned against Witness for Peace. The State Department refused to acknowledge that the Witnesses had ever been held against their will. Dennis Marker was told by one reporter that the State Department insinuated at a briefing the day after the kidnapping that the whole event was a show put on by Witness for Peace and the Sandinistas.

Reporting from the second day on, with a few notable exceptions, turned from sympathetic to downright hostile. Washington correspondents began grasping at straws to verify two damaging stories—that the Witnesses had either kidnapped themselves or had been kidnapped by Sandinistas dressed as contras. The press seized on minor points such as the fact that Witness had changed the numbers of captives in two consecutive press statements, not recognizing that the confusion was due to journalists boarding at the last minute.

In Managua the press corps complained that Witness was too disorganized. In Washington they complained that they were too well prepared. At a Washington press conference on the day the boat was seized, Dick Taylor was introduced as the head of the Kidnap Negotiation Team; several reporters found the existence of such a team to be evidence that Witness had been eager for such an event, if they hadn't planned it outright.

The press corps demanded to know why Witness contended in the early moments that they had heard machine-gun fire over the radio, even though their own colleagues, when they listened to the tape of the radio broadcast, concurred with the Managua staff's grim assessment.

It was a sickening performance by media professionals. Tiny inconsistencies in stories were used to destroy the credibility of the Witness. A pile-on mentality developed. The worst was an ABC-TV report from San Carlos by Peter Collins, who alleged that the Sandinistas were preparing a reception in San Carlos before the group was ever released. By the time the Witnesses made their way back to San Carlos, it was mid-afternoon on August 9, and no one was on the docks waiting for them.

Not even the journalists on the boat got a chance to tell their own story—they got to San Carlos to find that the story was over. It had been told by reporters who were never on the scene. The television eye had turned to a plane crash in Japan and the major league baseball strike.

The tired Witnesses were mistaken in thinking that their ordeal was over. A contra attack on the road to San Carlos prevented the Witness bus from getting to San Miguelito to retrieve them. Getting out of San Carlos proved to be a logistical nightmare, and it took nearly three days to arrange air transportation to move the delegation, three by three, back to Managua.

When the delegates returned home, they found their local press to be much more sympathetic, as had been the case since the very first delegation. Kathy Maire, Geralyn McDowell, and long–term witness Nancy Eckel immediately began a speaking tour to dispel the lies that had been told thus far.

It was to be years before Witness regained the credibility lost in those few days. But the organization no longer had to worry about people not knowing who they were.

THE SAN JUAN SEQUEL

Captain Enrique Reyes Gonzales changed the name of his barge from "Yegua Hambriente" (the hungry mare) to "Yegua por la Paz" (the mare for peace). But there was no peace. Sporadic fighting continued along the river and stepped up after the U.S. congress approved $100 million in contra aid in 1986.

For the moment the goal of demilitarizing the San Juan River was not achieved. No country or third party came forward to form a peace monitoring force. The goal of attracting attention to the area was met, but that attention focused more on the Witnesses than on the threat to peace.

The attention given to the Peace Flotilla did make it harder for Costa Rica to deny that the contras used their territory as a base. The kidnapping provoked the first phone conversation in months between Presidents Monge and Ortega, a positive step brought about through the mediation of Panama's Manuel Antonio Noriega. That rapprochement was short-lived, and a frustrated Nicaragua sued its southern neighbor in the World Court.

The threat of the United States using Costa Rica as a flash point, of seeking an incident to provoke an invasion, continued, latent but unutilized. With the election of Oscar Arias, a candidate interested in preserving Costa Rican neutrality, an airstrip and several hospitals operated by the contras in his country's territory were shut down. Nicaragua agreed to withdraw the lawsuit when the Central American Presidents' Peace Plan was signed in August 1987.

The act of taking U.S. citizens prisoner was a high-profile black eye for the contras. Press attention to contra terrorism did not last very long, however. When the tortured bodies of thirteen kidnapped campesinos were discovered in a dry streambed near Achuapa a week later, their fate didn't merit a ripple in the U.S. media.

Witness for Peace suffered a few black eyes of its own at the hands of headline writers and columnists who portrayed them as Sandinista dupes, and cartoonists who portrayed them as "Witless for Peace." An internal analysis in the wake of the crisis concluded that the incident had raised the organization's profile while simultaneously undermining its credibility.

Serious questions emerged about the wisdom and efficacy of nonviolent direct intervention in a hot war situation. While some pressed to accelerate the use of nonviolent direct action in ever more visible and risky ways, others interpreted the Rio San Juan events as a call to caution.

The event was the high-water mark for such actions. The ease with which the administration controlled the press made any future trips much more risky. After months of analysis Witness concluded that it would be too easy, on a future trip, for the contras to harm the Witnesses and then blame the Sandinistas. Continuing the presence ran the risk of giving the administration exactly the kind of pretext the Peace Flotilla was aimed at preventing.

If Witness had continued the presence on the San Juan, they might have stumbled on evidence of the Iran-contra scandal more than a year before it was revealed publicly. Just a few miles up the river from where the group was held, an Indiana farmer named John Hull housed a contra field hospital and training grounds on his ranch in northern Costa Rica. During the Congressional ban on direct U.S. military aid to the contras, Hull's ranch became an important link in the chain of illegal dollars, weapons, and drugs that Oliver North, William Casey, and the National Security Council used to keep their "neat idea" of war against Nicaragua alive. A permanent presence of pesky Witnesses on the shores of the Rio San Juan would have been a nightmare for the contras and their U.S. backers, and risky beyond what the Peace Flotilla planners had ever imagined.

9

INVISIBLE WAR

How can a country that has Bibles in every hotel room persuade people to pay taxes for the killing of their brothers and
sisters? Don't you read it?
　　—Nicaraguan campesino's question to a U.S. delegation of
　　　　　　seminary students in Jinotega, January 1986

Manuel Morales worked for everything he had, which wasn't
much, just a piece of a mountain where he could grow corn and coffee
and tend a few cows. He was a grateful believer who never failed to
thank God for each rainfall, and a proud man who never asked for
charity.

But one damp night, October 24, 1985, he found himself barefoot and half dressed, hobbling on a muddy trail after a group of men,
pleading with them to give back what was most precious to him—his
three sons.

The contras had gone from home to home in El Chile, where
Morales lived, and taken every young man they found. Morales loved
his boys. He needed his boys. He pulled on his pants and followed the
armed men into the darkness.

"For the love of God in heaven," he cried. "Let them go."

One of the contras stopped, turned angrily and leveled his rifle
at Manuel's chest. "Shut up old man," he shouted, "or you die right
here."

Morales persisted until his oldest son turned to him and insisted
that he go back to the house. "They will kill us all, Papa. Go back and
be with my mother."

Morales was lucky. That same night, on the other side of the
mountain, a grandmother trying to protect her young had her throat

158

slashed and was left to die on the mountain trail. She was eighty-one years old.

In all, fifteen boys were kidnapped. Their absence created more than an emotional loss. They represented the bulk of the labor force for the area. With the coffee and corn harvests fast approaching, the contras had taken them in order to strangle the area economically. Without them, the corn would likely rot, the coffee beans fall to the ground, and more farmers would be forced to migrate to the city.

A few days after the kidnapping, Peter Kemmerle, a long-term Witness from Ohio, showed up at the Morales home. Manuel Morales trusted him because the parish priest, Father Douglas Araica, had told him the Witnesses were good people. He told Kemmerle what had happened and asked for help.

A delegation from Colorado arrived a few weeks later. They included a priest, a lay minister, a retired real estate agent, a public official from Wyoming, and a Jewish judge from Los Angeles who had been appointed twenty years earlier by Governor Ronald Reagan. Most of the delegation members knew corn only as a picnic treat and coffee as a warm way to begin the day. Yet each morning they hiked up into the hillside cornfields singing as they went through areas where the contras frequently roamed.

Their objective was to harvest the corn for three people, including Morales and a woman whose husband had been taken. They started slowly but once they got the hang of it, the corn piled up, and they made a serious dent in all three *milpas*. Against the backdrop of a beautiful mountain panorama, the silence, the steady motion of harvesting, and the dry splash of each ear landing in the pile took on a rhythm that invited silent prayer, and soon, as if by signal, the peacemakers turned cornpickers were praying silently for peace and for each of the fifteen kidnapped boys with each ear of corn they picked.

The decades of technological development that separated the campesinos from their guests vanished as they worked together, just as a jet plane had erased the miles that once kept them apart. The simplicity, generosity, and poverty of the Nicaraguan people left deep impressions. Most short-term delegates regarded the contact with the poor as even greater in impact than the contact with the war.

"Experiencing the daily life and hospitality of the poor was a tremendous spiritual experience," recalled Albert Winn, a pastor from Georgia, after another Witness trip. "You recognize just how much energy it takes to be poor and how much effort the tasks which we middle-class people perform almost effortlessly take. . . . To see them operating with such humanity under such conditions was just inspiring."

This gap in life-styles also had its humorous side. Long-term volunteer Aynn Setright was washing her clothes in the riverbed at Bocana de Paiwas when a friend asked her how people in the United States wash their clothes. "Oh, we just put them in a big machine and push a few buttons," she answered. Her friend was quiet for a few minutes. Then she asked, "How do you get the machine down to the river?"

At the end of the week in El Chile, the delegation and their hosts gathered for an ecumenical celebration. The women and children wore their finest clothes. An altar was decorated with palms, and people lined the fence surrounding the neighboring corral. As the service ended, Irving Levine, the judge from Los Angeles, stepped to the improvised altar to chant an ancient Hebrew song for the dead. At least two hundred people gathered in the circle, and quite possibly Sandinista and contra troops in the surrounding hillsides heard his mournful cry for peace.

For every dramatic action like the Rio San Juan Peace Flotilla, there were a thousand of these simple acts of presence. Witnesses accompanied the people in hundreds of communities like El Chile.

MANUEL, YOUR BOYS ARE BACK

When a campesino told Kemmerle that the sons of Manuel Morales had escaped, Kemmerle went to Pantasma to meet them and then rode with them to Jinotega. The boys told him of months spent in Honduran camps, of battles and executions, and of their escape. Fearing contra reprisal, Morales gathered his sons, abandoned the farm, and moved to Jinotega. Kemmerle borrowed a truck and drove out to bring the family's possessions into town. For Manuel Morales the war was over, his sons all still alive. The Witnesses had seen this tiny piece of the war through from beginning to end.

But for the rest of Nicaragua the war did not end. The U.S. strategy of aggression became ever more subtle and less visible, more devastating to Nicaragua, and more elusive for activists trying to get a handle on it and put a stop to it.

Witness for Peace delegates could accompany the Morales family through danger and hardship. They could help them harvest crops and move belongings, document what happened to the boys, and use the information about their kidnapping to rebut administration claims about the contras. Perhaps their presence averted more contra attacks.

But another war was going on in those mountains, an invisible war known to its proponents as low-intensity war. Witnesses on the scene came to call it high-intensity aggression. It involved economic strangulation, diplomatic isolation, psychological and ideological bombardment of the civilian population, and a collection of measures designed, in conjunction with the military assault by the contras and the threat of invasion, to eat away at Nicaragua from within, to make the country ungovernable—in short, to put an end to the revolution.

It was a masterful strategy that had evolved in the post–World War II period to deal with third-world insurgencies and leftist governments. A cardinal rule was to wage the war with minimal visibility and to avoid sending U.S. troops. It is called total war, because it attacks every organ and limb in a society's body—the brain, the stomach, the arms and legs, the eyes and ears—slowly and relentlessly.

Alma Blount, a long-term volunteer and later executive director of Witness, wrote of this new strategy:

> We always talked about the war as the contra war, the military threat of the contras, the way the contras were attacking civilians, the way the Sandinistas had to devote half the national budget toward fighting the contra war. But the real war had to do with a new strategy of war, called "low intensity conflict" (LIC). The average American doesn't know anything about it.
>
> LIC is like the Cheshire Cat. The genius of the strategy is that it's "now you see it, now you don't." And when you can't quite decipher the strategy completely, what always remains in place is the mocking smile. . . . According to LIC theory, psychological warfare is more critical than actual combat.

Careful attention is to be paid to nurturing and shaping public opinion, winning the "hearts and minds" of both the local population and the U.S. public, who were after all footing the bill. The objective of invisible warfare is not all-out military victory—in Nicaragua it was to bring the Sandinistas and the people to their knees. In the United States, the objective was to win over the public to the notion that Washington had the right and the duty to dictate the politics of small neighbors in its "own backyard." Jack Nelson-Pallmeyer, in his book *War Against the Poor*, calls low-intensity conflict "a totalitarianlike strategy that is incompatible with authentic democracy. . . . We may be entering, or may in fact already have entered, a period in which democracy in the United States is more illusionary than real."*

This invisible war produced infinitely better results for U.S. policymakers in Nicaragua than the contra war alone ever could have. Whereas the contra war involved putting resources into the hands of uncontrolled peasants and warriors, undercover efforts could be carried out by Unilaterally Controlled Assets, as the CIA liked to call them. While the contra war had to be funded by act of Congress, other steps in the invisible war, such as the economic embargo, pressure on Nicaragua's neighbors to sink peace initiatives, and intimidating military exercises in the region, could be carried out single-handedly by the administration.

Best of all for the national security planners, the tactics of the invisible war rouse little opposition back home. It is the stealth bomber of third-world warfare. Mere mention of the contras evoked images of human rights violations that contradicted most people's concept of what the United States stands for, but other aggressive steps against Nicaragua either went unnoticed or did not provoke the same sense of outrage.

In the mountains of Jinotega where the Morales family used to live, the invisible war and the Sandinista response to it—especially the military draft and forcible relocation of peasants—worked to turn the population against the government.

The invisible war relied for its success not merely on creating difficult conditions but on interpreting them to the people in a way that cast a negative light on the government. Political and ideological support for the counterrevolution was nurtured by the constant broadcasts by powerful radio stations, paid for by the United States, blasting the contra message from Honduras every day. A study in 1986 by the Nicaraguan Foreign Ministry showed that nearly seventy pro-contra transmitters were audible in Nicaraguan territory.

Long-termers lived in those communities and traveled those mountain paths. Delegations stayed with families and rode trucks on the same dirt roads. The Witnesses began to see all around them a society imploding, falling in on itself, but were frustrated as they tried

*Jack Nelson-Pallmeyer, *War Against the Poor: Low Intensity Conflict and Christian Faith* (Maryknoll, N.Y.: Orbis Books, 1989), p. 67.

to convey the evil of that back to the United States. In part it was because low-intensity warfare was complex and novel; in part because it is, by definition, invisible.

In their letters home and their talks and slide shows on Sunday mornings, the Witnesses tried, with some success, to convey the true nature of the war. On the public policy level, however, the reality in Central America was becoming increasingly irrelevant. The issue as understood by members of Congress was never *whether* the United States should intervene, but *how* to intervene. Only one issue was up for grabs—funding for the contras. Congress was obsessed with contra aid, and in time Witness became obsessed with Congress.

In the early years David Sweet argued that Witness should do nothing to try to persuade Congress or the media. He regarded them as part of the problem. Yet over time both Congress and the media became the battlefields for the domestic side of the invisible war. Witness fought its fight against the war on the terms defined by the Reagan administration.

MEETING THE PRESS

Working with the media was a crucial element of peacemaking in the '80s. In the case of Nicaragua, perceptions translated into votes, which translated into dollars for the contras and more death for the Nicaraguan people. The Reagan administration media team were masters at managing public perceptions.

Witness for Peace, with its sizeable number of people on the ground, was in a position to challenge the many myths about Nicaragua that came floating out of the White House, if it could figure out how. The main strategy in the early years was to turn loose the "living media," the returned Witnesses, to speak to their own communities. This grass-roots work, it was hoped, would "trickle up" to the nationwide media. The information being conveyed varied with each individual, though the message was the same: stop the contra war. As the shooting war in Nicaragua and the war of words in Washington dragged on, Witness developed a more systematic approach to the media. In May 1984, the Hotline was established, and all returned Witnesses had access to weekly updates by calling Washington.

At the end of 1985, the long-term team assisted the Washington Office on Latin America in preparing an in-depth report entitled "Violations of the Laws of War by Both Sides, February–December,

1985." Mary Dutcher, an attorney and a long-term volunteer, directed the investigation on behalf of WOLA. The wide acceptance of the report and its potential for influencing votes on contra aid convinced Witness that it could make a contribution to the antiwar effort by continuing to carefully document as many attacks against civilians as time would permit. Witness continued to collect hundreds of eyewitness reports of contra violence. Just the titles of the reports were enough to make the most serious contra supporter reconsider:

> Small Cooperative Attacked, Pregnant Woman and Child Killed (9/8/86. Wilikon, Matagalpa. Report by Anne Woehrle)

> Farm Union Organizer Assassinated at San Esteban (9/20/86. San Esteban, Chontales. Report by Bard Montgomery)

> Pregnant Woman Bayonetted (9/22/86. El Juste, Chontales. Report by Daniel Erdman and Marci Ameluxen)

> Elderly Farmer Brutally Killed by Contras near Honduran Border (9/23/86. Palo Blanco, Chinandega. Report by Martha Swan)

> Six Civilians Killed, 43 Injured When Public Transport Hits Contra Mine (10/20/86. Pantasma, Jinotega. Report by Patricia Manning and Marci Ameluxen)

Beginning at the time of the WOLA investigation in 1985, every long-term volunteer received training in documentation skills. Short-term delegates as well as long-termers learned tips on how to deal with the press. A three-person mobile reporting team was later established. Equipped with a pick-up truck, radio, and portable video and still cameras, they chased the contras from one end of the country to the other, trying to document the war and get news and footage out in a timely way. They set up a network of ham radios across the country linked to Managua. When a contra attack occurred, field reports could be conveyed to the capital from the most remote locations, then relayed by phone or computer modem to Washington. The Washington office then passed on the information to editors and reporters stateside, while the Managua media staff alerted the press corps there.

The media office in Managua aggressively presented their documentation to journalists, diplomats, human rights investigators, and the various and sundry missions that came through almost daily. All over the United States, local media contacts passed on the Hotline information to reporters and editors at their local newspapers and TV and radio stations.

The Witness for Peace information-gathering operation on the contra war, with the possible exceptions of Nicaraguan state security and the CIA, became perhaps the best source of facts about the war. They had a network in the countryside that no news outlet could hope to match. And they had a network in the United States, anchored by the Washington office, geared up to get this information out. By mid-1986, seventy-eight media contacts were working in thirty-two states.

The press corps in Managua came to rely on Witness for tips on what was happening in the countryside, editors in Washington and New York followed reports from the Washington office, and local news outlets around the United States turned to Witnesses who had been on the scene to comment from a local angle whenever Nicaragua was in the news.

It was an uphill battle for credibility, but little by little Witness for Peace material found its way into most of the major newspapers and magazines that shape public opinion. Witness reports of contra attacks found their way into the congressional record. The reports were regularly quoted by diplomats, academics, and authors and became the raw material used by America's Watch and other human rights groups as a basis for their own investigations and reports. The Western diplomats so often quoted by the press came to Witness for Peace for information, as did former President Jimmy Carter when he visited Nicaragua in 1986. When the *New York Times* blamed the Sandinistas for a mine explosion that killed thirty-four people in July 1986, Witness investigators challenged the reporter and forced a retraction of sorts. From that point on the press corps had to contend with Witness as one more watchdog on their reporting.

Important articles in *Newsweek,* the *Christian Science Monitor,* the *Philadelphia Inquirer,* and the *New York Times* relied heavily on Witness for Peace materials. When correspondents from these journals expressed confidence in Witness reporting, their colleagues soon followed. The *New York Times* described Witness as the "only organization which seeks to document every armed encounter." It was a far cry from earlier, less flattering references.

A February 1987 report describing thirty contra attacks that caused more than 350 casualties was released at a Washington press conference by Representative David Bonior and Bishop Thomas Gumbleton of Detroit, along with Pastor Amancio Sanchez, a victim of a contra mine.* A September 1987 follow-up report was released at a Capitol press conference by Senator Claiborne Pell and Representative Lane Evans of Indiana, and at more than two dozen local press conferences around the country. Witness kept the evidence of contra terrorism in the public eye despite administration attempts to make it fade away.

Like any advocacy group, Witness faced skepticism from the media, which it only slowly overcame. Witness reporting was specific, reliable, and responded to a need within the press corps. Witness did not attempt to become known as an authority on all aspects of life in Nicaragua; instead, they focused on documenting the contra abuses of the civilian population.

The conversion of the media image of Witness for Peace from Sandalista peaceniks to reliable source was traumatic and costly. The long-term team had always suffered what Sharon Hostetler called "the painful privilege" of sharing with the Nicaraguan people some of their most difficult moments. At Santa Clara, in Ocotal, with the women of El Coco, the long-termers and visiting delegates accompanied the people and learned the details of the contra attacks as part of a process of accompaniment.

The pressures of time and the emphasis on detail in reporting that came with broader acceptance imposed a dynamic that sometimes strained the relationship between Witnesses and Nicaraguan communities. The mobile reporting team especially felt the pain and exhaustion of rushing from town to town, sitting with people as they related the worst experience of their lives, and then getting back in the truck and moving on. Investigators faced enormous difficulties entering politically divided communities, understanding cultural differences (such as the politeness of Nicaraguans that prompted them to answer yes no matter what the question), and converting heart-rending and blood-curdling stories into straightforward "Dragnet"-style prose designed to convince even the most skeptical.

In this role, they became a voice for those who could not speak. Their presence insured that the deaths of so many poor campesinos would not pass unrecognized. They formed a human and technologi-

---

*Amancio Sanchez and his seven-year-old daughter, Elda, were in the United States for treatment of their wounds suffered in an October 20, 1987, mine explosion south of Pantasma, Jinotega. Six people were killed in that blast. The Sanchezes were the first amputees brought to the United States by Walk for Peace, a Georgia-based Christian ministry that provided prosthetic devices to Nicaraguan amputees. Walk for Peace is part of Jubilee Ministries and was in part inspired by Witness for Peace member Don Mosley.

cal chain from the mountains and jungles where campesinos discreetly passed information to long-term volunteers, a chain stretching all the way to Washington and to the hearts and minds of activists all over the world who cared deeply about Nicaragua.

Many observers credit Witness for Peace with exposing mainstream America to the hidden story of the contra war. As time went on they faced the greater challenge of exposing the invisible low-intensity war, a war designed to remain hidden.

10

"STOP THE LIES, STOP THE KILLING"

If Tip O'Neill didn't have Maryknoll nuns who wrote letters,
we would have a contra program.
> —the late CIA Director William Casey, lamenting the
> activities of religious people opposed to
> the war in Central America.*

A delegation from Indiana, freshly scrubbed after a week of planting coffee seedlings and sleeping on the floors of peasant huts in the mountains of Jinotega, was celebrating their last night in Nicaragua, in obedience to Witness custom, with a going-away party on the porch of the house where delegations were lodged. There was Flor de Caña rum, fruit drinks and soft drinks, cold Victoria beer, and dancing to taped music that alternated between Caribbean salsa and ZZ Top.

A guest sat in a wooden rocking chair, sipping a Coke from a plastic cup and chatting politely. His name was Robert Fretz, the U.S. consul who regularly met with Witness groups as they passed through the embassy.

Visiting the embassy had become part of the ritual for short-term delegates, a sobering reminder of the thinking of policymakers they would face back home. Most delegations found the embassy meeting more upsetting than the mosquito bites, the bumpy roads, and the change in diet combined. The difference between what they thought they saw in the countryside and what they heard in the embassy was enough to drive many delegations to tears. Nonetheless

*Bob Woodward, *Veil: The Secret Wars of the C.I.A. 1981–1987* (New York: Simon & Schuster, 1987), p. 402.

this delegation invited Fretz to their party. It was April 23, 1985. The House was to pass judgment on a request for $14 million in contra aid, which Witness members had been working furiously to defeat. An ABC-*Washington Post* poll found that 70 percent of the public opposed contra aid.

After 10:00 P.M. the Voice of Nicaragua announced that the aid had been defeated. Fretz sat smiling, an unrevealing island in the midst of a sea of dancing long-termers, short-termers, and Nicaraguan neighbors. From the porch they could hear fireworks and shouting as Managua exploded in celebration.

In the morning, as the groggy delegates gathered themselves for their trip back to the States, President Ortega left for Moscow to visit the new Soviet leader, Mikhail Gorbachev. President Reagan, declaring a state of national emergency, imposed a trade embargo with Nicaragua. Congressional leaders on both sides of the contra question expressed outrage at Ortega. Democrats who felt they had taken a political risk to oppose the president felt betrayed by the Sandinistas. The long-term team held a fast and vigil outside the U.S. Embassy in Managua, and Witness in the United States began plans to defy the embargo.

Within six weeks Fretz had the last laugh. The slim House majority opposing contra aid collapsed, and in June a $27 million package, labeled "humanitarian aid," was passed. It was a turning point in the three-year-old battle on contra aid. Up until this point, the House had been holding firm. By painting his liberal Democrats as Ortega supporters and portraying Ortega as a Soviet puppet, Reagan resurrected a tried-and-true Cold War formula. By promising not to forsake the possibility of negotiations with Nicaragua, he courted moderate Democrats and solidified a majority that would hold for three years.

In vain, Witnesses tried to refocus the question. The issue, they insisted, was not who the Sandinistas are, but who the contras are. But it was to no avail—Congressmen flashing pictures of Ortega with Gorbachev were demanding blood, and that's exactly what they got. Not until February 1988 was military aid to the contras finally defeated, and then only by a margin of eight votes.

IN THE BELLY OF THE BEAST

Witness for Peace and so many Central America and peace groups had given their all in the effort to beat both the April and the

June '85 contra aid packages. They held vigils night and day at district offices around the country and sent torrents of letters and phone messages; delegations of prominent church people descended on Washington to make their views known. When victory slipped so quickly through their hands, many Witnesses soured on the congressional process and despaired of ever arriving at a fair policy through legislative means. Others rolled up their sleeves and kept working on the same representatives who had just voted to send contra aid.

From the earliest days it was clear that the real struggle for peace and a just U.S. policy had to go on within the United States. Yet Witness had never been of one mind about dealing with the legislative process. The founders advocated a grass-roots approach. They deliberately opted not to hire a lobbyist in Washington, preferring instead to go the longer, slower route of mobilizing people to apply pressure back home that would eventually be felt "on the hill."

Many activists were instinctively wary of Congress. Some were ideologically disposed to distrust and attempt to bypass the halls of power. Others became quickly annoyed with politician's talk of geopolitics and national security, feeling that their representatives were missing the boat. While the Witnesses talked of the palpable desire for peace that they felt among the people, their congressional representatives spoke of Soviet arms and airstrips.

Heavily briefed by the State Department and, in many cases, by their own visits to the region, legislators were not always keen to believe their constituents, and some went so far as to suggest the Witnesses had been brainwashed. Congressional staffers grew weary of hearing "the marvels of Nicaragua" as told to them by returned Witnesses.

Congress never debated an alternative to aggression against Nicaragua; the debate was only about different ways of applying "pressure" to make Nicaragua conform to the U.S. image of how it should look and behave. Witness was taking on a very tall order, essentially asking Congress to buck the tide and look at Nicaragua and the third world on its own terms, free of the lenses imposed by the Cold War.

Many in the movement concluded that Congress was just one piece of the puzzle and putting all their efforts into legislative change would be a mistake. Reagan held all the cards, they argued, and he could play most of them without even asking Congress. Only massive mobilization and resistance could stop him, and a considerable segment of the movement saw it as their goal to make it clear that, in the event of any invasion or escalation of the war, they could make the United States ungovernable.

Just how many cards the administration held became frighteningly clear in the early months of 1985 when the Pentagon mobilized up to ten thousand troops at a time in war games and exercises in Honduras, Panama, and the Caribbean. National Guard units from several states were called up to participate. At the same time, information was coming to light about private organizations, many of them religious, carrying on fund-raising activities for the contras. The contras were not the only weapon in the Reagan arsenal, and the president, brandishing his newly won "mandate," could launch a stinging attack on Nicaragua or actually invade, whether Congress liked it or not. Organizers devised public education and legal strategies to keep the National Guard from going to Central America, and to expose and protest the growing use of private organizations to fund the contras. These efforts served to complement more traditional forms of pressure aimed at Congress.

Gail Phares organized "Witness Wednesdays" to bring Carolinians every week to Washington to lobby their congressional delegations. Returned Witnesses in Syracuse, New York, held a weekly vigil at the office of contra backer George Wortley, their congressman. Around the country, members of Congress continued to feel the heat, though the Witness organization maintained ambivalent feelings toward Congress, the way one feels when confronted with a relationship you need but wish you didn't. Congress became to Witness what eggs were to Woody Allen.

The April '85 newsletter expressed the longing that many Witnesses felt to get to the heart of the matter and deal with the attitudes, the morality questions of why the United States was involved in this war.

> Even if contra aid is not approved, the hardest work for peace is still ahead of us. Not only has the President said, "We're not going to quit and walk away from [the contras] no matter what happens" . . . there is the more pervasive problem in Congress of basic hostility toward the revolutionary process in Nicaragua. The leaders of our nation are deeply uncomfortable with a Third World country which has "tried U.S. control and found it wanting." We have yet to deal with all the fears and all the ambitions for control that are expressed in the Monroe Doctrine. . . . We don't yet see how successful struggles of poor majorities can contribute to our peace rather

than disturb it." Quite possibly the greatest contribution WFP and others of conscience in this nation can make in the days ahead is to help replace fear by faith: fear of losing control by faith in sharing power.

The long-term team wrote in a memo before the April '85 vote, "It must be urgently reiterated from the Nicaraguan perspective that it will not be a major victory if the contra aid is defeated—however, it will be an unmitigated disaster if aid is approved."

BLOWING OUT THE CANDLES

Battling contra aid was like blowing out trick candles on a birthday cake. Each time the movement wore itself out snuffing the flames, it turned around to find them lit again and began to puff itself up for one more big blow. This endless series of votes, anticipated votes, and parliamentary finagling nibbled away at the Pledge of Resistance, which was originally designed as a massive, all-out response to a massive, all-out threat.

The list below itemizes the numerous votes taken and their outcomes.

December 1, 1981	Ronald Reagan signs the first presidential "finding" authorizing $19 million in aid to the contras.
December 1982	First Boland amendment passes, bars aid to overthrow Nicaraguan government.
May 1983	Second Boland amendment passes, bars aid "which would have the effect of supporting, directly or indirectly, military or paramilitary operations in Nicaragua by any nation, group, organization, movement, or individual." The amendment authorizes funds for interdicting alleged arms shipments from Nicaragua to El Salvador.
October 20, 1983	House votes $24 million in covert aid, by a margin of 227 to 194.
October 1984	Angered by mining of the harbors, the House votes to bar funding for the contras until December 1985.

April 1985	$14 million in contra aid is defeated in the House.
June 1985	$27 million in "humanitarian aid" passes the House, 248 to 184.
March 1986	House rejects request for military aid to contras, 222–210. Senate approves the request, 53–47.
June 1986	Military aid resumes as Congress votes to approve president's $100 million request. Aid can be channeled through the CIA.
August 1987	Reagan-Wright plan, Esquipulas II.
September/October 1987	Expected vote on military aid is postponed, administration concedes it does not have the votes.
October–December 1987	Three separate votes provide $21 million in stop-gap aid to the contras, pending debate on larger Presidential request.
February 3, 1988	House votes, 219–211, against a Reagan proposal for more military aid.
April 13, 1989	Congress approves $49 million in non-military aid as part of bipartisan agreement to sustain the contras through the election period.

The Pledge of Resistance expanded and grew more flexible, asking for signers who would engage in legal forms of protest as well as more stringent forms of civil disobedience. Pledge actions were not only in response to contra aid requests but were also protesting a number of aggressive measures, such as the use of U.S. Army helicopters to transport Honduran troops to the Nicaraguan border, the sending of emergency military aid to Honduras, and so on.

Organizers had to constantly adjust what they would ask the pledgers to do in response to the latest administration maneuvers, and after a while they had to conduct a head count of who was in prison, who was out on bail, who was on probation, and whose family would disown them if they went to jail one more time. At several key junctures they also had to face the frustrating phenomenon of police officers who would not arrest them.

These regular "fire drills" were perhaps the most effective training exercises Witness for Peace and the broader movement ever conducted, in an ironic way paralleling the exercises being run by the

Pentagon. People who had barely heard of Robert's *Rules of Order* were finding themselves legislative activists immersed in the minutiae of congressional committee proceedings, continuing resolutions, and budget appropriations. Street activists, many of whom had never received a parking ticket, were learning the feel of handcuffs on their wrists and the dank odor of an overnight lock-up.

Albert C. Winn was one of them. Winn was the perfect Southern gentleman, a one-time president of Louisville Presbyterian Theological Seminary and was General Moderator of the General Assembly of the Presbyterian Church (U.S.) in 1979. He was well known in Southern church circles.

The grandson of missionaries, Winn had served as a Navy chaplain during World War II, then became a pastor of rural churches in Virginia where, as Winn puts it, "I opened my mouth about the race situation." That earned him an invitation to teach Bible study at Tuscaloosa, a predominantly black college, where he involved himself in the Montgomery bus boycott. In 1986, he had just retired, and Nicaragua caught his attention. His family was not surprised when he signed up for a delegation. "My wife was very supportive, and my children have come to expect that kind of erratic behavior from their father. My siblings thought it was a mild form of insanity."

He felt so moved by his experience that, after six and one-half decades of doing things "in good order," he found himself compelled to break the law. In March 1987, on the steps of the U.S. Capitol, Winn told the story of a friend he'd made in El Serrano, near Nueva Guinea.

> I dare say that no one who hears these words has ever heard of Justo Herrera. That is the real name of a poor peasant in Nicaragua, a subsistence farmer with a wife and three children and an aged father-in-law, a campesino. I lived in his home for a week last November.
>
> Justo was a proud man, a quiet man. But on Saturday his tongue was loosed with a few beers, and he backed me in a corner with a volley of vociferous Spanish. I could understand enough to get the drift. Why was the U.S. government trying to kill him and his children? Why were they paying remnants of the Somoza guard to wage war on his poor village? His wife had already lost two brothers killed plus another brother and a sister kidnapped. Why was it routine to find the mutilated bodies of schoolteachers, health workers, agricultural experts—everyone that was trying to help him in his poverty?

Justo had given Winn a message as he left El Serrano. "Justo spoke, expressing the desire of the village for peace, for friendship with our people, for an end of war. He urged us to deliver this message to our government."

Winn and his companions tried delivering that message in letters to the editor, visits to Congress, sermons, at church suppers, Sunday school, anywhere and anyhow they could. Then he got a phone call that pushed him to go just a little bit further. One hundred and fifty contras had attacked El Serrano. Eight villagers had been killed. Justo was among them.

> Justo was killed by my tax dollars, killed by order of the President with the approval of the Congress. Justo's death places on me an obligation, more urgent than ever, to deliver his message to my government. I have tried. I have written my elected representatives. I have come to Washington and visited their busy offices. I am speaking on these steps to whoever will listen. In a few moments I am going into the rotunda, I am going to disobey a lawful order, and I am going to be arrested. Justo would gladly have gone to prison or to his death for a chance to speak out, so I feel I must do this on his behalf.

He spoke calmly but forcefully, echoing the conflicting feelings of thousands like him across the country torn between loyalty to an older order and a profoundly disturbing reality newly discovered.

> I do not do this lightly. I have a profound respect for law and have never stood before a judge before, not even in traffic court. But if Justo's message is not getting through by ordinary channels, the least I can do is to put my body on the line, my personal freedom on the line, in the hope that such a seemingly foolish action may open at least one pair of ears that has thus far been stopped. Maybe one person in a position of power will hear from my lips and my body the message of my dead friend and host: "Stop the war. Stop killing our children. We want to be your friends. We want to live in peace."

After Winn read his statement, he and eleven others knelt and prayed in the Capitol Rotunda. When they refused to leave, they were arrested by guards as they sang "We Shall Overcome." They spent a night in jail, until they were dumped unceremoniously onto the street at 2:00 A.M.

They were among thousands arrested for civil disobedience in the battle to end the congressional funding for the contras who killed people like Justo. Most of them, like Reverend Winn, would not have considered doing such a thing until the faraway war became a very personal issue for them. "I don't know if it changed American foreign policy," he says. "It was just one little drop of resistance."

CROSSES OF SORROW AND HOPE

By mid-1985, Yvonne Dilling, still managing the Washington Witness office, was spending almost half her time working on the Pledge of Resistance. The office was also producing a weekly tape-recorded message of field reports from the long-termers (the Hotline) and sending a monthly Newsbrief to a mailing list of two thousand. For the contra aid vote in April, she and several helpers edited and printed a booklet with the simple title "What We Have Seen and Heard" depicting the horrors of war, as reported by the long-term team, in human terms.

Witness had precious little staff time to dedicate to developing its own programs and resources. Dilling left shortly after the San Juan River kidnapping. Her cancer in remission, she was looking for a challenge a bit closer to Central America and farther from the Beltway.

In her place, the steering committee (now grown to include fifteen members) hired Jean Walsh, a founder of NISGUA, the Guatemala solidarity network, and Sam Hope, a Southern Presbyterian minister. Walsh and Hope went to work on an idea to remind the public and Congress in a very personal way of the names of the men, women, and children killed in our name. The campaign, called Crosses of Sorrow and Hope, envisioned Witnesses planting crosses in church courtyards, along highways, on front lawns and in town squares all across America. Crosses were the form of commemoration used in Nicaragua, but Witness adopted other forms of markers as well to respect its interfaith nature.

The administration was clearly winding up for a new push for contra aid in early 1986. The congressional Democratic leadership planned to oppose Reagan, but they couldn't predict the outcome. (A solid core of two hundred mostly Democratic members of the House could be counted on to oppose contra aid, and a roughly equal number were solidly pro-contra. The struggle was for the hearts and minds of the forty or so "swing votes").

The showdown was expected in early March, when Congress had to vote on passage of $100 million for the contras. As the vote drew near, Nicaragua came to dominate the press and television in a more sustained way than ever before. Joe Eldridge of WOLA called it the most acrimonious debate he had ever seen in Washington.

The Witnesses were well organized. Local chapters marched to congressional offices carrying the crosses, and left them planted, cemetery style, on the lawns of churches and in public parks. Thousands of local religious leaders signed a statement calling for an end to the contra war. In San Jose, California, three hundred people planted crosses bearing the names of people killed in the war along the roadside leading to a fund-raising event for representative Ed Zschau, who had met with Witness delegations but was still on record in favor of the contras. At a Milwaukee press conference ten religious leaders released a statement signed by 125 of their colleagues condemning the immorality of continued aid to the contras. One hundred people from across Vermont marched on the state capital in Montpelier and planted fifty crosses, one by one, in a service commemorating fifty recent victims of contra terrorism.

Nearly two hundred religious leaders signed a statement headed "In the Name of God—Stop the Lies—Stop the Killing."

> A scaffold of deception is being constructed around Nicaragua. Exaggeration, misinformation, and outright falsehood form the heart of the Reagan administration's case against Nicaragua. The purpose of the government's distortion campaign is to prepare the American people for further U.S. military action in Nicaragua. . . .
>
> If the present lying continues unchallenged, and has its intended effect, it is certain that yet more killing will result.
>
> We in the religious community feel compelled to speak out now about Nicaragua before many more lives are lost. We refuse to allow the deception to go unchallenged or to accept the senseless violence that is deception's companion. Together we say, "In the name of God, Stop the Lies, Stop the Killing!"

On March 5, front pages all over the country carried a spectacular photo of hundreds of people on the Capitol steps holding crosses and markers with the names of victims of the policy that was being debated just inside. Among them were Nicaraguan church leaders—CEPAD's Gilberto Aguirre and Moravian pastor Norman Bent. The protesters, formed into the shape of a giant cross, made network news that night, giving rare nationwide exposure to the existence of a broad opposition to the war.

The crosses and markers became one of the few symbols of the war that penetrated national consciousness on a mass level. That night Thomas Gumbleton, a Roman Catholic bishop from Detroit, debated Elliot Abrams, the overeager assistant secretary for contra affairs, on the MacNeil Lehrer news show. Gumbleton enraged Abrams by charging the administration with deliberately deceiving the American people by covering up contra atrocities with rhetoric calling them "freedom fighters." He challenged the administration's insistence that Nicaragua was a Marxist-Leninist Soviet puppet, and he went beyond anything a network audience had heard for a long time by suggesting that the Sandinistas enjoyed popular support.

"We should listen," Gumbleton said, "to people like Miguel D'Escoto, the foreign minister down there, who has very carefully explained the philosophy of their government. It is not a Marxist Leninist government. They are trying to bring about a change so that the poor people for the first time . . . will be able to share in the resources . . . of the nation. They have brought about a revolution—land is being distributed, peasants are growing their own food."

The bishop defied the administration's carefully crafted stereotypes and rewrites of Nicaraguan history, reviving the ghost of the forgotten 1984 elections: "The people have spoken . . . saying they want this government. . . . We are not on the side of the people, . . . we are on the side of terrorists."

For Abrams, this was more than he could bear to hear, and he began to attack the serene, calm bishop for not defending the Nicaraguan Catholic hierarchy.

"You don't speak for the church," Abrams fumed, and he referred to a Carnegie Institute report on Nicaragua charging repression of the church.

Gumbleton replied, "We don't have to go to outside sources, because our reports are based on witnesses—thousands of Witness for Peace people who've gone down there, . . . religious communities throughout the whole country who report to us. . . . The church knows what is happening . . . the church is not closed, religious education is being given, priests are free to preach, people are being ministered to."

Then it got heated.

ABRAMS: I cannot permit you to pose as if you speak for the church of
    Nicaragua. You do not speak for Cardinal Obando . . .
GUMBLETON: Mr. Abrams, you don't have to tell me who is the church
    of Nicaragua. The church is the people.

ABRAMS: I always thought that the church had a hierarchy . . .

GUMBLETON: If you could only understand that the church is . . . those three million people, eighty percent of them Catholics, . . . and the people who are in the hospitals, the schools, the dispensaries, the people who minister, they are telling us that they are free.

ABRAMS: That is not the position of the Vatican, or the Holy Father . . .

GUMBLETON: No bishop is the church, Mr. Abrams. I don't claim to be the church of Detroit. We have one point five million people here who are the church. Cardinal Obando is not the church.

ABRAMS (furious): You won't even stand up for your own church! . . . The church in Nicaragua is under enormous pressure and you won't stand up for the church!

GUMBLETON (smiling): I am standing up for the church in Nicaragua. They are the people who are suffering because of the contras, they are the ones being killed by the weapons we are supplying.

Gumbleton was voicing what was in the hearts of so many who had been lobbying all day for several days in the halls of Congress. He cut past the judgments and the questions of members of Congress and aides and got to the core of the matter: The U.S. government was lying in order to sell to its people a murderous policy. And the people did not want to pay for murder.

Abrams exploded at the bishop's assertion that the administration was lying. "I would ask the Bishop," he said, "that as we go through what is a very significant foreign policy discussion, that we try not to call fellow citizens liars."*

Gumbleton concurred. He did not wish to call Mr. Abrams a liar. But if the government was going to cover its crimes, it had fallen on people of faith and conscience to reveal them.

"It is very discouraging that I have to say, and two hundred religious leaders are saying, that our government is lying. But in the documentation we published today, we showed at least fifteen areas where the facts say one thing and our government says another."

*Abrams had to get used to this type of treatment as the months went by. While testifying before a House committee on April 8, Rep. Peter Kostmayer told him, "Frankly, Mister Secretary, I'm not surprised at anything you say to this committee anymore. . . . I am not surprised at your level of audacity. . . . An increasingly large number of people are beginning to regard Administration statements as simply untruthful." *Miami Herald*, April 9, 1986.

Challenged by the moderator to show what he meant by the administration's lies, he recited a list of them so long that he had to be interrupted.

The bishop expressed well the feelings of the rank-and-file Witness for Peace people who wanted badly to be able to be proud of their government. Long-termers often remarked that they felt jealous of people from other countries who could visit development projects, housing, or water systems being built with their country's help. "To show people what my country is building here, I have to take them to the cemetery," said one long-termer.

Crosses of Sorrow and Hope was one way of bringing that experience back home, of allowing people who had seen the suffering of Nicaragua up close to communicate to their neighbors in a graphic way that we needed to stop the war. For Nicaraguans, it was a way to ensure that the names of those who were being killed, maimed, and left orphaned were at least mentioned in the public debate. Witness resolved, for political and spiritual reasons, to keep repeating the names, planting them on crosses all over Congress and anywhere that it would do any good.

Massive lobbying by Witness for Peace and other sympathetic groups went on for weeks. In March, the House voted no on contra aid. Yet, as so many times before, the Congress snatched defeat from the jaws of victory, managing to bring the issue up once again within just a few weeks. The administration still had all the power to set the terms of the debate. Occasional shows of force could not dent the relentless disinformation and lobbying effort being waged by the Reagan White House.

Abrams, in his debate with Bishop Gumbleton, dismissed the bishop's position as "isolated."

"There is no debate over who the Sandinistas are and what they're up to," he told the interviewer. "That question has been settled. The issue that's being debated is what to do about it." Abrams was right, and that was the heart of the problem. At the end of June the House voted $100 million in new military aid to the contras, by a 221–209 vote. The next day the Sandinistas closed La Prensa, the opposition newspaper, and exiled pro-contra Bishop Pablo Antonio Vega and the cardinal's spokesman, Bismarck Carballo. One day later the World Court ruled that the U.S. war against Nicaragua was illegal. On August 13, the Senate voted 53–47 to approve the $100 million, thus initiating a new contra offensive and a new offensive by the antiwar movement.

After the vote Dr. Parajon asked a question of North Americans working in Nicaragua. "What have you learned," he asked, "about your democracy?" The answer was obvious, and damning—a democracy does not make life-and-death decisions about innocent people who have no say in the process. Parajon was not suggesting abandoning the struggle to convince Congress to change its mind. Yet the need for escalated resistance, for more compelling and larger demonstrations of the opposition to the war, was more evident with each congressional flip-flop, with each vote for more millions and more murder.

The Witnesses knew they were in for a long haul. It would not be until February 1988 that Congress put an end to military aid, and even at that time more funds were allocated to support the contras in "humanitarian" ways. Regional coordinators began recruiting media and congressional contacts in every district and city in the country. A direct-mail campaign was begun, which reached almost one million households per year and raised $2 million in four years. The hope was to develop a capacity to lobby and protest at the grass-roots level nationwide, or at least in key states and districts where representatives had yet to decide one way or another on the contra aid issue—the so-called swing votes.

A group of veterans from Vietnam and other wars decided they had had enough of the legislative process and took a different tack. On September 1, 1986, Charlie Litkey, the only chaplain to win the Congressional Medal of Honor in Vietnam, returned the medal in protest of the war in Nicaragua. Litkey, a former priest, had earned the medal by rescuing men under fire while he himself was unarmed. His time in Vietnam had made a pacifist of him, and recent visits to Central America with Witness filled him with a sense of déjà vu.

George Mizo, another Vietnam veteran, joined Litkey, along with Duncan Murphy, a veteran of World War II and of the first Action for Peace trip to Nicaragua in July 1983. A fourth man joined them, a veteran by the name of Brian Willson, who was destined to lose his legs when trying to stop a Navy freight train a year later. For more than a month they fasted, and their fast generated support from people all over the country, recruited more members for the movement, and stimulated new thinking about the uses of creative nonviolence. The Witness office in Washington became a center for activities related to the fast, and Witness activists around the country immersed themselves in support activities. The fast revitalized a movement that had been devastated by the reverses of the summer's votes for more contra arms.

Witness supported the fast but continued its more conventional organizing work. For a while national Witness for Peace seemed in danger of developing a split personality. One part of its life, one part of its personnel and its mission, immersed itself deeply in the reality of the poor, while the other half walked the halls of power and mingled with the rich. The interface with power, the petitioning on behalf of the poor was as much a part of the mission, but it carried with it new and serious dangers.

During October 1986, Witness held its first and last $250-per-plate fund-raising dinner in the posh Marriott hotel on Capitol Hill. The dinner actually lost money; drew negative press; sparked complaints from Nicaraguan participants as well as congressional leaders, including House Speaker Jim Wright, whose names appeared on the host committee but who had not been consulted; and raised eyebrows in the movement about a segment of the peace movement suiting itself in black tie while others were on their deathbed from fasting. By late 1986, the movement was willing to try almost anything to bring the spiral of war to an end.

11

KEEPING FAITH

Facing a war of low intensity, the response must be a solidarity of high intensity.

—Arnaldo Zenteno,
Mexican priest working in Nicaragua

The dollars approved in the summer of '86 were disbursed by the U.S. treasury in the fall, and by year's end had been converted into machine guns and grenades and boots that then found their way to the contra camps in southern Honduras. As winter gripped Washington, the newly outfitted contras began to reinfiltrate Nicaragua, and within weeks the bloody results began to make themselves apparent to Witness for Peace.

Near Waslala, in northern Zelaya, returning contras kidnapped dozens of farmers, including thirty-six taken on one night from a religious celebration. In the southern region near Nueva Guinea contra troops set up areas of control from which they regularly attacked the nearby communities and kept traffic on the roads hostage to their will. Cooperatives everywhere were destroyed as if on a hit list—at least nineteen were attacked between February and July.

Ambushes occurred with greater frequency on the rural roads. Random attacks were designed to discourage travel and commerce; selective ambushes, like the one on June 28 that killed an agrarian reform worker and his teacher wife in Jinotega, had a dual purpose: to deprive the communities of Sandinista-linked services and to frighten anyone who might collaborate with them.

It was the heaviest and most widespread contra offensive since early 1985. At that time the Sandinista army, launching its first major offensive operations of the war, had successfully cleared the contras out of their bases in northern and central Zelaya, in the Segovias, and on the Rio San Juan in a matter of five months. Prior to 1985 the brunt of the defense had been borne by local militias, while the Sandinista Army (EPS) was being organized, trained, and outfitted. The EPS "debut" in early 1985 was impressive, and by year's end Sandinista Defense Minister Humberto Ortega proclaimed "the strategic defeat of the contras."

Through late 1985 and most of 1986 the routed contras languished in camps in Honduras. Small bands inside the country remained to create havoc and make life treacherous and miserable for civilians. They maintained a presence for propaganda's sake, but they posed no military threat to the government. An indicator of the temporary lull in the war was the coffee harvest, which the contras tried to disrupt every year. In the 1984–85 coffee harvest, 138 coffee pickers were killed. The 1985–86 crop was brought in without a single war-related fatality. The "strategic defeat" didn't mean that the contras had stopped ambushing and attacking civilian vehicles and settlements, planting mines in the roads, kidnapping young people, and raping women. It meant only that as a military force their forward progress had been contained and they posed no threat of taking power.

In a New Year's Day, 1987, interview, Elliot Abrams, Assistant Secretary of State and Washington's point man for the contras, gleefully alerted the world that a new and improved version of the contras was about to take the field in Nicaragua.

Paul Dix, a photographer with Witness for Peace, had been trailing the contras for four years. He had probably seen and recorded the images of more human suffering than any other civilian observer of the war. Contrary to Abrams's opinion, the contras that he saw were not all that different from the contras of a year ago or five years ago.

Dix's New Year began by traveling to the scene of a series of ambushes and attacks on cooperatives in southern Chontales. He talked to the survivors of an attack on the El Chaguite cooperative, where two brothers were killed and two women from the same family were taken and raped by the contras. There was nothing left of the farm, which had no military significance.

In February, teams of commandos trained by the CIA parachuted deep into Nicaragua to carry out sabotage missions. They blew up telephone poles, electrical lines, grain silos, and a chemical storage tank—also targets with no military significance.

The persecution of farming cooperatives escalated. From March through June, Witness for Peace investigators were constantly on the run from one smoldering cooperative to the next, visiting survivors in hospitals, attending funerals, interviewing, documenting, and trying to call the attention of the media to the attacks. Some of the coopera- tives had been hit two and three times. Customarily, Nicaraguans named schools, health clinics, and cooperatives after people who had been killed in the war. Witnesses found themselves investigating the destruction of schools and communities named after people whose deaths had been documented by an earlier generation of Witnesses for Peace.

The war had gone on longer than the first group at El Porvenir would ever have imagined. More than one hundred long-term volun- teers had come and gone, and more than three thousand short-term delegates had visited Nicaragua. Not one had been killed or injured.

On April 28, 1987, a contra patrol near San Jose de Bocay am- bushed a group of workers preparing the site of a tiny hydroelectric dam. Among the dead was Benjamin Linder, a twenty-eight-year-old engineer committed to the revolution and to bringing electricity to Bocay. Linder was the first U.S. citizen killed by the contras.

Witness and church workers around Rio Blanco and Paiwas were frequently stopped and questioned. Ambushes threatened the road to Limay for the first time in more than two years. Near Achuapa, Leon, a relatively tranquil spot, the Las Mercedes coopera- tive was attacked and five adults and two children were killed. A Chilean agronomist was ambushed and killed, his throat slit, in the same area the next day.

Though contra behavior had changed little, the context in which they operated was vastly different. The Nicaragua that Wit- ness for Peace knew in 1987 would be scarcely recognizable to the earliest pilgrims in 1983. Thirty-five Witness volunteers were work- ing in almost every province that the war had touched, from the jun- gles of Central Zelaya to the Atlantic coast and the dry hills of Somotillo on the Honduran border. Three or four delegations arrived each month to live with the people for two weeks and take the mes- sage home.

The message they heard from their Nicaraguan host had radi- cally changed from the early days in Jalapa. The people were getting tired. Instead of hearing of the people's determination to resist the U.S. aggression, they heard from people who were simply tired of the war. The spirit of the heroic early days in Jalapa and the talk of building the new society was scarce. Church leaders who in earlier days had taken visible roles in support of the revolution were now playing mediator and conciliator roles in divided communities, or just trying to help their people survive.

Sandinista leaders spoke less of their achievements in health care, education, and land reform, and instead focused on the most basic achievement of all—survival. Inflation reached incomprehensible five-digit levels by 1988. Shortages of basic goods became a fact of life, so common that the first words learned by foreigners was often *no hay* (there is none). Factories were idled for lack of fuel and spare parts. The military consumed an ever greater share of what little there was to go around. Every family had someone in the army and someone who had died in the war. The people were weary of burying loved ones and the sons of strangers who died fighting in their fields, weary of competing claims on their loyalties. This war weariness affected the Witnesses who accompanied them. It had been six years since the first attacks began.

Long-term witness Inanna LeFevre visited a friend, Lucila Incer Tellez, in a Managua hospital. Lucila had been nearly killed in a contra ambush and had been hospitalized, unable to walk, for more than a year. "When will they stop, Inana?" Lucila pleaded with her friend. "When will they stop? When they've killed every man, woman, and child in Nicaragua?"

Ultimately the war was a political struggle for the hearts and minds of Nicaraguans. Would the Reagan administration's drive to crush Nicaragua run out of time or be ground to a halt by the Iran-contra scandal, or would the Sandinista attempt to build a new society falter under the weight of too much death and deprivation?

Long-term volunteers found themselves living in places that had never had a strong identification with the revolution, with religious communities whose otherworldly or sacramental views brought on a passive attitude toward God and life that most of the Witnesses did not share. Delegation members found themselves in deeply divided communities as Witness moved to places like Nueva Guinea, Chontales, and Boaco. Even in the north, it was not uncommon for delegates to learn that the family they were staying with had a son or a cousin fighting with the contras.

Campesinos challenged Witnesses who came to Nicaragua seeing the revolution as a source of hope. Anyone who came to Nicaragua expecting to see a people lifted out of poverty by the revolution was shocked to find a people slammed back into worsening poverty. The benefits that had been the product of so much struggle in the early years were slipping away. Anne Woehrle traveled with a parish priest to the community of San Pablo near Waslala in 1986. On that trip the priest was asked to say prayers for 153 children who had died in recent months of measles. There was no vaccine or no one brave enough to carry it from the Sandinista health clinic through contra lines.

The long-term team held monthly retreats to regroup, reflect, pray, and plan their response to the ever-changing war. They decided to make it a priority to accompany health workers on vaccination missions in risky areas. In Jinotega, the Witnesses were asked to travel with doctors on dangerous rounds giving tests for tuberculosis. TB was running at epidemic proportions, and the doctors were especially vulnerable, since contra spies knew they had to return two days after administering the tests in order to read the results. Long-term volunteer Julieta Martinez stayed in Jinotega, permanently assigned to working on the vaccination and TB testing programs. Tom Loudon was assigned to work with an organization of lay religious leaders in Somotillo after contras killed Mauricio Demierre, a Swiss volunteer working in the area.

As time went on the campesinos cared less and less about who was winning the military struggle or who was right or wrong. The hand of the United States behind the contras was obscured as more and more the campesinos came to view the fighting as a national war, even a local problem. It was a war to make Nicaragua "cry uncle." And it was working.

THE WAR AT HOME

The struggle against contra aid came to a climax in the second half of 1987. Witness for Peace and the Pledge of Resistance were joined by a small army of organizations working to defeat what was expected to be a crucial vote in late summer, just before Congress left on vacation.

Nothing seemed to shame the contras and their backers. The Linder killing, the Iran-contra scandal, the World Court condemnation of the United States for mining the harbors—they did not seem to matter. The contras had killed thousands in one of the most thoroughly documented cases of government-sponsored savagery in history. Respectable senators watched thousands of Central Americans die, knew the details of their deaths in gruesome detail, and listened in silence while their conservative colleagues questioned the loyalty of anyone who opposed the president. Congress nickled and dimed, compromised and vacillated, while the killing in our name proceeded apace. No one put the question to the administration straightforwardly—have you no sense of decency?

Two months after Ben Linder's murder, the president was seeking more millions in aid to the contras, who had spent most of the $100 million allotted to them in June of '86. Rather than oppose him outright, the Democrats sought to preempt the president, and offered a compromise, the Reagan-Wright plan, which essentially bought time for the administration while it pressured the Sandinistas to negotiate with the contras.

But the plans of both parties were upended by a declaration of independence from the Central American presidents. The five Central American presidents, meeting in Guatemala, stunned the world by signing a historic agreement that became the cornerstone of the regional peace efforts.

The Esquipulas II plan, also known as the Central American Presidents' Peace Plan, or the Arias Plan, called for

- —negotiated cease fires in El Salvador, Guatemala, and Nicaragua
- —an end to the use of the territory of one country by guerrilla groups threatening their neighbors
- —internal democratization and national reconciliation in each country
- —amnesty for insurgents
- —an end to all foreign aid to irregular forces

It was perhaps the single most important development in the region since independence from Spain. The signing of the peace pact threw everything up in the air. The contras didn't know how to react. Democrats expressed pleasure, Republicans disdain. Ronald Reagan dismissed it as fatally flawed.

The Sandinistas saw it as a way out of a war they could no longer afford. If all five countries complied, it would mean an end to U.S. aid to the contras and their ouster from their Honduran sanctuaries. But the administration was not about to let peace get in the way of its dirty little war. As summer turned to autumn in Washington, the administration planned another major contra aid request.

The movement to stop contra aid saw in Esquipulas II a golden opportunity for peace. Witness sought to capitalize on the momentum toward peace to put an end to contra aid once and for all. The key was in the House of Representatives. The administration could count on roughly two hundred votes for contra aid; opponents counted an equal number on their side. Thirty swing votes would make the difference.

The movement was working closely with the media, congressional leadership, religious leaders, and grass-roots organizing efforts and had never been stronger. Numerous antiwar organizations came together to forge a campaign with a dramatic name that reflected their sense of the urgency of the times—"Countdown '87." Countdown embraced a broader constituency than Witness for Peace ever could. They raised funds through concerts by Jackson Browne and Peter, Paul, and Mary and hired staff people who felt as at home at Capitol Hill cocktail parties as Witnesses were in a church pew. Countdown prepared slick television commercials and punchy newspaper advertisements. They were represented by George Miller, an influential congressman from California. It was a state-of-the-art, issue-oriented political machine.

In response to the communications explosion of the '80s, the Central America movement was growing wiser in dealing with the media all the time. While the heart of the Witness for Peace experience was the face-to-face encounter at the grass-roots level, the influence of the mass media on public opinion was too great to ignore. The Reagan administration was giving a lesson in how to control public policy debate by adept media manipulation, and the movement was playing catch-up all the way.

Witness came to play a role in the broader Central America movement, supplying information that other groups used in their media work. The photos by Paul Dix plus the Hotline, newsbriefs, and letters from long-term volunteers, and special Witness publications were reproduced and quoted. Witness offices held training sessions to maximize the effectiveness of grass-roots media work by helping the activists understand and work with the media.

Organizations working on Central America and the media proliferated. The pioneering organizing work of Neighbor to Neighbor promoted the showing of the film *Faces of War* on seventy-five television stations around the country. Neighbor to Neighbor organized local groups to raise money to buy air time to show the documentary, which included a segment on Dr. Ed Myer, on commercial stations.

Fairness and Accuracy in Media (FAIR) grew from a small Los Angeles office into a national watchdog group that often challenged coverage of Central America and assisted local groups, including Witness chapters, in their analysis of and work with the media.

By mid-decade, Peacenet, a computer network for peace groups, connected seven thousand subscribers nationwide and established a modem link with Managua to get the news out quickly. The film *Witness to War*, about the experience of Dr. Charlie Clements in El Salvador, won an Oscar in 1986, and Clements accepted the award on national TV in the name of Archbishop Romero. Fenton Communications, an East Coast public relations firm, formed a Central America media project to handle publicity for many groups within the Central America movement, including the Countdown '87 campaign to stop contra aid.

It was impressive, but in a decade when media magicians became kingmakers and communications technology mushroomed, it was still not enough. Witness for Peace worked with Countdown and also served as one of the leading groups in a coalition preparing an action campaign called "Days of Decision." "Days" was organized to keep up the pressure on Congress from the religious sector. Local Witness activists teamed with the grass-roots efforts of Neighbor to Neighbor to hold house meetings, conduct petition and letter-writing campaigns, make visits to Congress, raise funds, and place newspaper ads in "swing" congressional districts. An August national call-in day to congressional offices was followed by two days of nationally coordinated actions in September.

In August, Oliver North swayed public opinion by showing his emotional slide show on behalf of the contras at the Iran-contra hearings. In response, twenty-two Democrats held up Witness for Peace photographs in the well of the House and read from testimony about the victims of the war. In September, when Witness unveiled its latest findings on contra attacks against civilians, nearly one hundred press conferences were held across the country to present the report. Momentum was building.

The movement was on alert as Congress came back on September 8. As soon as the president formally introduced his plan for contra aid, they planned to start a forty-eight-hour blitz of phone calls, to be repeated when the vote was about to take place. Two hundred National Religious Leaders signed a statement calling for an end to contra aid, entitled "In the Name of God—Stop U.S. Contra Terrorism!"

Released at a September 15 press conference, the statement noted that the Iran-contra hearings had not challenged the essence of U.S. policy toward Nicaragua and called for a new way of looking at foreign policy.

Insisting that "Nicaragua is not our enemy," the leaders concluded that "the time has come for our nation to repent, to run from the path of war and terrorism . . . and to seek reconciliation with a small country our nation has brought to the edge of ruin."

In California, a group of Vietnam veterans was organizing "Nuremberg Actions" at the Concord Naval Weapons Station, where arms were loaded onto ships destined for Central America. They planned to fast and pray and block the train tracks with their bodies, physically stopping the arms from getting to their destination.

The actions began on June 10. David Hartsough wrote, "We can ask ourselves—what good will it do to literally put our bodies in the way of these trains? . . . Or, we can see that we have a moral responsibility to act in the strongest nonviolent way we can to stop the killing of innocent men, women and children in Central America."

On September 1, a U.S. Navy munitions train ran over Brian Willson, one of the Vietnam veterans who had fasted the year before on the Capitol steps. Willson's legs were severed, and the loss of blood nearly killed him.

Just before the train hit him, Willson had spoken these words: "One thing seems clear: If the munitions train moves past our blockade, other human beings will be killed and maimed. We are not worth more. They are not worth less. Let us commit to ourselves and to the world that we will claim our dignity, self-respect, and honor by resisting with our lives and dollars, no matter what it takes."

The train hit Willson and dragged him down the tracks. His near-murder enraged and energized the movement. Willson was in the hospital for weeks, was outfitted with a prosthetic device, and campaigned from coast to coast for people to take up the cause of risky peacemaking. Witness for Peace called for long-term volunteers to maintain a permanent vigil at the tracks.

The administration was unmoved, but they could count. Clearly they did not have the votes to pass a major contra aid package. Instead, they asked for and received new packages of "humanitarian" aid. Opponents of contra aid had hoped for a showdown in the autumn. But the administration, like the guerrilla fighters they fielded in the Nicaraguan mountains and jungles, knew the value of not meeting the enemy head-on. Over the next five months Congress approved three measures extending $21 million. Countdown '87 became Countdown '88. In those five months of "humanitarian" aid, Witness documented ninety contra violations against unarmed civilians. Ninety-seven civilians died, 143 were wounded, and 135 were kidnapped.

In the Nicaraguan countryside, the Sandinistas organized 250 local peace commissions all over the country. Originally formed to encourage contras to return to civil life, their work soon expanded. Local people asked them to address their own problems with the army, or to press for changes in how the draft worked in their town, and to ask the contras to release kidnappees. Many of the members were local priests and pastors. Witness volunteers were often asked to accompany the peace commissions. Witness documented the impact of the peace process and introduced a new publication called "Peace Watch," which tracked compliance with or violations of the peace process.

Paradoxically, as the peace process advanced, life in the countryside became more dangerous for the Witnesses and the people they accompanied. In Condega, Moises Cordova, an FSLN leader, was shot from his motorcycle and killed on September 7. Cordova was on his way home from a meeting in an outlying community where he had been explaining the amnesty law to relatives of the contras.

In October, during the first days of a unilateral cease fire declared by the government, long-term Witness Mardy Townsend wrote from Quilali that "everyone is holding their breath and praying." There was a reduction in fighting but not in tension for most of the people living near the designated cease-fire zones. The contras used the zones for rest and relaxation and as bases to conduct forced recruitment missions and receive supplies from the air. Still, some of the peace commissions kept trying to do their work. The local priest was, in most towns, asked to head the peace commission. In Waslala, the local priest was Father Enrique Blandon.

Enrique Blandon was a city kid who rode a horse as if he were born on one, he was an intellectual who talked like a street-wise kid, and a priest who looked like a Don Juan. His preferred habit was a pair of blue jeans, his favorite hymns were Beatle songs, and his sense of humor reached out both to men and women, not an easy feat in rural Central America. Ann Dohrmann once said that Blandon "looks like he should be in the movies and not in the jungles of Nicaragua."

More to the point, Blandon was a believer in Sandinismo, and he labored in mountains that by and large belonged to the contras. His parish included fifty-three remote communities, and he visited each one of them on horseback once a year. He supported cooperatives, health campaigns, community militias "not because I am a Sandinista," he would say, "but because this work of building community is the work of God." He had been threatened innumerable times, shot at more than once, and kidnapped for nearly a month. The lay leaders in his parish were at the mercy of the contras and were constant targets. Rather than tone down his message, the danger emboldened Father Blandon. His straightforward retorts in the face of contra interrogations were the stuff of legend, and that legend was widely credited with keeping him alive.

A group of contras once woke him out of his hammock and began to search his bags for "subversive" materials. As they leafed through his Bible, he warned them to be careful, for the book was more powerful than anything that came in their daily air supply drops. Frustrated, they warned him not to be preaching politics. As they left, he reminded them that he had only one boss, his bishop, and one mission—the mission of the church, which was to work for peace, as Jesus says in the Sermon on the Mount.

His was the kind of faith that energized Nicaraguan campesinos who wanted to make a difference. They were usually the same kind of people who supported the revolution. A hymn they often sang inadvertently said a great deal about him.

> All I ask of God
> is that I not become indifferent
> facing the pain of so many people
> I just don't want to be indifferent.

He also held great appeal for the kind of people who joined Witness for Peace.

Conscious of the risks he and his pastoral team faced, Father Blandon asked that a Witness volunteer accompany him on mission trips into the mountains. The pastoral visits were the biggest events of the year in the tiny communities. Work stopped and people from miles around gathered and camped out in the fields surrounding the thatched-roof, open-air chapels. Twelve months' worth of newborns were baptized, the year's dead remembered, and couples who so desired had their marriages blessed at the day-long celebration. Outside the chapel, clusters of contras wearing rosaries as necklaces waited and listened.

Greg Hessel, a long-term volunteer from Wisconsin, accompanied Blandon on a twelve-day trip in October 1987. As they arrived at the parish house in Waslala on October 9, the priest met Sister Roseanne of the local peace commission and an evangelical pastor named Gustavo Tiffer. The two were about to head out of town. They had gotten a note from a local contra commander, inviting them to a dialogue about amnesty. Blandon was concerned about Sister Roseanne's health and offered to take her place. When Blandon and Tiffer arrived at the appointed meeting place they were kidnapped and forced to hike farther into the mountains.

On October 17 Paul Fisher, a long-term volunteer working in Chontales, was kidnapped. Fisher was on his way to investigate reports of contra kidnappings near La Libertad. A group of contras boarded his bus and forced him and three men to get off. As the contras marched them to the north they separated them into groups of two. Fisher's companion was a tall, thin agronomy student named Rolando Mena.

When the long-term team called Washington with the news of the kidnapping, no one was there to answer the phone. They were all at the Capitol steps, holding a vigil while, inside, the Congress debated another package of contra aid.

The Fisher kidnapping became one of the most bizarre chapters in the history of Witness for Peace. Fisher was taken on what he later called "a guided tour of contra-land." It lasted two weeks. After the second day, a high-ranking contra leader named Pirata was brought in to take command of the squad. Pirata gave Fisher, who was probably the first non-journalist foreigner to spend that much time inside Nicaragua with the contras, special attention. The contras tried to demonstrate that their cause enjoyed popular support and that they treated the campesinos well.

The contras tried to make a convert out of him by using the Witness for Peace methodology. "I think they were hoping," Fisher later said, "that I would go back to Managua, hold a press conference and tell the world, 'These are nice guys—like the Boy Scouts.' " Paul Fisher was the first contra short-term delegate, except that he was not there of his own free will. He barely was able to sleep because of the combination of stress and harsh conditions, and was allowed to talk to people only in the presence of the contras. An elaborate game of psychological manipulation was played on him. Pirata had personal information about Fisher that could have been obtained only through espionage or if Fisher inadvertently released it. The contras invented stories telling him his ex-wife had been on the radio pleading for his release and saying she wanted to get back together again, that the pope had intervened in his case, and other exaggerations and falsehoods.

Rolando Mena stayed as close as he could to Fisher, helping him out when he could, explaining where they were and how they should act, trying to ground him in reality and help him weather the psychological assault. The two men quickly became friends. They both knew that Mena's life depended on the fact that the North American happened to be on that bus. If the contras were hoping to impress their gringo visitor, they would hurt their image badly if they harmed the young Nicaraguan.

On his twelfth day of captivity, Fisher was taken to meet Quiche, a top contra field commander. Quiche gave him a message to take back to Managua—a plea to Daniel Ortega for negotiations. Fisher agreed to take the message to Radio Catolica and *La Prensa** in exchange for assurances that Mena would be freed along with him.

Eighty miles to the north, Enrique Blandon and Gustavo Tiffer were still being held. The people of Waslala held daily prayer vigils for the return of their pastors. One day more than one thousand people jammed the town's main road in a procession from the evangelical to the Catholic church.

When the contra radio station began announcing on October 14 that the two had been freed, but they still did not show up, the mood in Waslala turned grim. Many thought that the brash young priest's luck had finally run out. Greg Hessel walked into the mountains with five Catholic lay leaders on that day, seeking word of Blandon's fate. They were forced by contra threats to return to Waslala empty-handed.

Father Blandon and Pastor Tiffer had no "shield" except the priest's forceful manner—and the intervention of Bishop Salvador Schlaeffer. A gruff, enigmatic, Wisconsin-born Capuchin priest who came from what Catholics call "the old school," Schlaeffer spoke with the loping, circular Spanish of the eastern jungles and plains he had come to know and love during forty years of mission work. Schlaefer was not the kind to rock the boat—in all likelihood, he had baptized the men who were holding his priest captive. Like his fellow bishops, he never paid much attention to Witness for Peace, but if pressed, would probably have registered a negative opinion of them.

The only link to Waslala, and to news of Blandon's fate, was the radio in the Witness Managua office. Each day the bishop came by to listen and to talk to people in Waslala, and he came to appreciate the work of the Witnesses. He took an interest in the Paul Fisher case. When Louis Stokes, the congressional representative from Cleveland,

---

*Both *La Prensa* and the Catholic radio station had been reopened shortly after the Esquipulas II Peace Plan.

where Fisher's mother lived, announced on October 20 that the contras had promised him to release Fisher, along with Blandon and Tiffer, as soon as they could find a trusted third party to receive them, Schlaeffer offered himself to be that person.

Back in the United States, protest vigils, phone banks, and prayer services demanded the release of all the captives. Gail Phares led a group to visit the State Department's William Walker, who was decidedly uncooperative. The delegation then went to the FDN* offices in Washington. The FDN spokespeople were furious with the Witnesses, which helped confirm their belief that their presence was making a difference.

Bishop Schlaeffer made his own contacts with the contra leadership and made it clear that the irascible and impulsive young priest was still one of his ordained servants and should be let free. The bishop never said so, but many believe that he also told the contras to release Paul Fisher unharmed. This was only the second time that Witness had had such close cooperation from the Roman Catholic hierarchy. The other occasion was in July 1985, when Paul Schmidt of Bluefields, another Wisconsin Capuchin, endorsed the idea of a Peace Guard on the Bluefields Express.

On October 21, Tiffer and Blandon walked into Waslala. They held a long and rousing service giving thanks to God for their safe return and informing the community of what had happened. The priest promised to keep preaching the gospel of peace "to the ultimate consequences." It was clear to everyone in the church that ten days with the contras had not changed Padre Enrique.

The campaign to have these captives released had to impress the State Department. As many as five thousand civilians had been kidnapped by the contras thus far in the war, but the Blandon kidnapping was one of the first to make headlines, largely because it coincided with the Fisher kidnapping. Calls poured into the State Department. Vigils and protests took place all over the country.

The long-term team deployed itself throughout the countryside, and Witness made it known where their people were, in case the contras should want to drop him off. As it happened, they delivered him to Father Jim Feltz, the parish priest of Paiwas. A call from the State Department informed Witness for Peace on October 30 that Fisher had been turned over to Feltz and an unidentified North American journalist in the hamlet of El Negro, a full day's hike from the

*Nicaraguan Democratic Force, one of many names used by the contras.

nearest road (there was no mention of Mena). The "unidentified journalist" was Paul Dix, at the time in his third year with Witness for Peace. The contras made Dix and Feltz sign a paper attesting that "We received the two kidnapped people Paul Fisher and Rolando Mena Hernandez on the 30th of October 1987, in El Negro, municipality of Bocana de Paiwas, Zelaya Central."

When they got back to Managua two days later, fifteen members of Mena's family and his girlfriend were waiting at the Witness house. The reunion brought tears to the eyes of the long-term team standing by. The question they had lived with for two weeks was *when* would Fisher be released. As Mena's family embraced him and broke down in sobs and cries, the different value placed on Nicaraguan and North American lives became clear once again. The Mena family had not known *if* they would ever see Rolando alive again. "Our hope," his mother said, "was knowing that he was with a foreigner. That was his salvation." In other words, Witness for Peace was his shield.

Fisher gave a press conference the next morning. He spoke of being forced to walk and ride for days, being kept against his will, uncertain if and when they would be freed, of taunts and threats, the psychological manipulation. He told the story of the two men who had escaped after seeing another man tortured. At the press conference it was revealed that Quiche, who had presented himself as a simple campesino, was in fact a former sergeant in the National Guard of Somoza. Few of these details made it into the newspapers. The little attention given focused on Quiche's plea for peace talks and on Fisher's description of the contras holding control of vast zones of territory.

Fisher and Blandon went to Washington to tell what had happened to them, and an exhausted long-term team gathered for a retreat in Managua later that month. As they listened to one another's stories, it became abundantly clear that the road to peace was not going to be smooth, even with the Esquipulas peace plan signed.

As the world talked more about peace, Witnesses in Nicaragua were at the greatest risk ever.

Long-term volunteer Cathy Thomas was riding a truck from Jinotega to Pantasma when the sounds of gunfire and grenades exploded all around her. Along with the other passengers, she and her dog jumped and ran for safety on the side of the road. When the shooting stopped, she came out to find that the contras had ambushed a vehicle coming the other way. Five victims lay on the roadway. One of them was her roommate, a nurse in Pantasma.

A few weeks later Thomas was sitting on the porch of the home
of friends. In the next house a friend of Thomas's, a ten-year-old girl
named Mercedes, played. A mortar shell fell. Gunfire shattered the
night. Rhett Doumitt and Sue Delahunt, who had come to work with
Thomas, collected some children and ran for a bomb shelter. When
the firing stopped, they went to the site of the mortar explosion. It
was a direct hit. Mercedes was dead. Doumitt helped the girl's father
remove her body from the post that she had been blown against.
There was nothing left of the little girl who just half an hour ago had
been playing with them.

On December 2, 1987, a contra ambush killed thirty-four-year-
old Carmen Mendieta, a community leader well known to Witness for
Peace. She was hit by hundreds of pieces of shrapnel from a mine and
bled to death before help arrived.

Carmen Mendieta had hosted many Witness delegates in her
thatch-roofed home in Paiwas. Long-term volunteers lived with her.
She had learned to read and write in the 1980 literacy crusade, and
since then had served as a lay church leader and as an organizer for
the Sandinista women's organization. She also raised seven children.
She loved her community and the revolution that was bringing hope
and progress to it. A tiny dynamo, she worked with the parish's development project to build housing, a day-care center, and sewing
cooperatives for the women to make a living. Strong-minded and curious, Mendieta was intrigued by the visitors from the United States
and often asked them why they had left the comfort of their own
homes to come to Paiwas.

Most of the Witnesses thought they had an answer to her question, but by the time they left, they had a much clearer vision of what
had brought them there. Faithful people like Mendieta who tried to
incarnate the struggle for justice helped to teach them.

The power unleashed by contact with the Carmen Mendietas of
Nicaragua was a force that the administration simply had not
counted on. People like Mendieta became the commitment. "The
cause I came here crusading," wrote Aynn Setright, "has been re-
placed by the people, the individuals I've met." The personal relationships built in long truck rides on mined roads and in quiet
evenings under thatched roofs, struggling with the language barrier,
drinking dark coffee, and sharing have unleashed a love force in communities all across the United States. The impact of familiarizing
people with a faith and commitment that does not fear death, and
with the people who practice that faith, will be influencing religious

communities for decades to come. Thousands of U.S. religious people who have perhaps read about liberation theology have, through Witness, engaged in dialogue with its practitioners, and that will be making a difference in U.S. religious communities for a long time.

"WHEN WILL THE KILLING END?"

Peace was as illusory as ever. Mardy Townsend, Eric Nicholson, and Jerry McKinney, long-term witnesses, were caught in the middle of fighting on the road outside Quilali. They transported two wounded soldiers back to town, probably saving the life of one of them by applying a tourniquet to his leg. The boy, a nineteen-year-old named Martin, had his right foot completely blown off.

Will Prior, a long-termer who drove the ambulance in Paiwas, drove Carmen Mendieta's daughter to her mother's funeral. He went to a cooperative named David Tejada near Paiwas to celebrate Christmas. "The Christmas service featured 12 first communions and 21 new babies to baptize," Prior later wrote. "How everyone appeared in spanking clean shirts and blouses amid all that rainy season mud is still a mystery to me. One little girl was wearing a t-shirt that said LOVE, and Padre Jaime . . . related this concept to our love of family and to God's love for us. . . . I will never forget the communion, community and peace of David Tejada."

But the peace in their hearts did not extend to the nearby jungle. Even during the service, the men of the community held their rifles at the ready, and gunfire and explosions kept Prior awake most of the night. The next day he wrote:

> Dec. 26. The grinding sound of an antique generator kept reminding us all through the night of the wake being held in our little church for the boy (14 years old) . . . killed on Christmas Day. . . . The generator's sad droning kept the feeble lights glowing while the women made coffee and baked rolls for the mourners. . . .
>
> We drove the wounded man to the hospital in Matiguas. The wound was very severe and I could hear the boy's moaning increase each time we got the ambulance lodged in a gulley or bumped against a rock. . . . Each moan was a reminder of this painful and useless suffering that goes on daily in Nicaragua.

The cover of the year-end Witness for Peace newsletter carried a plaintive headline—"When Will the Killing End?"

12

A BLOODY PEACE

In January 1988, the five Central American presidents met again, this time in Costa Rica. They signed a follow-up agreement that kept the Esquipulas process alive but weakened provisions that required all countries to comply simultaneously. What had been a plan for peace in the region was being converted into a tool to force concessions from Nicaragua. The Sandinistas agreed to open indirect cease-fire talks with the contras.

This satisfied the most serious stated condition of U.S. policy-makers, and many reasonable observers believed that the five presidents had killed off any hopes for renewed contra aid. Yet the administration refused to say die. They made a request for more millions in contra funding, asking for military and nonmilitary aid. As they usually did before each vote in Congress, the contras stepped up their attacks in January.

Witness puffed itself up for one more attempt to defeat contra aid. By now their presence was felt in almost every congressional district. Some legislators regarded them as pests, others saw them as valuable allies, and there was a whole range in between. There was no denying that Witness for Peace was now an important player. The Washington office was an information and resource center for activists around the country. Rather than hiring Washington lobbyists, Witness believed that by getting timely information on the situation in Nicaragua to its thousands of members, they could enable the grass roots to speak out, organize, and pressure Congress.

This "trickle down" approach produced some amazing results.

Bard Montgomery, a West Virginia beekeeper, was a long-term volunteer. He and another long-term volunteer, Veronica Gunther, had been at the scene of a contra attack on the town of La Victoria. Montgomery's report about the attack was disseminated to the press, and eventually the attack became the subject of a National Public Radio report. Montgomery had it taped and sent it to members of a delegation that had visited La Victoria just after the attack. One of the delegates, Joe Chasnoff, sent copies to dozens of "swing votes" in Congress.

Clark Webb, a member of the delegation from Blacksburg, Virginia, used the tape as part of his slide show. He showed the slides to a number of groups, including a gathering of taxi drivers in Washington, D.C. One of his friends, a taxi driver, later told him this story. A cab driver got a call to pick up a fare at the State Department. The passenger was a man wearing a conservative suit and carrying a briefcase. He directed the driver to Capitol Hill. They chatted, and it turned out the man was on his way to testify to a congressional committee about Central America.

So the cab driver told him about La Victoria. The passenger's face fell. He groaned. "Oh, no, not La Victoria again! We're getting all these calls on La Victoria. Everyone in Congress wants to know what happened there."

The culmination of eighteen months of Iran-contra revelations, the progress in the peace process, and years of pressure by a public disgusted with the contras led to a vote, on February 3, 1988, against President Reagan's request for more contra funding. The margin was only eight votes—four votes either way could have made the difference. Witness for Peace and the Central America movement celebrated a victory.

The day after the vote, Will Prior wrote in his diary: "What a glorious morn for Nicaragua. . . . We woke up at 4:00 A.M. to hear the shortwave news from Padre Jaime's radio—what a joy. . . . Congress repudiated Reagan's "dirty" war . . . it's a BIG small victory for peace.

"At this moment I am waiting in the ambulance for the 'all clear' message on our road. The Contra are still very much in evidence. . . . It's still scary, but we all feel so good that one small victory for peace has been won."

Prior, one in a line of Witnesses who drove the ambulance on the Paiwas road, was a beloved figure in the mountains. A former vaudeville song-and-dance man, minor league baseball player, and one of the earliest Peace Corps volunteers, Prior always had a song and a story to share. As he drove past the David Tejada cooperative, his friend Leopoldo came down the hill toward the road, waving his arms in the air. Leopoldo was jubilant. The two men embraced, tears in their eyes. "Will" shouted Leopoldo, "it's a step on the road to peace!" There on the rutted jungle road, witnessed only by the rolling green hills and a moist breeze that blew in all the way from the Atlantic, the two men danced together, the aging vaudevillian and the hardscrabble campesino, celebrating a tiny victory in their common struggle.

REACTION IN NICARAGUA

That victory seemed distant and hollow in the mountains of the Segovias, where resentful contras unleashed a wave of assaults as soon as the votes came in. Long-term Witness Tom Eby was traveling to El Jicaro in a cargo truck. He hopped off to walk to Jicaro, and the truck continued down the road toward Quilali. As he got into town, an ambulance was already racing in the opposite direction. Five miles from the point where he had gotten off, the truck hit a mine and nineteen people were killed. Two days later, Eby sat by a stream near Jicaro and wrote in a letter: "I was fortunate that I had decided to go to Jicaro rather than on to Quilali that day. 50 other Nicaraguans were not so fortunate. . . . I saw three women from the truck who were taken to the Jicaro Health Center. Two were incoherent, yelling and screaming with shrapnel wounds covering their bodies. The other woman looked at me and said, 'Didn't I see you on the truck?' That was when it hit me that the ambushed truck really was the one I had been riding on."

At a demonstration held in Wiwili a few days later to protest the killings, a grenade was thrown at the crowd. Ten people died—six of them were children. Erik Nicholson, a long-term Witness working in Wiwili, attended seven funerals in two days.

It was in this twilight-zone moment between war and peace that Richard Boren was kidnapped.

Boren was a clearheaded, easy-going young man who had worked three years in rural Ecuador as a Peace Corps volunteer. He returned home to North Carolina to study for a graduate degree in industrial technology at Appalachian State University in Boone, North Carolina. There was an active chapter of CITCA working in Boone, and one of its leaders was Jefferson Boyer, whose anguished suggestion at El Porvenir and his organizing work in the spring of 1983 had given impetus to the founding of Witness for Peace. By the time Boren finished his degree he had become so concerned about the war in Central America that he applied to be a Witness long-term volunteer.

It was a natural fit. A hiker and enthusiastic white-water kay-aker, his past had prepared him well for his new role. He was rugged and adapted easily to the long rides on dusty roads in trucks with no springs and the long mountain hikes from the end of the road to campesino's homes. Campesinos felt at home with his easygoing Southern manner, his gentle laughter, and his inclination to look for ways to be helpful. He tried not to ask a lot of questions, but he usu-ally got the job done—whether it was setting up a delegation or inves-tigating a reported contra attack. He felt keenly the need to get the testimonies of the campesinos to the U.S. public.

On February 29, the priest in Jinotega gave Boren the names of four people kidnapped near Mancotal. The next day he hopped a ride on a truck to the cooperative, fifteen miles north of the city. He visited the frightened families of the victims. The body of a twenty-five-year-old man kidnapped from a neighboring community had just been dis-covered, hands tied behind his back, with signs of torture.

For cooperative members, the risk of such a gruesome death was especially high. To a visitor, Mancotal was just a collection of forty homes on the shores of Lake Apanas. In the eyes of the contras, however, farm cooperatives epitomized the communist society the Sandinistas had imported from Russia and Cuba and were trying to impose on the whole country.

In order to save the people from this menace, the contra logic went, cooperatives had to be destroyed. Contra spokesmen said their attacks were justified because of the presence of army units at the coops. Yet documentation by Witness for Peace had shown that the contras usually attacked when the defense of the communities was minimal, and the army was nowhere in sight. Such was the case at Mancotal on the night of March 1. The cooperative president com-plained to Boren that he had requested help from the army to defend the settlement but had gotten no response.

That afternoon Boren attended a prayer service. At the end of the service, he introduced himself to the congregation and discussed the possibility of establishing a permanent presence in the endan-gered community.

He had supper at the home of the Ramos family. Only the mother, Leonor Ramos Mercado, and her thirteen-year-old daughter, Reina Isabel, were left. Leonor Ramos told Boren that two of her sons had been killed by the contras, one during an attack on Mancotal, another while in military service. She was glad to have Boren there, she said. No, she wouldn't accept money for room and board. "You're welcome here anytime." Reina Isabel read a book quietly for most of the evening. and by 9:00 P.M. they were all asleep.

At 11:00 P.M. they awoke to what sounded like fireworks. Then the sky lit up. Twenty mortar shells exploded in the next ten minutes. The air filled with thick smoke. Boren threw on his clothes, pulled on his socks and boots. Terror rising in his throat, he cried out to the woman, "What are we going to do?" She was frozen. The little girl was awake now, too, trying to crawl into a hole in the floor. Boren thought to take his notes and a pile of reports about other contra abuses from his backpack. Rather than have them fall into the hands of the contras, he searched for somewhere to hide the incriminating papers. Unable to bury them, he dropped them over the wall, behind the house.

Shrapnel and bullets were hitting the roof of the house. His eyes shifted from side to side in the darkness, struggling to make sense of the shadows and the outlines before him. Suddenly Reina jumped up, then fell on the floor. Boren groped in the darkness until he found her. Already he could feel the blood gushing out of her, and he searched for something to stanch the flow. In desperation he wrapped a piece of his sleeping bag around her leg. Minutes later he was ordered out of the house and marched away, a prisoner of the Larry McDonald Task Force of the FDN, led by Comandante Wilmer. As he was marched away, he heard one of the contras explaining to the people that "We are Reagan's freedom fighters." As the contras prepared their retreat, they sacked and then set fire to the storage shed, pulled the boots off the bodies of the dead, and began to interrogate Boren.

For the next four days he was forced to march continuously as the contra patrol zigzagged through the mountains in its retreat. They made him carry twenty pounds of milk and a thirty-pound pack of supplies. The others were forced to carry supplies and the bodies of the contras killed in the attack. Of the ten Nicaraguans taken prisoner with Boren that night, all but one, Victor Rodriguez, escaped or were freed when they were no longer needed as beasts of burden. They accused Rodriguez of being a Sandinista collaborator because he had been part of the military reserves. He defended himself by saying that military service was obligatory, not his choice.

Boren and Rodriguez were marched thirty miles north to a contra hideout in La Vigia, near the Rio Coco.

The first report to reach the long-term team in Managua said that a North American named Richard Boren had been killed at

Mancotal. Within the hour, another call corrected that version but confirmed his kidnapping. In the middle of the call, the phone lines went dead. All three phone lines in the Witness office went dead at that same moment. The team used a ham radio to get the news to Joe Moran in Durham, who relayed the information to Washington.

Paul Dix, Rose O'Donnell, and Doug Schirch were working on the mobile reporting team and headed to Mancotal as soon as they got word. They interviewed survivors, including Reina's mother, who told them of Boren's efforts to save her daughter's life. The girl was in the hospital. She was going to live but it was too early to know if the leg could be saved.

The team met and decided to remain at their posts. They did not want to give their Nicaraguan hosts or the contras the impression that their work would stop if one of their number was in danger. They decided to actively press for Richard's release—not just in the newspapers and in the streets, but out in the countryside, in places where the contras were likely to be.

Witnesses working in the Pantasma Valley and in El Cua began walking the mountain trails asking startled campesinos if they had seen a contra patrol going by with a gringo in tow. Within a few days, more than ten Witnesses were carrying photos of Boren and knocking on doors in areas where the contra squad that hit Mancotal might be.

Back in the states, thousands of people were pressuring the U.S. government to order his release and the release of all contra captives. The Witnesses kept up the pressure with vigils, letters, and phone calls.

The mobile reporting team continued to crisscross the mountains of Jinotega, trying to find Boren and to get word to the contras that they were available to pick him up. At times they were within miles of the farm where he was being held.

Meanwhile Boren was conducting his own campaign of resistance. In the early hours of captivity he became concerned that verbal abuse by some of the contras could escalate into physical abuse unless he won their respect. From that point on he refused to answer their questions or to talk with them. He refused to carry anything unless given a direct order, and he made them repeat their orders.

Boren was made to hike all day and got little sleep at night. On some nights he heard explosions and fighting. Other nights he was too cold or had to sleep on hard, wood floors. He heard a radio report about his capture that mentioned that he had "tried to give first aid" to a little girl who was shot. The report didn't mention what happened to Reina, and Boren interpreted it to mean that she was dead.

On the fifth day, the contras crossed into La Vigia, where they maintained a social base. At one point the contras separated the two men, and Boren refused to eat until Rodriguez was brought back to where he could see him. The contra leader, Wilmer, met with Boren to explain that Rodriguez had committed some crimes and he had to pay for them. In the jargon of the war, this meant they suspected Rodriguez of collaborating with the Sandinistas and planned to kill him. Boren decided to take control of the situation. Instead of negotiating for his own release, he dictated to Wilmer the conditions under which he would allow them to release him.

He asked where the other kidnap victims were, how they were being treated, and when they were going to be released. Wilmer at first denied he was holding any other prisoners, but eventually relented and said they were with the rest of his troops and they had to undergo an investigation before they could be released.

"Listen," Boren told the contra commander. "I've got a problem. I'm a prisoner. You've got a problem. You get your supplies from the United States, and you're holding a U.S. citizen prisoner. I want you to release all your prisoners at the same time I am released."

"No way," said Wilmer.

"I absolutely won't accept being released unless Victor is released with me."

"You can't intervene in this situation," protested Wilmer. "If we let you do this, then you'd have to go tell the Sandinistas to release all their prisoners."

"I've gotten to know Victor too well," responded Boren. "I can't leave him, knowing his life is in danger."

Wilmer was paying attention now. "There must be an investigation and he [Rodriguez] has to be punished. If you want to wait, you can see how the investigation turns out, and then if you want you can receive the same punishment." The commander was trying to intimidate him and looked surprised when his captive accepted the deal.

"I accept," said Boren.

"It could be a very long sentence."

"I'll take whatever he is given."

"Even if it is ten years?"

"Yes."

On the morning of March 10, Rose O'Donnell, along with Paul

Dix and Doug Schirch, drove east from Quilali toward La Vigia. It took two attempts to get past an army roadblock just outside of town. When they did, they came upon a civilian pickup truck that had just been ambushed by the contras. They recognized it as one they had seen earlier in the morning, with two children riding in the back. Blood dripped from the pickup bed where just hours ago two children had played. They later learned that the two children were badly wounded and a passenger was killed.

From the troops at the roadblock they learned that the civilian truck had been allowed to go up the road only after the army had sent several military vehicles and a foot patrol to make sure it was safe. The contras had allowed two military trucks and a foot patrol to pass by before opening fire on the civilian vehicle. What Schirch and his companions didn't yet know was the most frightening detail of all— that the contra group that had shot up this pickup with two children in plain view in broad daylight was the same group that was holding their friend captive.

They continued up the road, stopped at a house beside the Rio Coco, where a man claiming to have seen a North American with the contras agreed to take them to where he was. Across the river, four contras met them and took them for a thirty-minute walk. They acknowledged that they had Boren and were in radio contact with Wilmer. The contras never asked the identity of the Witness for Peace crew.

After a forty-minute walk, they stopped at a house where thirty well-armed contras awaited them. Half an hour later the contras tried to hand Boren over. Exhausted by the ordeal and stunned and relieved to see his friends and coworkers coming to get him, Boren insisted he wasn't going anywhere without Rodriguez.

He turned on Wilmer and accused him of breaking his word. "We had a deal," he reminded the chief. Wilmer argued that Rodriguez had yet to be tried and punished for his "crimes."

"We had a deal," said Boren.

Paul Dix, running about snapping pictures, started to doubt whether anyone was going to be freed at all. It was getting late, and they still had a long walk back to the truck, and a drive down the road where the ambush had just occurred.

Several contras bragged to Dix about an ambush they had committed earlier in the day against an army truck. He realized they were talking about the truck he had seen. "On the road near Panali?" he asked. "Yes," they answered proudly. "No. They were children. Those were your victims." They didn't want to believe him, but they fell silent.

Wilmer promised Boren to hold the trial first thing in the morning, and to let Rodriguez go as soon as it was over. By now it was clear that the three Witnesses who had just arrived weren't leaving without Boren, and Boren wasn't leaving without Rodriguez. Wilmer hesitated. Dix mentioned that it would look very bad for the contras if Boren were released and told the press that they were holding Rodriguez, since the contras claimed they didn't kidnap people. Faced with the choice between relieving himself of one pesky gringo or acquiring three more, Wilmer finally relented. He ordered his men to go get Rodriguez, and they brought him to where the truck had been left.

"Halcon," the contra who brought Rodriguez, made Schirch write out a receipt for him and dictated that it was to say that the two had been taken from the "base" at Mancotal. Like a defense lawyer, Boren objected to the use of the term "base." "There were only houses there," he said.

Objection sustained. The objectionable term was removed, the preposterous receipts signed and handed out, and in a few moments the frustrated contras were standing by the house overlooking the river, shaking their heads as the truck with its two additions waddled west on the dirt road toward Quilali.

It was already dark and explosions shook the night. Schirch later wrote: "What lay ahead of us was the drive along the road to Panali, past the ambush site. It was tense. We drove back slowly through the dark, shining a flashlight beam on the white flag flapping over the truck. The trip seemed to take forever, but we reached Panali. In the morning we called the Managua office on our portable radio to inform them that we had Richard and Victor. We were going home."

That night they attended the wake for the passenger killed in the ambush of the pickup truck. Boren broke down when Rose O'Donnell told him Reina was alive. During his long march with the contras the little girl whose blood was all over his clothes had been constantly on his mind.

Reina spent more than a year hospitalized, and doctors performed numerous operations on her knee. They saved the leg, but she will always walk with a limp. Victor Rodriguez went back to Mancotal with his parish priest two days later, collected all his belongings, and moved to the city of Jinotega. It was too dangerous for him to continue living in Mancotal.

Just after the February 1988 vote to end contra military aid, the administration sent thirty-two hundred troops to Honduras to counter an alleged Nicaraguan incursion into that country in pursuit of the contras. While the move had little military significance, it signaled the administration's willingness to act unilaterally, defying Congress, and to risk direct military confrontation. Witness and the Pledge of Resistance responded with acts of civil disobedience from coast to coast.

During Holy Week a group of five hundred conducted a week-long Via Crucis march through the Carolinas, protesting the war and remembering those killed by contra bullets supplied by the United States.

SAPOA

The peace process inched forward even as the fighting in the countryside continued. Two negotiating sessions with Cardinal Miguel Obando y Bravo as intermediary produced nothing. The government announced it would meet directly with the contras in the town of Sapoa.

Sapoa, a tiny border post, all but abandoned since Eden Pastora's troops shot up the customs station more than five years earlier, became the repository of the hopes of three million Nicaraguans for two days in March 1988.

After fourteen hours of negotiations, both sides signed an agreement calling for a sixty-day cease fire. They agreed that outstanding issues would be settled in a political dialogue with the internal unarmed opposition, which contras were free to join if they laid down their arms. They agreed to meet in Managua to finalize a definitive cease fire. President Ortega called on President Reagan to respect "this spirit of peace that we Nicaraguans have signed here in Sapoa."

The impact of Sapoa was immediate. Michael Skinner of the long-term team wrote in a letter home: "The first two months of the cease fire . . . were dreamlike: the fighting . . . all but stopped, and the contra fighters came down from the mountains to meet in open discussions with the Sandinistas. People had hope, for the first time in eight years."

Instead of documenting contra atrocities, the long-term volunteers found themselves spending time with the contras in the cease-fire zones. Dozens of meetings between Sandinista and contra troops, called *encuentros* in Spanish, brought together the foot soldiers who previously had communicated only with rifle and artillery fire.

Will Prior wrote, in a May 30, 1988, letter to a friend, about an informal *encuentro* on the road to Paiwas:

> . . . a big camion [truck] from Boaco was winding its way down our infamous rocky Paiwas road with a load of goods, and "fortunately" stalled just outside of town. A group of wandering contra chanced by and surrounded the truck, which they soon discovered (to their sheer delight) was also carrying a cache of precious Eskimo helados [ice cream]—the first such treasure bound for Paiwas in six months. Of course, the contra began enjoying an ice cream party, and "surprise" they even dutifully paid the owner for his treats. In the middle of this "dessert fiesta" along came a group of local militia and Sandinista soldiers. They were welcomed, cordially, to join the helado encuentro, con amistad, y paz [with friendship and peace]. I was hoping this ice cream peace special would at least make *Time* magazine—it was a beautiful happening.

During the period of the sixty-day cease fire agreed upon at Sapoa, Witness for Peace documented only twenty-three incidents, in which five civilians were killed. But on June 9, the talks broke down. The government agreed to continue the cease fire but the contras refused. In the first six weeks after the Sapoa cease fire broke down, twenty-one civilians were killed by the contras in attacks documented by Witness for Peace.

The floundering peace talks and resumed killing gave new life to the administration's unending crusade for contra aid. In July an opposition rally in Nicaragua was broken up by the police, and U.S. Ambassador Richard Melton was expelled. On August 10, an administration request for $27 million in nonmilitary aid passed the Senate.

Most of the contras had already retreated into Honduras. The last two weeks of August 1988 were historic. For the first time since the initiation of the Hotline, no killings, injuries, or kidnappings by contra forces were reported by the twenty-five long-term Witnesses scattered around the countryside.

NO MERCY

But Nicaragua was to know no mercy.

On October 21, 1988, the worst tropical storm to hit Central

America in a century slammed across Nicaragua, leveling the Atlantic coast town of Bluefields, cutting through Nueva Guinea and across the rest of the country. One hundred and sixteen people died, nearly two hundred thousand were left homeless; crops, roads, and electrical power lines were lost to the 100-mile-per-hour winds and devastating floods. Sixty-seven bridges were ripped out by the storm— more than the contras had managed to disable in seven years of war.* Bluefields was battered, Rama inundated, and Corn Island leveled. Roads in the north washed out, and floods destroyed refugee communities near Rio Blanco. Estimates of the economic damage caused by the storm started at $1 billion—three times the value of the country's annual exports.

In Nueva Guinea, 350 families crowded into the Catholic church. There they talked about the complete loss of their crops and their homes. After listening to them, long-term volunteer Barb Wenger echoed the laments of Job in a letter home: "Many people . . . had already lost their land, homes and family members to the violence. Now . . . just as they were getting back on their feet, BAM! . . . this hurricane pounds them back down to their knees again. Now they can't even feed themselves for at least several months. I'm angry. If God is supposed to be a God of the poor then how come it's the poor who are always pounded the hardest?"

Politics governed the U.S. response to the hurricane. The United States offered no aid, and Marlin Fitzwater, President Reagan's spokesman, suggested that the Sandinistas were exaggerating the storm's impact. This "[puts] Americans in the unusual situation of watching a human disaster unfold just off U.S. shores while Washington offers absolutely no relief," according to the *Miami Herald*.**

Witness for Peace raised $26,000 for CEPAD's relief efforts, and a vast array of organizations provided housing materials, foodstuffs, tools, and technical assistance to an already battered country. Nicaragua's economy was heading toward levels of inflation unheard of since the introduction of money. Desperate measures were tried but failed to stem the rise. Earlier in the year the government laid off twenty thousand state workers. Ministries merged to save money, and services were cut even further. In February, the government se-

---

*Government figures quoted in Witness for Peace Hotline, November 3, 1988.

**"Storm Deepens Nicaraguan Crisis," by Sam Dillon, *Miami Herald*, October 30, 1988. The death toll was surprisingly low for a storm of such magnitude, and observers on all sides credited the government evacuation of 325,000 people with saving many lives.

cretly printed new currency, the new cordova, and withdrew all money from circulation for three days. The new cordova was substituted for the old at an exchange rate of 1,000 to 1, and the dollar exchange rate was slashed in half. But shortages of almost everything spurred inflation even higher until the markets were full of products priced out of the reach of ordinary people. Hundreds of thousands of Nicaraguans survived on dollars sent from relatives living abroad. The dollar was becoming an unofficial second currency, and professionals were leaving public service to become black-market peddlers or to leave the country.

The Nicaraguans had a capacity to adapt and to overcome that amazed most of the Witnesses. Barb Wenger wrote from Nueva Guinea that the people there "woke up the day after the hurricane with hammers in their hands and with a determination to rebuild and survive." A new class of technicians known as "innovators" had learned to fashion spare parts for machinery from scrap material. Rural health-care workers came to rely on available herbs and traditional medicine. Everyone became a mechanic, learning to keep their aging vehicles running, and everyone became an economist, learning to make the most of the regular currency swings.

There are limits to the amount of stress any people can endure. The stress manifested itself in physical illnesses—people told Witnesses of *los nervios* (nerves) and *psicosis de guerra* (war psychosis) that kept them awake at night and agitated all day. Alcoholism, always a problem, blossomed into an epidemic. Young boys drank until they cried their eyes out retelling the horrors of battles. Old men drank and talked of the past as being a paradise of plenty. Robbery and theft, comparatively rare in years past, became a major social problem as standards of living for the poor dropped below Somoza-era levels.

In the countryside the threat of death was constant, nutrition was poor, and sleep was rare. Watching people stay up half the night on guard duty, lose loved ones, and see nothing but war and hardship on the horizon—the Witnesses had to wonder when the breaking point would come. This form of "pressure," a sophisticated torture, was more barbaric than the worst of the contra war.

Finding the breaking point was the key to low-intensity, invisible warfare. The administration strategy of wearing down Nicaragua counted on finding that point and pressing it relentlessly, like a boxer flicking away at an opponent, wearing him down round by round, waiting for the moment when the towel is thrown in.

Erik Nicholson, in a letter written to a friend after more than a year living in Wiwili, analyzed how the contras fit into the broader strategy of trying to make Nicaragua "cry uncle."

> While the contra have failed as a military force, they have been an effective political force. Many government programs designed to help the general population have been shut down because of the contra. In Wiwili, of the 64 schools in the area (only 11 existed during Somoza's era) only 31 were open in 1988. . . . Four teachers were kidnapped last year; the rest were basically scared away . . . by contra threats. . . . As a result, hundreds of children no longer have access to education.
>
> The National Development Bank, the Ministry of Agrarian Reform, and the hospitals in Wiwili all also suffer from a dramatic lack of trained personnel. . . . The contras have killed enough workers in all the above offices to scare potential personnel away from Wiwili. As a result, a little less than half of the 46,000 people [here] . . . live without seeing the direct benefits of the revolution: teachers, agricultural engineers, doctors and nurses.
>
> The war forced choices on the government that left it in a no-win situation: People blame the government for forcing them into fighting a war that no one wants. While the contras regularly kidnap civilians . . . people . . . blame the government for not better protecting them from the contra.

Michael Skinner measured the decline in the economy and the success of low-intensity warfare in Nicaragua in stark terms in a February 1989 letter home: "Every Nicaraguan I meet talks about leaving—a 180 degree switch since I first came in 1987." Nicaragua's most precious resources were going north, and only weapons flowed south in return.

Witness resisted the urgings of many other groups to get involved in direct material aid. Except for a few tools or medical supplies left by each delegation with the community they stayed in, and the symbolic contribution of labor, Witness tried to avoid being seen as an aid source, for three reasons.

First, aware of how difficult the work of rural development was and how much the involvement of outsiders could complicate matters in small communities, they did not feel they had the expertise to carry out such projects. Second, they wanted to avoid creating divisions in Nicaraguan communities by creating competition for donated goods. Third, Witness consciously wanted to have a different kind of impact within the U.S. communities of faith. "The easiest thing for church people to do when they are moved by the suffering of poor people is to give charity," said Bob Bonthius. "We . . . told people that when they went down there they would see things that would make them want to give whatever they had. But we asked them to resist that urge and to instead direct their energies into changing the policy that had created that suffering."

The Hurricane Joan relief fund was the first time that Witness had officially raised funds for direct aid. In 1989, after much controversy, the delegation program adopted a dual focus: repair the damage/change the policy. Several delegations carried out specific reconstruction tasks, but the organization resisted shifting gears too much, not wanting to give supporters the mistaken impression that the war was over.

Many projects had evolved as spin-offs of Witness for Peace delegations, such as the Leon–New Haven sister city project, a sister city project between Jicaro and Yellow Springs, Ohio, and the Proyecto Minnesota/Leon. An early delegation from Arkansas started a project called "Puente de Paz" to provide potable water in Jalapa and Waslala. "Walk in Peace," which gave prosthetic devices and medical services to amputees, drew its initial inspiration from Witness, and the Cristo Rey project in Rio Blanco, started by Jim Feltz, was staffed largely by former Witness long-termers. Several dozen Witnesses stayed in Nicaragua working with religious groups or development projects, and many who returned to the United States worked full-time with Central American organizations.

Other organizations were coming to Nicaragua's aid with much-needed supplies. Quest for Peace shipped dozens of container loads of medical and school supplies collected as part of a drive to match the administration's aid to the contras with real "humanitarian aid." Pastors for Peace sent truckloads of aid. Veterans set up their own convoys, and a Veterans for Peace group began construction projects in Jinotega. The Linder family raised more than $250,000 to carry on the electrification of El Cua and Bocay, where Ben Linder was working when he was killed.

The Abraham Lincoln Brigades from the Spanish Civil War sent ambulances. Sister city projects, more than one hundred of them by mid-1988, sent dollars, supplies, love, and labor. TecNica helped link up technicians with tasks in the field of computers and engineering. APSNICA (Architects and Planners in Solidarity with Nicaragua) designed and built houses, and, like Habitat for Humanity, redoubled their efforts in the wake of the hurricane. Thousands of U.S. citizens, Europeans, Canadians, and Latin American volunteers were working on projects all over the country.

As the year came to a close, the Reagan era drawing to its constitutionally mandated end, Witness took one last opportunity to remind the American public of what this jolly old man and his zealous underlings had brought to Nicaragua. It was called EyeWitness Week, and the theme was "Our Eyes Don't Lie About Nicaragua." Just before the U.S. presidential elections, dozens of local Witness groups placed ads in newspapers, held public forums, and sponsored readings of reports of contra atrocities. The week of activities demanded an end to the U.S. financing of the contra war, an end to the embargo, and normalization of relations and war reparations.

Some Witness supporters began to believe that Reagan's departure and the Sapoa accords spelled the end of U.S. attempts to control Nicaragua. For the first time in its history, Witness for Peace had to cut back on its staff due to a shortage of funds. Fighting contra aid had required enormous expenditures, and now that the public saw the peace process moving along and the Congress had voted no to more military aid, many people lost interest in Nicaragua.

Letter after letter from Nicaragua pleaded with people to remember that "the war is not over!"

A poignant reminder came from six-year-old Tito of Nueva Guinea. Barbara Wenger, a long-term Witness from Pennsylvania, asked him to draw a Christmas picture.

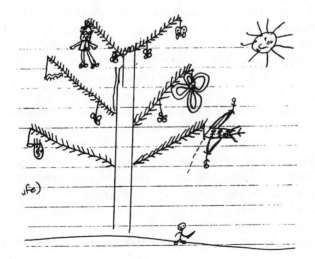

He tells me it's a Christmas tree with a doll, a snake, a pot of beans, a butterfly, a flower and an airplane.

I ask him what is under the tree. "A boy with an AK [an AK-47 rifle]," he matter of factly tells me.

Not my idea of Christmas. But to a kid who's never had a Christmas free from war—well . . . I'll write again. In hopes of the Peace and Justice that Christmas calls us to.

                                                                                          Barb

On January 20, 1989, Ronald Reagan moved back to California and parties erupted in the streets of Managua. Daniel Ortega was still president of Nicaragua, the revolution was still in power, and Reagan's beloved contras were languishing in Honduras. Reagan's most cherished foreign policy prize had eluded him. The military aims of one of the most popular presidents in U.S. history had been thwarted by a determined Nicaraguan people and their friends in solidarity.

But the war wasn't over.

Marie Clark
Rio Blanco, Nicaragua
Sunday, January 22

Dear Friends:

The health center was a scene of panic and confusion. Hundreds of people were gathered outside, some shouting orders, others weeping uncontrollably, and still others staring in shock and disbelief. The crowd converged on the trucks as we backed up to the emergency entrance.

We had barely come to a full stop as they loaded the first victim, Alfredo Suarez, 21, into the back. I watched as the life drained from his face and his skin color changed to sallow yellow . . .

As I jumped out of the truck I heard someone calling my name. It was Jilma Zelaya. "Maria. Oh my God, Maria. Help me. I can't feel my hands. Oh my God, I can't feel my hands . . . "

I rushed over to her as they laid her in the back of the truck. She was reaching out for me. Her hands were covered with blood and her head swung back and forth violently from shock and pain. I tried to comfort her as they brought out her five-year-old son, who was also wounded, and placed him beside her.

I turned around and saw Denis Artiles, the highest ranking

government official in the zone. . . . His body was filled with shrapnel . . . and his clothes were torn and spattered with blood. He stared lifelessly, unable to blink because of shrapnel in his eyes.

A . . . truck pulled up . . . [and] unloaded the blood soaked sheets that contained the remains of the dead.

Only minutes before I had been lounging in my pajamas, enjoying a springlike Sunday morning. We heard an explosion. . . . Anita came running . . . screaming for help. We bolted down the stairs. . . . She caught her breath enough to tell us that a mine had gone off [in] the center of town.

She leaned against the wall, tears streaming down her face. "Oh you guys, Raoul's dead. I saw his body. The mine . . . Oh my God, it blew his head off."

We all ran in different directions. My stomach knotted and my whole body began to shake violently. I started saying to myself, "Don't think, just move . . . I dove into the back of one of the pickups as it was pulling out."

Raoul had become a friend to many of the long-term volunteers. His death touched them. It made little or no difference to the press or to the opinion shapers, the movers and shakers and policymakers. His death was an accident in a way; he was killed as he examined a land mine that supposedly had been deactivated. Yet he would not have died if the contras hadn't planted the mine that was given to them by the United States. He wasn't a civilian casualty, because he worked for state security (usually referred to in congressional debates as "the dreaded state security"), but he was a victim of the war as much as anyone else. Marie's letter continued:

. . . The force was so great that Anita . . . was blown out of her hammock. . . .

Four people were killed . . . eight others were seriously wounded. In the days following, we mourned individually and together as a town. . . . It was a turning point in my experience here.

I've been living in Rio Blanco for eight months now, and I've seen a lot of suffering. . . . In sympathizing with the pain [of others] I've always felt something; this time the pain was my own.

A week later on a transport truck, I was talking with a fellow passenger. He asked me where I lived and I answered, Rio Blanco. I realized later that there was something different about the way I had said it that time. Like by living through this experience, I had earned the right to say it.

By this time, Witness, like Marie Clark in Rio Blanco, was a fixture, a regular part of life in Nicaragua. More than thirty-seven hundred people had come on more than one hundred eighty delegations by early 1990. One hundred sixty long-term Witnesses had served on the team, some for as long as three years. Most of the original Witnesses, with notable exceptions like Sharon Hostetler, who was married with two children and continued to work in Managua, had returned to their lives in the United States.

Nicaragua had changed their lives, and Nicaragua had changed the Witness. *En carne propia,* in their own flesh and blood, the Witnesses were experiencing the effects of a dragged out, multilayered conflict where the sides were increasingly blurred—and they were also experiencing the hope and the inspiration that somehow kept raising up leaders in the remote communities where they worked, leaders who inspired their own people and their visitors from the United States.

For most of 1989, they continued to travel in the war zones, to document killings that at times seemed as much like blood feuds as they did the outgrowth of a war that had earlier in the decade been defined as pivotal to superpower relations. Now Nicaragua was being forgotten. The press corps was pulling out, the world's eye was turning to Eastern Europe. The long-term team, which at its peak numbered forty, had been reduced to only sixteen.

Leslie Toser became a long-term Witness as part of an odyssey that began in Chicago. After visiting Nicaragua with a short-term delegation, she went back to Chicago, resigned her high-level job with the commodities exchange, and moved to Nicaragua by way of Guatemala and El Salvador. She was in Juigalpa when a man came over to her who had been a friend of an earlier Witness volunteer.

> He had met others from WFP before when his wife and three kids were killed when the contra attacked their farm. He too, . . . [once] a farmer, is now a city person. He hates it and awaits peace so he can return to his farm.
> I feel sad and guilty seeing this man all alone. Everything has been taken away from him. I am, my country is, responsible for all this pain, this awful, awful pain—for what? . . . It hurts to look at him. We are discussing our work. How we cannot stay longer and play the guitar and sing with them like

we often do. We explain that the team used to be forty volunteers and now we have only sixteen. They ask why. I am unable to tell them the truth. The raw truth that donations are down, the U.S. is no longer interested in Nicaragua, many say the war is over here. We don't have the money to support more volunteers. I can not say it, I can not hurt them anymore. I am struck by my own silence.

The Bush administration promised a new tone in Central America, though its basic goal remained the same—getting rid of the Sandinistas. Secretary of State James Baker set about crafting a bipartisan agreement that met the concerns of supporters of the peace process while at the same time maintaining support for the contras.

On March 24 (Good Friday, and nine years to the day since Archbishop Romero was killed), the White House and congressional leaders announced the outline of such an agreement, and on April 13 both houses of Congress voted nearly $50 million in "nonlethal" aid to the contras. Provisions of the bill barred any funds to contra units that violated human rights or that were engaged in offensive military actions.

The president didn't request military aid for the contras. There was little need for it. The focus of their effort to oust the revolution had shifted to an electoral struggle. At a February meeting of the five presidents, Nicaragua, pressured by U.S. allies Honduras and El Salvador, agreed to change its electoral schedule and hold presidential and parliamentary elections in February rather than November of 1990. The Sandinistas released nearly nineteen hundred prisoners in March, most of them members of the National Guard from Somoza's time.

Witness for Peace strategy for 1989 was two-pronged. The first part was to mobilize to hold Congress and the administration to their agreement not to fund contra offensive actions. As continued reports of contra attacks were documented by the long-term team, activists throughout the United States publicized the attacks and demanded that their congressional representatives and senators cut off the aid as promised. In July, ninety-nine members of Congress wrote to Secretary of State Baker asking for an investigation and a cut-off of funds to any units involved in attacks and human-rights violations.

The second part of the strategy was called "Eyes on the Elections." It seemed likely the administration would accept the elections as valid only if the Sandinistas lost. The long-term team planned to document the election campaign from start to finish, and events stateside were planned to keep attention on the reality in Nicaragua, not the rhetoric coming from Washington. Seven delegations of nearly one hundred twenty people were organized to be present at the elections. Their purpose was to tell the world just what had happened.

No matter what the outcome, Witness was already looking to expand beyond Nicaragua. At the 1989 annual face-to-face meeting, the statement of purpose was amended to include the other countries of Central America. Many delegations were already visiting other countries in the region, and many activists had been involved in peace work related to El Salvador and Guatemala. By 1990, four long-termers were working in Guatemala and two more were accompanying communities of Guatemalan refugees in southern Mexico. A presence was begun in Honduras but discontinued. Eight fact-finding delegations visited Guatemala in 1990, including one that also toured Panama. Witness consolidated its U.S. offices in Washington, D.C., in August 1990, and hired an organizer for programs dealing with El Salvador and Guatemala.

Proposals to expand the presence into other parts of the world had been presented to Witness for Peace for years. Scott Kennedy, the Resource Center, and the Fellowship of Reconciliation began a program of delegations and nonviolent presence in Israel and Palestine in 1988 and asked Witness for Peace to adopt the project as its own. The organization declined, but it lent its support to the formation of MidEast Witness, which Kennedy sees as an extension of the model developed by Witness for Peace.

A survey of members of Witness for Peace conducted in 1987 showed that most respondents believed Witness could easily expand into other nations of Central America. The most frequently cited location for a future presence outside the region was South Africa. The steering committee has moved cautiously on requests to move into other areas, including third-world areas in the United States.

The policy goals for the year reflected the shift to a regional approach and a deeper awareness of the economic and political aspects of the war. In addition to halting contra aid and supporting the dismantling of contra camps, Witness called for an end to all military and police aid to El Salvador, Guatemala, and Honduras; bringing home all U.S. troops in Central America; and negotiated settlements to conflicts.

Witness called for support for the process of evaluating Nicaragua's elections, which had been set up by the United Nations and the

OAS, and for that support to be extended to elections throughout Central America. Witness pledged to work for free trade with Nicaragua, an end to the embargo, payment of war reparations, and emergency disaster relief.

On July 19, 1989, nearly half a million Nicaraguans jammed into the Plaza of the Revolution in Managua to celebrate the tenth anniversary of the revolution. It was a time of unity and celebration, which were growing more and more rare.

In a marathon session in August, President Ortega reached a political agreement with the internal opposition. The government altered the electoral law to account for the complaints of the opposition parties. In return, the opposition called for dismantling the contras. The five Central American presidents, meeting that same month, called for the contras to lay down their arms and return home before the elections.

Everyone seemed to be saying the contras' time was up—everyone except the new president of the United States. The administration never ceased to insist that the contras needed U.S. support so they could act as "pressure" on the Sandinistas. The administration adopted a two-track strategy of supporting the contras and the internal opposition. In October, Congress approved an administration request for $9 million to help the campaign of the Nicaraguan opposition (UNO). President Bush promised that the embargo and the contra war would be ended if the voters chose Violeta Chomorro, the UNO standard bearer.

Witness for Peace continued to document the many forms of pressure on Nicaragua. In the two months after the Central American presidents called for the contras to disband, Witness documented cases in which the contras victimized nearly seventy people. Witness tried, with some success, to get word into the media that the contras still represented a threat, but little ink was available for Nicaragua. As far as the press was concerned, Nicaragua was closed until election time.

Just before Christmas, when U.S. Marines repossessed Panama, it was page-one news all over the world. Many in Nicaragua believed the Panama action might be the precursor to the long-feared U.S. invasion of Nicaragua. But such was not to be the case.

The electoral process was observed more closely than any in history. The United Nations, which had never before observed elections in a sovereign state, sent a 300-person team. They worked closely with the OAS and a delegation headed by Jimmy Carter.

The Witness for Peace contingent was the largest private observer delegation. They split into more than forty small groups and visited hundreds of polling places in seven provinces, including the Atlantic coast. The voting, with rare exception, was conducted with scrupulous adherence to the electoral law. It would be very difficult for the administration to claim fraud.

THE 1990 ELECTION

As it turned out, there was no need. On the morning of February 26, 1990, Witness for Peace activists were as shocked as everyone else to learn that Violeta Chamorro had been elected president of Nicaragua. Leone Bicchierri, a long-term volunteer, cried for hours in his tiny room in Siuna. Sharon Hostetler, by now committed to Nicaragua for life, wondered aloud what the future would be for her two children. Was Nicaragua headed for a bloodbath? Civil War? Would the advances in public health, grass-roots organization, and education be maintained? Managua was overtaken by an eerie silence as everyone pondered the previously imponderable. No one, not even the winners, had thought seriously of the possibility of an UNO victory. All but one poll had predicted a Sandinista triumph.

"We should have listened to ourselves," concluded Paul Dix. Most of the long-term volunteers, who wanted to see the FSLN win, had believed the Sandinistas would lose in the area where they worked. But they believed the polls and the impressive demonstrations of support, especially a closing rally attended by as many as half a million people. But the results spoke otherwise, and the Sandinistas agreed to give up power on April 25.

The embargo was lifted, relations normalized, and President Bush, instead of lobbying for contra aid, asked Congress for $300 million in economic aid to the new Nicaraguan government. Political cartoonists and pundits mistakenly lumped Nicaragua in with "the emerging democracies of Eastern Europe." Witnesses had to endure the spectacle of Dan Quayle lecturing Daniel Ortega that he must turn over the armed forces as well as the presidency.

Analyzing the results a few weeks later, Charles Gray and Dorothy Granada, two former long-term volunteers who were still working in Nicaragua, wrote:

> Was the process fair?
> We would say that the process was and the context wasn't.

It may have been the most carefully prepared, thoroughly observed, and scrupulously carried out election in Latin American and, perhaps, world history.

. . . The context of the election was not fair. The United States was saying to the Nicaraguan people, "We will stop killing you when you vote for our candidate." Ten years of war. Ten years of torture. People crack under torture.

. . . In hindsight, the . . . war weariness of the people was underestimated. For too long [the Nicaraguans] had seen their loved ones kidnapped, tortured, maimed, and killed. They had seen their meagre standard of living cut in half. It now appears that hundreds of thousands of Nicaraguans simply couldn't stand it any longer. In the secrecy of the cardboard voting booth they finally cried "uncle."

Everyone who had gone to Nicaragua over the years had to spend hours rethinking and trying to understand the new situation, to figure out how it had happened and what it meant. But Witness was about action, about presence, about being with people, not just thinking about them. And without even deciding, Witness for Peace decided to stay. The communities and the parishes where Witness worked, along with CEPAD and the other partner agencies, felt that it was still important to have their presence at such a difficult and uncertain time.

An example of just how uncertain life became for Nicaraguans was the case of Reina, the little girl injured in the attack on Mancotal. After nearly two years of operations and hospitalizations she was finally at the point of being able to walk. But the doctor who had been treating her was Cuban. Would the new government allow him to stay? Would the military hospital that was her lifeline remain open? Almost every Nicaraguan family faced serious questions like these.

With Chamorro's inauguration on April 25, contra troops began moving into designated "security zones" to hand over their arms to the United Nations and return to civilian life. It wasn't the ending they had imagined, nor the ending Witness for Peace had envisioned.

As it happened, Mancotal was on the edge of one of the zones where the contras congregated. A few weeks after the Chamorro inauguration, Paul Dix and Dierdre Morano were visiting Mancotal, when a contra patrol came through, heavily armed and belligerent. The contras went from house to house, ransacking, threatening, intimidating, and interrogating the campesinos. The two Witnesses followed them around, dogging them, asking them questions, making their presence known. After the contras moved on, the people thanked them and said that if they had not been present, it might have been much much worse—instead of frightening them and leaving, the contras might have taken prisoners or hurt people.

In the countryside, the election results had produced only more uncertainty, more danger, and greater need for solidarity. "It was like an echo of Jalapa in the early days," said Doug Schirch. "People all around at the cooperatives and near the zones where the contras were congregating were asking us to stay with them, telling us they were safer if we were there." In a strange way, Witness had come full circle, from being a shield in Jalapa when the contra war was still an open secret, unknown to most of the world, to standing with the vulnerable people of Mancotal. They decided to maintain a permanent presence in eight communities still threatened by the contras.

Witnesses were also present for the beginnings of disarmament. Schirch traveled to El Almendro on May 8 and watched as eighty contras turned in their weapons and exchanged their camouflage uniforms for blue jeans. The U.N. forces, following Isaiah as much as the mandate from their secretary general, cut each of the rifles into three pieces with acetylene torches.

On June 9, contra commander-in-chief "Franklin" brought 3,000 troops to a Mass officiated by Cardinal Obando y Bravo and agreed to have his soldiers disarm. After a speech by Franklin, the contras began to turn in their weapons. The first soldier to do so handed his rifle to Mrs. Chamorro and gave her a kiss. It was Wilmer, the field commander who had led the raid on Mancotal, wounded Reina Isabel Ramos and kidnapped Richard Boren. Doug Schirch, attending the ceremony, wrote from Managua that "unreal as it may seem, the war as Nicaragua has known it for the last eight years may be over."

_____ **13**

LOOKING TO THE FUTURE: "WE HAVE ONLY STARTED"

The enemy of love is not hate but indifference.
—Elie Wiesel

Some might judge the work of Witness a failure. Forty thousand Nicaraguans were killed or wounded in the six years following the first border vigil. Ten percent of the population fled the country during those years, and an equal number lived as war refugees in their own homeland. The economy was lumbering in reverse, and the nation that had entered the 1980s as a Latin American symbol of national independence entered the '90s waiting in line for aid from the United States.

The U.S.–backed candidate had won the presidency, and the contras and their supporters were claiming victory. A majority of the U.S. Congress had come to accept the administration's view that Nicaragua was a threat to our national security, and an even greater majority scoffed at the Witness assertion that the Nicaraguan revolution should inspire hope rather than fear. Critics of Witness gloated at the election results, claiming vindication of their charge that Witness had been blind to Nicaraguan realities.

Over the years Witness had evolved into much more than a third-world tour service or a Washington advocacy group. Witness was many things to many people. Asking the question What is Witness for Peace? is like the story of the three blind men touching an elephant. Depending on whom one talks to, Witness is a radicalizing political experience, a life-changing religious experience, an exercise in moral courage, a warning to U.S. national security planners, an experiment in nonviolent action, a prayer put into action, or all of the above.

If an organization can be so many things, then on what grounds can it be judged? Let us examine its own statement of purpose. The statement commits Witness to "stand with the Nicaraguan people." The decision to stay in Nicaragua after the elections was really not a decision at all but rather a foregone conclusion. A thousand and more stories of people like Reina Ramos made the need for a continued presence compelling on a human level. The communities of Paiwas, Waslala, Yali, Nueva Guinea, and others still expected the volunteers to remain with them and delegations to keep visiting. Witness entered a long process of reflection and analysis about the meaning of its continued work, but to Nicaraguans there was no question but that the accompaniment should continue.

The very presence of Witness was good news for many in Latin America. For the North Americans who went, the acceptance and the forgiveness extended to them by Nicaraguans was very good news. By their presence in Nicaragua, four thousand Witnesses for Peace defied the prevalent assumption that the lives of the brown- and black- and yellow-skinned people of the third world are somehow worth less than the lives of people from the first world. By their open-armed welcome to the Witnesses, the Nicaraguan people resisted all attempts to divide them from their brothers and sisters in the United States.

The four thousand U.S. citizens risking their lives in Nicaragua and thousands more going to jail back home all sent a visible sign to Latin Americans that there are people who care about their struggle for justice and are willing to accept the consequences of standing with them. Dozens of communities in Latin America, the Middle East, and Africa have contacted Witness requesting a supportive presence. A Nicaraguan student, Amelia Mallona, expressed the human impact when she said, "Witness for Peace showed that two peoples can love each other." As this book goes to press, Witness is continuing its presence in Nicaragua and expanding its work in Guatemala and elsewhere in Central America and Panama. An exploratory delegation is planning to visit South Africa in 1991, and several Witness for Peace members traveled to Iraq on peace delegations as war loomed in the Persian Gulf.

Nineteen ninety-one may be the year that the Witness came home in a new way. Black pastors in Charlotte, North Carolina, established a nonviolent presence patterned after Witness for Peace in a heavy drug-buying area of the city. They were led by Rev. Jim Barnett, a Witness veteran. Witness delegations were visiting farm worker coops in Oregon and other third world areas within the United States, and the organization struggled to become more inclusive in terms of the racial and ethnic background of its members. While keeping its anchor in Nicaragua, Witness began to address other aspects of U.S. policy.

The stated purpose committed the Witnesses to work "to change U.S. policy to one which promotes friendship, justice and peace with Nicaragua." In an ironic twist, this goal was achieved in a single day when the Bush administration ended contra aid, lifted the economic embargo, and announced a $300 million aid package to the Chamorro government. However, that was not what most people within Witness considered friendly or just. The intent had been to push the administration to deal justly with revolutionary Nicaragua, not harass and make war on the people until they elected a government acceptable in Washington's sight. The new Nicaraguan government is as politically and economically dependent on the United States as any government in the world.

Witness did help to promote the peace that communities are now feeling after nearly a decade of war. In addition to lives that may have been saved by the presence in the war zones, Witness for Peace can take some credit for being part of the movement that finally put a stop to contra military aid. In doing so, Witness and its partners in coalition prevented the imposition of a military solution and helped, along with many efforts around the world, buy time for the Contadora process to eventually give birth to the Esquipulas II Peace Plan. CEPAD's Gilberto Aguirre has said that in its efforts both in the field and in Washington Witness "saved lives."

Tracing cause and effect between political activity and its impact can be deceptive. Some have argued credibly that the contra policy was so full of inconsistencies and illegalities that it collapsed of its own weight. Joe Eldridge, who has worked on Latin American issues for nearly two decades, believes that Witness has been "incredibly successful." "Witness has responded to an incredible need in the American people to be more than armchair philosophizers writing Congress. [It has] given ways to lots of people to express convictions in ways they hadn't imagined."

Tim Rieser, a Senate aide close to the debate on contra aid, believes Witness for Peace was successful in stimulating pressure from the grass roots and at providing information on contra activities that no one else was getting. "As far as affecting the outcome," says Rieser, "I would not say Witness for Peace was very effective, but then again nobody else was." He believes it was the Esquipulas II Peace Plan more than anything else that led Congress to cut off military aid. "I'm not sure Congress would have stopped this war if Arias had not taken his initiative," says Rieser. "The Congress continued to send weapons and ammunition even when it knew the contras included ex-National Guardsmen, and they were attacking civilians."

As a partial measure of the Witness impact, Eldridge notes that, "In 1980, there were no more than twenty [Capitol] Hill people conversant with Latin America issues. Now there must be five hundred or more. Those people need to have information that comes from agencies other than the State Department, the Defense Department, and the CIA. They need another view—the view from underneath." By bringing back their intimate experience of living with the poorest of Nicaragua's poor, Witness provided that missing dimension to the public discussion. Illinois Representative Lane Evans, a contra aid opponent, says Witness helped generate awareness and outrage, while other groups, particularly Neighbor to Neighbor, were more effective at channeling public sentiment into effective political pressure.

One way to evaluate Witness is to ask what might have happened if Witness had not existed. What would have happened to Nicaragua if there had not been a solid body of people who cared deeply, vocally, and visibly? While it is impossible to say for sure, it is not hard to imagine what Nicaragua's fate might have been.

The products of past silence are visible in Chile, in Guatemala, in Grenada, and in Panama, all victims of U.S. interventions.

In Guatemala in 1954, the United States overthrew a freely elected president and no one raised a voice (in fact, Cardinal Spellman helped the CIA make contacts with Guatemalan Catholics supportive of the coup).

In 1965, twenty thousand U.S. Marines landed in the Dominican Republic, and there was a mild protest but not much of a public outcry. The churches, with the exception of the protests of a few missionaries and campus ministers, were subdued.

The Green Berets were at war in Guatemala for most of the duration of the Vietnam War, chasing reports of guerrillas in the highlands. There was a mild protest now and again, and occasional mentions at protests against the Vietnam War, but nothing near the level needed to force a change in the policy.

In 1973, the Nixon administration overthrew a freely elected government in Chile, and there was no serious dissent until it was too late.

Yet in the allegedly self-centered 1980s, the most powerful and popular president in this century was challenged and beaten time and again as he pursued his most cherished foreign policy objective, the defeat of the Nicaraguan revolution. The challenge came from a movement largely based in religious communities. Powerful figures in the administration wanted to invade, but the activities of Witness for Peace, the Pledge, and others helped prevent their getting their wish. The administration was never able to build the patriotic consensus it needed to prosecute a full-scale war, and part of that was because each pretext they used was refuted by the testimony of people on the scene.

The statement of purpose also committed Witness to maintaining a prayerful, faith-based presence, and in this they were very faithful. The reflections shared by Witnesses and the Nicaraguan communities they stayed with have life-changing and society-shaking implications for North Americans. The Latin American church has spent two decades calling on their North American brothers and sisters to look at U.S. economic, political, and military domination of their continent as if North American lives depended on it. Nicaraguan communities of faith, by inviting Witnesses to come live with them, allowed thousands to experience what that means, *en carne propia*, in their own flesh, as the saying goes in Spanish. Witness is changing churches and other religious communities by bringing people of faith into contact with Latin American liberation theology, with its attempt to read scripture and understand faith from the viewpoint of the struggling poor.

The core experience of Witness for Peace is this encounter between U.S. citizens and the victims of their country's policies. Witness provided the opportunity for thousands of people to begin a journey, a relationship with the poor of Latin America, a journey with profound implications for their own faith and politics. It provided many more with what the Presbyterian church called "a communication link distinctive from that of the state." The news coming in through this alternative means gave individuals and institutions the strength to dare more. It reminded many churches and synagogues of the importance of creating public discomfort and disorder if the actions of society don't square with its stated norms of morality. Witness took people away from their comforts and their safety, away from books and round tables that often protect as much as they inform.

Many who returned talked of their experience as a personal conversion, of a triumph of hope over fear. Hundreds of lives have been changed and new ministries begun after the experience in Nicaragua with Witness for Peace. A similar radicalization at the grass roots is what began to change the Latin American church. It remains to be seen what changes are in store as the leaven left in the bread of U.S. religious communities slowly rises in the years to come.

Witness went beyond motivating people, to train them for effective action. Thousands were trained in the tactics of nonviolence, in more conventional political organizing, in working with the media. Nearly two hundred long-term volunteers received a unique brand of training for cross-cultural service and advocacy work. This training continues. Its impact will be felt not just within Witness but in the many struggles that Witness veterans will be involved in over the coming years.

The statement of purpose committed Witness to a nonviolent presence. Witness became a pioneer in the use of nonviolence. No one had maintained an intentional nonviolent presence of such magnitude in a war zone for any length of time. Witness set up a truly permanent, flexible presence and has spent six years in the war zones. Witness expanded the uses of and explored the limits of interposition, learning that such a tactic must always be tied to a larger strategic conception of social change if it is to be effective. The nonviolent presence came to include symbolic marches and vigils, accompaniment of individuals and communities in danger, fasting, work projects, peace flotillas, and a host of other actions.

Witness combined prophetic, dramatic actions with analysis and political work to capitalize on the attention generated, and it did so *on a sustained basis.* As the situation in the war zones changed, the response changed as well. Two crucial lessons for the future can be learned from this: Prepare for the long haul, and be prepared to be flexible and to àdapt to circumstance. If Witness had been married to a given tactical notion at the outset, it would have fizzled as soon as the contra offensive against Jalapa did. And if the organizers had not been willing to stick it out for the long haul, the early actions would have remained isolated gestures having little or no impact. From the people's struggle in Central America they learned that work for social change cannot be conceived in terms of single actions or campaigns. In a struggle that has gone on for centuries and where the work of a lifetime can barely be measured, we are either in it for the long haul or we are not in it at all.

Witness is not a model that can be exactly duplicated. Nicaragua was a revolutionary society open to the presence of U.S. citizens, willing to allow them to risk, and one in which long-standing ties between the churches existed. Particular circumstances in El Salvador and Guatemala have called forth different responses, such as the accompaniment of refugees going back to El Salvador, Peace Brigades' accompaniment of human rights workers. Central American governments, with the exception of Nicaragua, have been hostile to the presence of such groups. Yet openings occur and determined people can find ways to do meaningful work.

Some elements of the Witness experience can be generalized, such as the need for careful screening, training, and sensitivity to the local culture. The development of partner relationships with local people and agencies and ongoing consultation is also key. Importantly, practitioners of their own brand of nonviolence must recognize that people of other cultures have their own experiences that can teach us about creative nonviolence.

A number of proponents of nonviolent action were disappointed in Witness for Peace in that it did not go far enough. Brian Willson expressed dismay that the organization seemed to grow more conservative with time, becoming less willing to risk both its people and its prestige. Others within the organization still feel that the focus should have been on actions right in the field in Nicaragua to confront the contras directly, rather than on public education and changing votes in Congress.

CHALLENGE FOR THE FUTURE

The statement of purpose mentions opposition to all forms of U.S. intervention, overt and covert, in Nicaragua. In 1989, the focus was broadened to include all of Central America. The next challenge Witness faces is not fighting the visible wars but struggling against the invisible, low-intensity wars the Pentagon promises for Latin America and the third world into the foreseeable future.

Richard Barnet writes that what the U.S. public is really being asked to buy when the president requests aid to the contras is "protection for their sons." This is the essence of the domestic agenda of low-intensity conflict—to keep our wars of empire invisible and to keep the blood of North America's "best and brightest" from being shed. This is the lesson the national security establishment learned from Vietnam.

The Pentagon's belief that invisible wars will work in the third world is based on an extraordinary assumption—that the people of the United States, sprung forth in large part from the Judeo-Christian heritage, will not become concerned so long as the blood being shed is not their own. The national security planners have taken a moral inventory of the U.S. public and found the shelves to be all but empty. Only steadfast resistance to such wars of domination can prove how out of step they are with the ordinary person's capacity for caring.

And then there is the question at the heart of the matter: How can Witness for Peace contribute to changing the United States into a nation that no longer relies on such forms of intervention in order to preserve its privileged stature and "way of life"? Panama is only one example of how frustrating it can be for a movement that works to oppose a specific example of U.S. intervention to watch the same attitudes fuel a policy of intervention in another country. As long-termer Greg Hessel put it, "The problem is not how we think about Nicaragua; the problem is how we think."

On the one hand, the flowering of a movement like Witness is a tribute to the U.S. people's love of justice, but on the other hand, that such a war could even be debated is a measure of the sickness of U.S. society. All the Witnesses did was reject the anesthetics of our society long enough to feel the pain we were inflicting on others. All they did was remove, for just a moment, but, in a sense, forever, a bit of the protection that keeps the nonpoor in our society from experiencing the violence our society exports.

While Witness for Peace can regard its work to date as successful in many respects, it cannot forget that the low-intensity conflict planners at the Pentagon consider their little war in Nicaragua very successful too.

Invisible warfare is the modern method for the accomplishment of a century-old goal of U.S. foreign policy: continued control of Latin America. Even when the guns are still, a silent war goes on. Children die of poverty in countries making huge debt payments to U.S. banks. Terms of trade slip year by year and greater numbers of campesinos and urban workers slip from poverty to desperation. Witness for Peace was able to make an invisible war on the Nicaraguan/Honduran border visible, and to incite many people to action. How can the ongoing, built-in injustice of U.S.–Latin American relations be similarly brought home to our consciousness and changed?

It will not be easy. It is the American way to react to the dramatic, and the low-intensity conflict planners strive to avoid situations that appear dramatic. Many of the issues that will form the crux of U.S.–Latin American issues are economic issues of little interest to ordinary people. Yet the example of Witness shows that people can care even when the forces of evil are gambling they will not.

Finally, the key word in the statement of purpose is "continuous." The Witnesses commit themselves to "continuous nonviolent resistance." Now that the end of the Cold War has taken attention away from Central America, we will see how serious that pledge is. There is a danger that those who cared will also turn elsewhere. For Central America, the crisis threatens only to get worse. If Witness has really learned the lesson from Latin America that the struggle lasts for lifetimes and not just for a day, then indeed something radical will have happened. The poor majorities of Latin America are watching and waiting.

APPENDIX

WITNESS FOR PEACE
ORIGINAL STATEMENT OF PURPOSE

To develop an ever-broadening, prayerful, biblically based community of United States citizens who stand with the Nicaraguan people by acting in continuous nonviolent resistance to U.S. policy. To mobilize public opinion and help change U.S. foreign policy to one which fosters justice, peace and friendship with our Nicaraguan neighbors. To welcome others in this endeavor who vary in spiritual approach, but are one with us in purpose.

THE COVENANT OF
WITNESS FOR PEACE

Together, we make the following Covenant:

- We commit ourselves to a prayerful, biblical approach and unity with one another as the foundation for this project.
- We commit ourselves to nonviolence in word and deed as the essential operating principle of Witness for Peace.
- We commit ourselves to act in solidarity with the people of Nicaragua, respecting their lives, their culture, and their decisions.
- We commit ourselves to maintaining the political independence of Witness for Peace.
- We commit ourselves to honesty, openness and inclusiveness in our relationships with one another.
- We commit significant time and financial resources to Witness for Peace.

• We commit ourselves to circulating our documentation as widely as possible.

THE ORIGINAL TEXT OF THE
PLEDGE OF RESISTANCE

In the event of a U.S. invasion of Nicaragua, the following will happen:

1) A signal for action will go out to regional, state and local contact people and groups.

2) People across the country will gather at a previously designated church in their local community (at least one in every congressional district). These churches will be the gathering points for receiving and sharing information, for prayer and mutual support, for preparing and commissioning one another for action.

3) A nonviolent vigil will be established at the congressional field offices of each U.S. senator and representative. Each office will be peacefully occupied until that congressperson votes to end the invasion.

4) A large number of people will come to Washington, D.C. (in delegations from every area of the country) to engage in nonviolent civil disobedience at the White House to demand an end to the invasion.

5) The United States citizens who are in active partnership with us (Witness for Peace, Maryknoll, the Committee of U.S. Citizens in Nicaragua, etc.) will launch their own plan of action in Nicaragua in concert with us. Depending on the political situation, the timing of the invasion, and the possibility of getting into Nicaragua before or during an invasion, we will send other people to Nicaragua to join in the actions of the United States citizens already there, if our partners in Nicaragua feel such an action would be advisable.

For more information on Witness for Peace, contact:

Witness for Peace
2201 P. Street N.W.
Room 109
Washington, DC 20037
(202) 797-1160

For a biweekly taped message of news from Central America, call (202) 797-1531.

Other peacemaking groups:

Peace Brigades International
Box 1233
Harvard Square
Cambridge, MA 02238
(617) 491-4226

Pledge of Resistance
4228 Telegraph, Suite 100
Oakland, CA 94609
(415) 655-1181

MidEast Witness
515 Broadway
Santa Cruz, CA 95060
(408) 423-1626

Fellowship of Reconciliation
Box 271
Nyack, NY 10960
(914) 358-4601